110

DATE DUE

DEC 5 1998		
JAN - 8 1999	JAN 1 7 2001	
JAN 2 9 1999	JAN 2 4 2001	
FEB 2 5 1999	JUN 1 4 2005 NOV 1 3 2007	
MAR 1 2 1999		
MAR 2 4 1999	JUL 1 0 2008	
APR 1 4 1999		
MAY 0 7 1999		
JUN 5 1999		
JUN - 9 1999 MAR 1 6 2000		
APR 1 9 2000		

GAYLORD   PRINTED IN U.S.A.

Also by Andrew Harvey

Andrew Harvey

Photographs by Eryk Hanut

Son of Man

The Mystical Path to Christ

Jeremy P. Tarcher / Putnam

a member of Penguin Putnam Inc. New York

Matthew Fox's *The Cosmic Christ* quoted by permission of HarperSanFrancisco.

Bede Griffith's *Return to the Centre* quoted by permission of Temple Gate Publishers.

Most Tarcher/Putnam books are available at special quantity
discounts for bulk purchases for sales promotions, premiums, fund-raising, and
educational needs. Special books or book excerpts also can be created to
fit specific needs. For details, write Putnam Special Markets,
375 Hudson Street, New York, NY 10014.

Jeremy P. Tarcher/Putnam
a member of Penguin Putnam Inc.
375 Hudson Street
New York, NY 10014
http://www.penguinputnam.com

Library of Congress Cataloging-in-Publication Data

Harvey, Andrew, date.
     Son of man:the mystical path to Christ /
   by Andrew Harvey;
   photographs by Eryk Hanut.
         p.   cm.
     ISBN 0-87477-912-X (alk. paper)
     1. Jesus Christ—Person and offices.   2. Mysticism.
   I. Title.
   BT205.H226   1998
   232—dc21   98-26665
                                               CIP

Printed in the United States of America
10   9   8   7   6   5   4   3   2   1

This book is printed on acid-free paper. ∞

Book design by Ralph Fowler

Acknowledgments

To my beloved Mother, for the fire of her passion for justice, and for all her years of love.

To my beloved husband, Eryk, for teaching me the truths of Sacred Marriage.

To Leila and Henry Luce, for the extravagance of their goodness.

To Gloria Cooper, for her trust and the unfailing refinement of her spirit.

To Lance and Susan Morrow, for hours of joy.

To Rose Solari, for her witness.

To Peggy Wright, for the warmth of her wild soul.

To Fran Bull, for the depth of her loyalty and the wisdom of her kindness.

To my agent, Tom Grady, for his stamina, belief, humor, and guidance.

To my fine editors, Joel Fotinos and Mitch Horowitz, for their patience and generous faith.

To Dorothy Walters, for her sweet height of being.

To Lauren Artress, for her solidarity and brave work.

To Mary Ford Grabowski, for her loving-kindness and for always being there.

To Karen Kellejian, for all her continual care.

To Caroline and Francoise Bouteraon, for their profound tenderness.

To Maria Todisco, for all her help and truth.

To Bridget Bell, for her gifts of sweetness.

To Lanore Fontes, for constant examples of selflessness, and for all her work.

To Ruth Fisher, for her high kindness.

To Purrball, for herself.

For Mollie K. Corcoran, my beloved friend and sister.

"Blessed are the pure in heart;
for they shall see God" (Matthew 5:8).

Contents

⊞ ⊞ ⊞

Preface

▨ ▨ ▨

This book is designed as an unfolding initiatory journey into the full nature of the Christ and into the vision and spiritual practices essential to embodying the Christ directly, without the need for intermediaries, and as completely as possible, in the heart of life.

It has four linked parts: "The Historical Christ"; "The Mystical Christ"; "Christ and the Sacred Feminine"; and "The Direct Path to Christ."

In the first part, "The Historical Christ," I try to present as vividly as possible the figure of Jesus that is emerging from contemporary biblical scholarship. This Jesus is startlingly more radical than that offered to us by any of the existing churches; he is a mystic revolutionary in every dimension, who wanted nothing less than the transformation of all the laws and conditions of this world into those of the Kingdom of God. The authentic historical Jesus never claimed divinity or unique status; on the contrary, it is clear that he wanted to empower all human beings, whatever their sex, race, or social status, with what he knew to be their essential divine identity so that, liberated from all the structures, shibboleths, and fantasies of the past, they could together create a new world, the world of the Kingdom. No other spiritual teacher had so comprehensive and radical a vision of the limitations of all forms of religious or political power; it is this vision that Jesus dedicated his life to promulgating, and it is for this vision, which threatened (and threatens) all elites, dogmas, and hierarchies of any kind, that he was killed. Reclaiming this vision in its full subversiveness is essential if the authentic Christ-force is to enter history at last to transform it.

In the second part, "The Mystical Christ," I try to show how Jesus himself *embodied* this revolutionary mystical and practical vision. In the section "The Eight Thresholds and Mysteries," the mystical Christ tells us of the stages of "Christing" and of the ordeals and possibilities of full divine human life. In the section that follows—"The Map"—these "eight thresholds and mysteries" are condensed into a "Map" of four stages: Purgation; Illumination; Sacred Marriage; and Birthing, which leads the seeker who undertakes the Christ-path through its essential rigors into the final mysteries and creative powers of Christhood. What I intend to show in this second part of the book is that Christ-consciousness waits in all of us to be evoked, realized, and lived out in passionate, mystical, and practical action in the world, and that when it is realized in us we become, as the historical Jesus was (and as the mystical Christ is both within and beyond "time" and "space"), "birthers" of the Kingdom in every aspect of life.

In the third part of the book, "Christ and the Sacred Feminine," I point at length to the necessity of restoring to awareness the Sacred Feminine in its full power, glory, and demand for justice if the full birth of Christ-consciousness is to be realized. Christ, I attempt to show, must be seen and known as the divine Child of the Mother as well as the Father and as the Sacred Androgyne, who fuses the "masculine" and "feminine" in his own being to engender a uniquely powerful and all-encompassing realization and to birth a new kind of divine human being. It is the birth of this androgynous, mystical, and practical Christ Child that the divine Mother as Mary is working to engender in all of us now. Unless this Cosmic Mary is known and invoked in her full splendor, this Christ cannot be born; "Christ and the Sacred Feminine" ends with a revelation of this splendor in all its transformatory aspects and demands.

When these first three parts of *Son of Man* are understood and "fused," what will emerge, I believe, is a comprehensive vision of the Christ as a total mystical and social revolutionary, the incendiary pioneer of a wholly new form of human divine life, whose critique of all forms of power, including so-called religious and "mystical" ones, is ruthless and whose teaching is perpetually menacing to every kind of limiting dogma and worldly authority. The historical Christ that emerges from the pages of the new biblical scholarship is not, as some Christians claim, a "diluted" one; for when seen and understood along with the mystical Christ and the Christ that is the Sacred Androgyne-divine-Child of the Cosmic Mary, as well as of the Father, the true nature of the Christ-force is revealed at last, stripped of the conservative and patriarchal accretions of two millennia of falsifying tradition. And it is revealed in all its radical glory, forensic brilliance, and in all the turbulent demand of its boundless love, becoming in the process what it was, I believe, always intended to be—a force for the most radical imaginable change in and of the world, a fire-mirror in which all the lies of power of every kind are finally unmasked, and the true face—and true challenge—of human divine possibility revealed.

In the last and fourth part of my book, "The Direct Path to Christ," I offer what I believe to be the most powerful spiritual exercises that enable us to sustain a direct relationship with Christ. *Son of Man* then ends with the thirty-one meditations on the mystical Christ taken from the full range of the Christian tradition, and designed to present as precisely as possible the glory of Christ-consciousness and to act as an inspiring source of sacred wisdom and passion.

At the beginning of this century, Albert Schweitzer wrote, "What has been passing for Christianity during these last nineteen centuries is merely a beginning, full of weakness and mistakes and not a full-grown Christianity springing from the spirit of Jesus." What I have attempted to present in *Son of Man* is this "full-grown Christianity, springing from the spirit of Jesus," for I believe that if it is not imagined, embraced, and realized in its complete vision, the human race cannot survive the horrors its arrogance and degradation of the environment have created. The extremity of the world-scale tragedy facing all of humanity demands a final birthing of the "full-grown" Christ, a final invocation and embodiment of his extreme passion, clarity, and unconditional, all-transforming, and radical love in every arena of the world.

The Second Coming will not be the return of an avatar or of a "person," but will be—if it is to be at all—the birth of the authentic "full-grown" Christ-consciousness in millions of beings who have realized, as the historical Jesus did, the journey into unconditional love for all humanity, the journey of the Christ. It is up to each one of us to take up the terrifying and glorious challenge of Jesus to "Christ" ourselves, so as to be part of this great birth; it is the responsibility of each one of us to imagine, risk, and give everything to participate as fully and fecundly as we can in the evolutionary leap that this birth makes possible.

The Second Coming and its great birth are not inevitable, and there is very little time left in which to co-create with the divine the conditions necessary for their realization. The world is in ultimate danger; on how urgently we dare to transform ourselves and on how wisely and passionately we act in all the areas of human life to secure justice for all beings and the safety and health of our natural and cultural environment depends the future of the planet. As the great Catholic mystic Bede Griffiths lay dying in the early months of 1993, he was heard one night to say over and over, "Serve the growing Christ, serve the growing Christ." Those who know the apocalyptic truth of our times know that there is nothing more necessary, or more potentially transformatory, than to serve the Christ that is everywhere and in every being, struggling against terrible odds to be born at last.

Andrew Harvey, Easter Day, April 12, 1998

A Vision

I was in despair at the murder of nature, at the horrible degradation of all things sacred, and at the coming suffering of millions of human beings and animals. All at once I heard all around me a voice, thrilling and loud as a trumpet, saying, between flashes of lightning and claps of soft thunder:

I am Alpha and Omega. I am the Christ, the first and the last. I am the one who lives within you and who wants to live you completely. I am the living one you are, the Sacred Androgyne longing to be born in you, the complete divine human, whose heart births and holds the whole cosmos in its fire. I am you, as you can and must become. I am your beginning and your end. I am your original and final face.

Worship me as separate from you and outside you and the tragic and horrible farce of history will continue; the forests will be destroyed and all the birds and animals will die and the entire world will become an external image of the inner poverty and desolation of your vision of yourself.

Know me as your deepest secret and innermost heart, know my power as your power, my love as your love, and you will come into the splendor of direct vision, which I, as Jesus on the earth, gave everything to try to give to you. And with that vision to inspire you, you will enter the whirlwind of my revolution of glory: you will become humble revolutionaries of glory, and the abundance of divine life that will flow to you from me will release you from all structures that contain you and free you from all social, sexual, political, and religious prisons. You will work with my passion that is your passion, my power that is your innermost power, in the center of the world, and spread the flames of my truth and justice everywhere.

Each of you will know yourselves in me and like me, a child of the Father-Mother, directly fed with wisdom and love from the source. Each of you will become the hands and feet and mouth—the body—of love itself and work and act with the tireless stamina of love to transform every facet of the injustice of the world into the compassion and justice of God's Kingdom.

And the reign of the evil one, who has reigned because of your delight in limitation, your embrace of failure, and of the small powers of reason, and your refusal of the great kingdom of the soul, shall be over forever; the great secret of the divinity of every human being and of the external sacredness of every human soul and of the right of each being to honor and justice and respect in the name of God's love will flame out. Then the whole of life shall be brought into harmony with this my voice and my love, and the new Jerusalem will descend in a fire of divine compassion from heaven on earth, and earth itself become the heaven it has always been in the heart of my Father-Mother.

For out of the sacred act of your recognition of yourselves as me and of me as yourselves will arise a great cry—a cry for justice—for an end to the psychic degradation of billions, the destruction of nature through greed, the domination of millions of seekers by false masters and mystic and religious systems drunk on body hatred, power, and evasion. This cry will have great agony in it, an agony of pain and rage at all the ways in which you have been enslaved and allowed yourselves to be enslaved—but it will also be a cry of light, a cry of resurrection on behalf of every being, a cry of rebirth that will echo around the world and shake the pillars of all the false temples of worldly power and bring them all down.

All the forces of evil and limitation will try everything to prevent this cry from being born in its full outrage and passion, for when it is born it will be a sign that the Christ is being born in humanity. And when I am born in humanity, all the structures of all the forms of political and religious authority will be changed forever to reflect the boundless glory and equality and justice and honor of the love of the Father-Mother, and to bring humanity at last into divine harmony with the earth and heaven.

This birth of me in you and you in me is the birth that the whole of history has been groaning for: to make it possible is the reason I loved and suffered on earth as Jesus—to birth myself and help all others birth themselves. Hunger to be born now! Hunger and strive with all your powers to realize and spread the power, humility, and ecstasy of this birth!

All those who claim that I am calling you to a "rapture" beyond this world and time and space are lying; I am calling you to enter time and body with divine love and knowledge and to enact the laws of God on earth so as to transform this earth and all aspects of human life. I am not calling you to an escape from the world, however glorious, but to an embrace of it, in the spirit of God, to a dying into life to become one with the life of life and so be humble and powerful enough to flood all things with the glory of love. One with me and the source of love, you will work with my power and my love to realize my great dream to bring all of creation—every human being and fern and dolphin and stone—into the glory of the divine, to take back all things into the all, transfigured by love and justice. This is the great dream of the Christ, the great plan, the deepest meaning of my Second Coming, and you are called upon to realize it with and in me—now, before it is too late—and with your whole heart and mind and body and soul gathered up and blazing in one flame of love.

I am the furnace of love you must burn away in and become one with; I am the passion that you must let kill and rebirth you; I am the Child waiting to be born when your feminine and masculine powers fuse in the core of your heart and love is born forever, radiant and invincible in you and as you. Every atom of the universe and every being is in me and I am in them, and all things are being drawn to me and in me up to the One in glory. This is the truth of all things and the hope and the beauty and the glory without end. Believe me, trust me, love me, enter me and discover yourself and act as me-in-you to transform all the conditions of the world into the Kingdom. As one world ends, be the beginning in me of the new world.

Part One

The Historical Christ

You have come with knowledge
That you might rebuke their forgetfullness.
You have come with recollection
That you might rebuke their ignorance . . .
You walked in mud
And your garments were not soiled,
And you have not been buried in their filth
And you have not been caught.

FIRST APOCALYPSE OF JAMES

Here is the Truth who does not lie.
Here is the One whom the Authorities fear when they see him.
Here is the One who confuses those in power.
The Authorities ask, "Who are you and where do you come from?"
They do not know the truth because they are the enemies of the truth.

ACTS OF THOMAS

Introduction

▩ ▩ ▩

Who was Jesus the man and what connection is there between the historical person and the Cosmic Christ? These are the two central questions that confront serious seekers now. They are, of course, connected. If Jesus is the world-teacher that Christianity and the Christian mystic tradition know him to be, then the form his ministry on earth took, the way he lived and expressed himself, the forces he summoned, and the causes he fought for are extremely important, because they show the movement of the Christ-force in time and give us clear clues as to how to act with that force now in the terrible problems that threaten the survival of the human race.

An inadequate, distanced, sentimental vision of who Christ is and what Christ stood for will limit the potentially all-transforming force of the Christ in history. We cannot afford that now, when everything depends on whether sufficient numbers of people can first be awakened to their innate divine truth and then empowered to act in the world to preserve the planet. How they should act in the name of Christ is known most clearly by a definite vision of what Christ stood for in his life and how he acted.

Many Christians are frightened by the new historical criticism that over the last sixty years has revolutionized our vision of the historical Christ. Its forensic, sometimes fiercely skeptical, methods of inquiry have challenged many of the most cherished myths and legends of the Christian faith, such as the Virgin Birth, the Last Supper, and the historical accuracy of the Gospels. This is not a disaster, however; it can be seen as a liberation—a liberation from manipulation and hysteria and religious superstition, a liberation, if you like, of the Gospel of Jesus from the Jesus of the Gospels, and so a freeing-up of a wholly new vision of Jesus himself, and our relationship to him. The Jesus that emerges from the "myth-cleansing process" of the best of the modern explorers of this field is not in any way a "diminished" figure with his majesty and mystery stripped from him: he is, in many crucial ways, a far more challenging, unnerving, and revolutionary guide and teacher than anything pious legend has made of him.

The Historical Jesus
and His Message of the Kingdom

❖ ❖ ❖

Historical criticism has proved, conclusively, that the Gospels are to be read not as Spirit-inspired, faithful eye-witness accounts of Jesus' life but as carefully sculpted *versions* of that life, arranged to suit or promote different spiritual interests, personalities, and factions within the dramatic years of early Christianity. The Gospels are neither directly inspired divine documents nor straight-forward historical records; neither divine revelations directly inspired by God nor eye-witness accounts written by people who had known Jesus and wanted only to report clearly what they had experienced with him. Written in the last third of the first century, they express and condense the traditions of different early Christian communities and were put into their current form slowly over a period of three hundred years.

The complexity that emerges from such an enterprise should not surprise any historian of comparative religion or biographer of a major religious figure. The factors that shape the narrative of a world-transforming religious life are always extremely various and rich, even contradictory. And someone as disturbingly radical as Christ, and as powerful in his actions, presence, and mystical legacy, could only excite differing interpretations, some of them tinged by denial or religious exaggeration or the needs of a particular group of "disciples" to see or interpret his life and message in a way that suited their claims to power.

What *is* surprising, as recent writers are starting to point out, is not how little we can know about the historical Christ but how much. If we cannot always know exactly what he said or did, we can know the kinds of things he said and did. A profound synthesis is now emerging as to exactly who Christ was in his social and political context, and what kind of teacher he was. When this vision is absorbed into Christian practice it will revolutionize everything about Christianity. It will not destroy it, as scandalized conservative critics claim, but renovate and reinspire it, in a way that, I believe, restores the full radical passion and revolutionary power of Christ's real path—one that combines the deepest mystical absorption in the divine with the most absolute and selfless work for justice and compassion in the world.

In other words, the essential Christ—the mystical, practical Christ, the one who dared not only to see and know the divine and its love in full truth but also to act in every arena to see that that truth became real in its full subversive splendor—will come again to be the inspiration of those who take the Christ-path. Christ's challenge to everyone—to enter into living communion with the Father-Mother, to pour out every skill and energy in a passion of adherence to the truths of that love and that fire in reality—will only grow in power as the courage, intelligence, and unstinting enactment of the sacred laws of unity and compassion of the historical Christ become ever-clearer.

Such clarity can only deepen the wonder of those who love Christ and increase the focus of their energies on the "actual"—on changing abusive relations of power and trying to realize the Kingdom on the earth. To follow Christ, the new vision of Christ makes clear, means to abandon all safeties and securities except those rooted in God, to subject not merely the self but also the world to ruthless analysis, to become clear about the deforming and betraying nature of power in all its forms, and to dedicate one's life to standing for justice and compassion in an uncompassionate and unjust world. Without millions of beings willing to make such a leap into authentic love, how can the forces that are destroying nature be reversed, or a bearable and livable life for the billions of beings suffering from actual and psychic poverty be created?

Trying to create an alternative Kingdom of love in the night of Roman patriarchy, the man Jesus of Nazareth has everything to teach us now. We have a great deal to learn not only from his humility and fearlessness but also from his analysis of the divine life of the Kingdom and of the nature of the world and of how to overcome evil within it and represent the healing transforming powers of love. And we have everything to learn, too, from the mysterious and poignant passion of his life itself—the life that burned itself away in service to the truth of divine love and justice and the potential glory of human beings who lived in dynamic harmony with them both.

◈ ◈ ◈

What then has contemporary historical criticism of the Gospels revealed of the life and teaching of the "real" Jesus? Many comforting myths have to be surrendered, along with the belief in the total veracity of the Gospels themselves. Jesus was probably not born in Bethlehem but in Nazareth; many modern scholars also believed he was almost certainly neither the firstborn nor the only child of Joseph and Mary. He did not belong to a learned middle class; he was a "tekton," an artisan maker of wooden products like doors and frames, at the lower end of the peasant class, who may have had on occasions to beg for his living and who came from a family who probably owned no land.

Modern scholarship also makes clear that there is no firm evidence to suggest that Jesus thought of himself as the Messiah, or as the "unique" Son of God; the only title we can safely say he gave himself is Son of Man (as in Matthew 11:19). He likely used this generic term to identify himself with those he was addressing and to emphasize that he shared with them a common destiny and destitution. The Jesus we see in the New Testament and Gnostic Gospels is not always omnipotent or omniscient, and does not think of himself as completely "divine."

The Savior Icon, in other words, is a later "inspiration" of the early Christian church, reeling under the impact of Jesus' life and of the transmission of his mystical force and essence that continued after the crucifixion and resurrection; it has nothing to do with Jesus' own vision of himself and of his mission. Jesus' self-understanding did not include thinking and speaking of himself as the Son of God, and his message was not about believing in him.

Knowing Jesus in this way challenges the beliefs not only of all "fundamentalist" churches but also of all those who place emphasis on Jesus Christ as the unique and all-powerful savior; the historical Jesus never claimed for himself such an honor, never saw himself in such inflated and exclusive terms, and never interpreted his crucifixion as a sacrifice for the sins of the world. Such interpretations represent the visions of later followers and have nothing authentic about them (except the wonder and enthusiasm that prompted their evolution in the first place).

It is also quite clear that Jesus never intended to establish a new set of religious dogmas or to inaugurate a church or found a new religion. All of the most reliable modern scholars and commentaries agree on one crucial point: Jesus was a Jew of his time, one of several charismatic healers in Palestine in the first century of Roman occupation. Jesus did not propose the scrapping or diminishing of Judaism in favor of a new vision (his own). He criticized Judaism with the passion of one who loved and honored it and from within an iconoclastic tradition of Judaism itself, the tradition of the prophets, the outspoken critics of political and religious power such as Isaiah, Joel, Jeremiah, and Amos.

Such a vision has the great advantage of seeing Jesus in the sociopolitical context of his time and of making us concentrate not so much on his human or divine status but on what we can see he actually said and did. This is not the scholarly distancing exercise that some might think: seeing how Jesus reacted to the crisis of violence and political and religious oppression in his time helps us to interpret how the Christ-force might act in ours, and with what passion and focus. Paying attention to how Jesus acted and in what context and to what he really said—and not on the dogmas surrounding his divinity—can have the paradoxical effect of making us take him and his actions and words even more seriously and, above all, and in the highest, most urgent sense, practically.

The Jesus we meet in the pages of historical scholars Robert Funk, Dominic Crossan, and Marcus Borg, among others, is a figure whose unwavering minute attention to all the deformities of power in the actual world around him and whose creative responses to his time's desolation can only focus and inspire our attempts to renovate our own era. Knowing and feeling this gives a wholly fresh element of urgency to the thirteenth-century Franciscan mystic Bonaventure's wonderful celebration of Jesus the man: "The manifold wisdom of God shines from him and in him as in a mirror containing the beauty of all forms and lights, and as in a book in which all things are written according to the deep secrets of God."

We cannot know what stages or visions or experiences led to the overwhelming enlightenment that illumines the whole of Jesus' teachings and life: we do not have any reliable records of his inner spiritual development; the Christian mystical tradition has preserved no accounts of the different aspects and ordeals of his awakening (perhaps because it came to assume Jesus' divinity from the start of his life so that he did not need to awaken); the apocryphal and Gnostic material that we do have about Jesus' childhood presents him unhelpfully as a frightening, frankly incredible, prodigy of insight and power from the beginning. Jesus himself—as far as we can tell—spoke rarely, if ever, of his own experiences; it was an inherent part of his message that actions and "presence" should speak louder than any words or metaphysical explanations, however inspiring.

Nevertheless, it is clear that at the heart of Jesus' life and teachings lay a continuous, living mystical experience of the universe ablaze in the glory of God and of his own (and everyone else's) inherent identity with that glory, and of the Kingdom that glory emanated on earth—a living, actual realm of adoration, ecstasy, charity, and radical empowerment that was open to anyone who dared risk every form of comfort, social status, and position to attain, enshrine, and enact it. Jesus saw and knew that the entire creation was alive with Godhead; he saw and knew that at the core of human consciousness lay a spark of divine consciousness in which the glory of the Godhead is always reflected and which is one with the Godhead; he saw and knew that in the mind of God this world was already transfigured into a living mirror of divine mercy and justice. For Jesus, it is clear, the entire task of the human being lay in living the life that would allow entry into so vast a vision and permit its force and intensity and passion for transformation to flow into "ordinary" reality, so that everything could be changed—and changed utterly—to reflect the hidden purposes of God and the hidden eternal laws of the Kingdom. For Jesus, the glory of being human was this chance to cocreate and coparticipate with God in the realization in actual terms of that Kingdom, which surrounded and infused all things with its potential truth. It was for that purpose that a merciful, all-loving God had endowed human beings with the most extraordinary powers and possibilities, which Jesus understood had to be released if the divine plan for the world was to unfold in its full splendor.

It cannot be emphasized too often that the vision of God that Jesus derived from this inner experience has very little to do with the gloomy, pathologically angry judge, which is one facet of the Jehovah of the Old Testament. And nothing whatever to do with the God that has survived in many of the Christian churches—a God who demands terrible sacrifices and deprivations in the name of purification, and who constantly "rewards" heroic acts of submission and self-denial. Jesus' God is a God of final mercy and forgiveness; the glory Jesus saw and knew in God was a glory not merely of omnipotent power and knowledge but, above and beyond that, a glory of love, a love so boundless, so overflowing, and so continually self-outpouring in every way that for Jesus it was a blasphemy to speak of it in narrow or judgmental terms.

The parable that most clearly reveals the originality and daring of Jesus' vision of the love of God is that of the Prodigal Son. It is important to remember the context in which Jesus tells it; "Then drew near unto him all the publicans and sinners for to hear him. And the Pharisees and scribes murmured saying, This man receiveth sinners, and eateth with them" (Luke 15:1–2). Before plunging into the long and elaborate narrative of the parable itself, Jesus tries to open the consciousness of the Pharisees and scribes (and to comfort the publicans and sinners) by speaking of God's great joy in the recovery of "sinners": "What man of you, having a hundred sheep, if he lose one of them, doth not leave the ninety and nine in the wilderness and go after that which is lost, until he find it? And when he hath found it, he layeth it on his shoulders, rejoicing. And when he cometh home, he calleth together his friends and neighbors, saying unto them, Rejoice with me; for I have found my sheep which was lost. I say unto you, that likewise joy shall be in heaven over one sinner that repenteth, more than over ninety and nine just persons, which need no repentance."

Already Jesus is announcing the supreme theme of his message to humanity—that God's love is extravagant beyond measure, infinitely tender-hearted, and far more ready to forgive and celebrate than to judge. After all, the shepherd does not leave the stray sheep to its fate but leaves the ninety-nine others to go out into the wilderness to look for it. God never abandons those who abandon him, the Father does not simply "wait" patiently; his love is passionate, and urgent; he goes out in search of the "lost" one.

Everyone who sins and abandons God, Jesus is implying, prompts God in his burning love to "go looking" for them. God's mercy is not passive; it is restlessly active in its desire to restore and renovate and renew. Surrounded on the one hand by "outcasts"—sinners and publicans—and on the other by so-called "righteous" and "arbiters of justice"—the "Pharisees and scribes"— Jesus is reminding both of the essential character of God, and of that divine mercy that transcends both sin and righteousness, that exists in a dimension of absolute love beyond the reach (and understanding) of either.

Jesus continues his exploration of God's mercy and joy by using a feminine example: "Either what woman having ten pieces of silver, if she lose one piece, doth not light a candle, and sweep the house, and seek diligently till she find it? And when she hath found it, she calleth her friends and her neighbors together, saying, Rejoice with me; for I have found the piece I had lost." Jesus' use of a feminine image here is not merely to "domesticate" what he is saying and make it more actual, even homely; it is, I believe, to point subtly to the maternal nature of God, to the "Mother" in the "Father." God is shepherd and housewife, masculine and feminine; the love of the Father, Jesus knows, has a maternal tenderness, and a loving, maternal anxiety.

Just as in the previous example of the shepherd rejoicing when he has found his stray sheep, Jesus has the woman who has found her missing silver piece invite all of her neighbors to a feast of celebration; the recovery of a "sinner" and the restoration of a lost soul to health is not merely an affair between human beings and God, but an occasion for rejoicing for a whole society and world. All beings (and this includes the Pharisees and scribes who hide behind "righteousness" and "judgment") are called to participate in the effulgence of God's mercy, and to bathe in its living fiery waters: to participate in God's all-inclusive joy is authentic life. A healthy world, Jesus is saying, would be one in which "sinners" and "outcasts" were not treated with scorn, judgment, and exclusion, but one in which every effort was made to help and "recover" them and draw them back into the living world of love and communion. Such effort would mirror, in human terms, the ceaseless effort of the love of God himself to help and "recover" all beings.

It is at this moment, with the ground of his vision prepared, and God's mercy and concern invoked and praised, that Jesus tells the parable of the Prodigal Son, in which all of his startling themes about the Father's infinite love are interwoven:

> And he said, A certain man had two sons: And the younger of them said to his father, Father, give me the portion of goods that falleth to me. And he divided unto them his living. And not many days after the younger son gathered all together, and took his journey into a far country, and there wasted his substance with riotous living. And when he had spent all, there arose a mighty famine in that land; and he began to be in want. And he went and joined himself to a citizen of that country; and he sent him into his fields to feed swine. And he would fain have filled his belly with the husks that the swine did eat: and no man gave unto him.
>
> And when he came to himself, he said, How many hired servants of my father's have bread enough and to spare, and I perish with hunger! I will arise and go to my father, and will say unto him, Father, I have sinned against heaven, and before thee, And am no more worthy to be called thy son: make me as one of thy hired servants.
>
> And he arose, and came to his father. But when he was yet a great way off, his father saw him, and had compassion, and ran, and fell on his neck, and kissed him. And the son said unto him, Father, I have sinned against heaven, and in thy sight, and am no more worthy to be called thy son. But the father said to his servants, Bring forth the best robe, and put it on him; and put a ring on his hand, and shoes on his feet: And bring hither the fatted calf, and kill it; and let us eat, and be merry: For this my son was dead, and is alive again; he was lost, and is found. And they began to be merry.
>
> Now his elder son was in the field: and as he came and drew nigh to the house, he heard music and dancing. And he called one of

the servants, and asked what these things meant. And he said unto him, Thy brother is come; and thy father hath killed the fatted calf, because he hath received him safe and sound. And he was angry, and would not go in: therefore came his father out, and entreated him.

And he answering said to his father, Lo, these many years do I serve thee, neither transgressed I at any time thy commandment: and yet thou never gavest me a kid, that I might make merry with my friends: But as soon as this thy son was come, which hath devoured thy living with harlots, thou hast killed for him the fatted calf. And he said unto him, Son, thou art ever with me, and all that I have is thine. It was meet that we should make merry, and be glad: for this thy brother was dead, and is alive again; and was lost, and is found (Luke 15:11–32).

What strikes any reader who meditates on this parable for long is the extremely unpatriarchal behavior of the father. His younger son demands his share of the inheritance (which in contemporary terms was shocking, tantamount, in fact, to wishing his father dead): not only does the father not upbraid him, he says nothing and hands it over, respecting the freedom of his son's choice and putting his family's wealth at risk. Then, when the father "saw" his battered and repentant son returning from "a great way off," he didn't stay where he was, waiting for his son to return to him and beg his forgiveness; he forgot all "patriarchal" dignity, any pain he might feel, and, almost shamelessly, "had compassion, and ran, and fell on his neck, and kissed him." He didn't wait for his son to embrace him, or even to apologize; with a full heart, he overrode all "blame" and enfolds him in a free and wild embrace. This "Father" is nothing like the stern and furious Jehovah of the Old Testament; nothing in his character clings to "righteousness" or "judgment"; the essence and core of his whole nature is compassion, a compassion that sees immediately that the son has judged himself by his abandonment of his father's love and by his terrible suffering in strange lands, and needs now only to be restored to his old "position" and essential dignity to be healed. The only authority this father claims is that of a love that desires only to bless.

At first the son is still too lost in his own guilt to be able to understand or even imagine the depth and all-embracing abandon of his father's forgiveness. Jesus beautifully illustrates here how the "sinful" soul, because of its own shame (which it brought upon itself by forgetting the laws of God and its own dignity), cannot comprehend the wildness of God's love, and still, half-consciously, hides from it in self-contempt. The son says, "I am no more worthy to be called thy son." The father doesn't say anything here; he acts; his compassion overflows in extravagant acts of welcome and blessing. The son is prepared to be treated as a "hired servant": the father calls for the robe of a distinguished guest. The son no longer feels worthy to be called "son": the father calls for a ring to be put on his finger, a ring of inheritance, and shoes to be brought for his feet. For God, every soul is sacred and blessed and always God's child; the soul may forget its home and inheritance and identity, but God never forgets and acts in thousands of secret and overt ways to remind the soul of its real nature, and rewards the slightest movement of "return" with lavish displays of honor and recognition.

Just like the shepherd and housewife, when they found what they had lost, the father in the parable now calls for a great feast to be made in his son's honor. "And bring hither the fatted calf, and kill it; and let us eat, and be merry." God wants the whole universe to rejoice with him when one of his children returns to him; his joy spills over into and illuminates the entire creation, creating ever-more abundant life.

At this point in the story, Jesus turns his attention to the elder brother, the righteous one, who had always been a "good child" and who, he reveals now, also needs healing. Just as the "scribes and Pharisees" hide behind rules and laws and their own sense of superior righteousness, and so miss the wildness of God's love for all beings and cannot participate in its unconditional forgiveness and rapture, so the elder brother is furious at the treatment his reprobate brother is now receiving. He points out to his father that he has always followed exactly what his father told him "and yet thou never gavest me a kid, that I might make merry with my friends." The elder son is enclosed in a "religious" world of law, responsibility, obligation, comparison; his soul is not free to love with his father's love or to be compassionate and know compassion's joy. He is trapped in the shadow of "righteousness" just as, Jesus is implying, the "scribes and Pharisees" are.

Just as he does not judge his younger son but embraces him, so the father does not judge his elder son but tries to open to him the wonder and passion of his own love. "And he said unto him, Son [in the Greek "tekton"—a tender diminutive, meaning baby or child], thou art ever with me, and all that I have is thine." This "all" means not only all the father's power and possessions but also "all" the glories of the father's inner being. The father is saying to his elder son, "You have in you everything that I have in me so you, too, can experience the great healing joy I am experiencing; you, too, can live in the sun of unconditional compassion."

The father then continues, "It was meet that we should make merry, and be glad; for this brother was dead, and is alive again; and was lost, and is found." The father has tried to heal the pain of his younger son by restoring him to the dignity of "sonship" with great love and happiness; the father now tries to heal the subtler but just as profound and limiting anguish of his elder son by revealing to him the true nature of the Kingdom of God—that boundless compassion is its core, and that "making merry," divine festivity, is its most accurate as well as its loveliest expression.

Jesus himself constantly expressed his love of beings and life in feasts, and again and again spoke of the Kingdom as a feast or banquet to which God was inviting everyone. In the parable of the Prodigal Son, Jesus demonstrates, with customary psychological brilliance, that this Kingdom has two main enemies—that "sin" that swerves the soul from the glory of its essential nature, and that man-made, limited "righteousness" that traps beings in a judgmental self-regard, which forbids any participation in God's limitless joy. Both belong to the realm of illusion; the reality is feast, the glory of compassion, the Kingdom on fire with the festivity of celebration. This reality is the only one, Jesus is saying, that is worth our attention because it is the reality of God's nature, it is the true Father's shining.

In giving this version of the "true" Father's mercy and compassion to an audience of "sinners" and "Pharisees," Jesus was symbolically, and with tremendous mystical courage, trying to heal the essential illness of his—and our—"patriarchal" culture, its fear of a God created in its own fierce, cruel, savage, punitive image. This "projection" had—and has—terrifying power and keeps humanity agonized, depressed, and obsessed by "rules," "laws," and "regulations"; it is this projection, after all, that has justified all forms of patriarchal hierarchy and systems of "purity" and "exclusion."

Jesus' vision of the Father, as the parable of the Prodigal Son makes clear, has nothing to do with the distant, all judging, vengeful, and terrifying Jehovah figure of the Old Testament, that terrible Father that kept the "publicans and sinners" convinced of their worthlessness and the "scribes and Pharisees" cowering behind a facade of frightened holiness. Jesus' Father is the Father met in deepest mystical experience, a Father who is also a Mother, whose nature is loving beyond all human imagination, whose profoundest longing is not for judgment but for the festive reconciliation and harmony between beings birthed from love. It is this Father that Jesus calls, with overwhelmed love, "Abba," Daddy: it is to this Father and his infinite tenderness that Jesus' whole life is dedicated; it is this Father to which Jesus wants to awaken the whole of his world. It is this vision of a Father who is also feminine that increasingly molds Jesus' own spiritual nature, drawing him deeper and deeper into sacrificial love, and makes of Jesus himself a supreme example of divine human balance between "masculine" and "feminine," a Father-Mother himself, the antithesis and radiant enemy of patriarchy in his every word, gesture, and loving movement.

For Jesus, it is clear, what was essential was to awaken to the extremity of the Father's love, the extremity of his passion for all beings and things, and the extremity, too, of his desire to see the world transformed by his holy power and in his eternal name. Any philosophy or custom however sanctified by tradition, any system of power or influence that prevented the experience of this love and blocked its expression in all the arenas of life, was destroying the plan of love and rebelling sadly or demonically against the truth of the Kingdom.

This truth of divine love and forgiveness—and the challenge to enact it with ever-greater focus and fervor—is not located by Jesus in the future. It is clear to most scholars now that Jesus was not an eschatological prophet preaching continually about an imminent end of the world: the passages in the Gospel of Matthew that deal with the Last Judgment are almost certainly later redactions.

For Jesus, the Kingdom was a present mystical reality, the only authentic reality to which all other loves and actions are to be directed; its splendor is always all around us, and only our blindness and driven desperate attachments to all the various forms of conventional wisdom prevent us from seeing the wonder of it, living in it, and living it out so that others can catch flame from its fire. In Logion 113 of the Gospel of Thomas, "His disciples said to him: 'When will the Kingdom come?' And Jesus answered 'It will not come by waiting for it. It will not be a matter of saying, "Here it is" or, "There it is." Rather, the Kingdom of the Father is spread out upon the earth, and men do not see it.' "

The door into the Kingdom—into a unitive, interconnected relationship of divine human charity with all things and beings and into the life of total service and celebration of others that must flow from it—lies always open. Again and again, as in the parable of the Prodigal Son, Jesus makes clear that reality is a banquet to which everyone is always invited—a wedding banquet at which the marriage between the spirit and matter, earth and heaven, reason and passion, intellect and divine love is always continually being celebrated in a blaze of divine beauty and glory.

It is clear, too, that Jesus knew that participation in this Kingdom of feast is open, without exception, to everyone. The universe is a sacred marriage between God and matter, spirit and flesh, an entirely sacred holy emanation of divine love; the destiny of human life is to live this sacred marriage here on earth, with as complete and compassionate a consciousness as possible.

In Logion 3 of the Gospel of Thomas, Jesus is reported as saying, "If those who lead you say to you, 'See the Kingdom is in the sky,' then the birds of the sky will precede you. If they say to you, 'It is in the sea,' then the fish will precede you. Rather the Kingdom is inside you and outside you. When you come to know yourselves, then you will become known, and you will realize that it is you who are the sons of the living Father. But if you will not know yourselves, you dwell in poverty, and it is you who are that poverty."

In this fiercely radical statement, Jesus is dismissing all past religious attempts to locate the Kingdom of God outside time, in space or in "heaven." It is these well-meaning but ignorant designations of God's presence to some "mystic other where" that has kept humanity enslaved to depression and all the games of depression. The Kingdom is not in the sky or the sea; if it is, then the "birds" and "fish" will "get there" first, and that is obviously an absurdity: in Jesus' overwhelming experience, the Kingdom is now, is here, is the inmost heart-core of reality itself, the fire of love and justice blazing at the heart of all things and beings. "The Kingdom is inside you," Jesus is telling all of us; it is our inmost consciousness, that divine consciousness in us that is our real consciousness, which, one with the Godhead, intuitively sees and knows the real as the play and work of love; looking for it anywhere else is to wander in darkness.

Yet Jesus doesn't simply say, "The Kingdom is inside you." Here, in the Gospel of Thomas, he reminds the human being that the Kingdom is also—and crucially—"outside."

Jesus' teaching works here on many different levels at once. On the highest mystical level, he is pointing to the obliteration of all categories of "inner and outer," "inside" and "outside," that occur once the unitive consciousness has been realized and the universe is experienced as the dance of divine consciousness and love; in such a consciousness, as the mystics of every tradition testify, what in ordinary consciousness is perceived as "outside" is known as one with the heart and in the heart; all things, without boundary or exception, are known to be alive in the flame of self-presence.

The Kingdom is, however, "outside you" in another way that is essential to Jesus' teaching. It is "outside you" not only because the whole universe is dancing in the fire of what is also inside our inmost consciousness, but also because the Kingdom is in the real, and must be seen in the relationships between beings in the real; and because not to see the Kingdom in the real is to be narcissistic and absorbed only with one's own spiritual progress (which is, in that case, neither authentically spiritual nor real progress). To wake up to the Kingdom "inside," then, is to wake up to the potential presence of the Kingdom in all of reality, to observe its hidden laws in all things, to watch for its signs, to encourage its increasing manifestation in the actual, and to participate in its creation through a dedication of the whole being to enacting its love and justice and mercy at every moment in the real.

For Jesus, mystical reality is not a private, inward affair only; once the soul or heart is awake to the truth of God's glory—and to the glory of the relationship of total love that God is offering everyone—then everything in the entire being has to be offered to that glory so that it can be changed into it, and so that the "external" world can partake more and more of its truth and reflect its laws. An authentic awakening, Jesus is saying (and says again and again elsewhere and proves by the tireless service of his life), has to begin by a purification of consciousness but must end, if it is to be fertile, with the fertility of the Sacred Marriage, in unstinting attention to the potential glory of "what is outside" and to a continual attempt to flood what is "outside" with its own innate glory so that all its structures and relations can be transfigured. This flooding of all aspects and structures of the real with glory is what Jesus undertook in his own life, and it is what he demands of everyone who has come into the Kingdom.

The reward of such a gigantic enterprise, Jesus makes clear, is nothing less than participating in the consciousness that he himself lived in—a conscious, continual recognition of inmost connection with God.

As Jesus says in Logion 3, "When you come to know yourselves, then you will become known." He means here that when a person awakens to their full divine human personhood, to the Kingdom within and without them, he or she simultaneously awakens to the divine ground that sustains and infuses at every level that personhood. As Mohammed said, "He who knows himself, knows his Lord." "Knows," in other words, beyond thought or dogma or any possible formulation, that "he and the Lord are one," or, as Jesus put it, "I and the Father are one." This knowing of oneself as divine and of being known (and knowing that one is being known) by the divine itself is the real birth into the Kingdom, the true and high initiation of life, the goal of all things, and the beginning of conscious divine human life in which "you will realize that it is you who are the sons [and daughters] of the living Father (Mother)." This conscious life in God is one of unimaginable wealth and abundance and energy and unwavering humble recognition of the sacredness of all things and beings, of the Kingdom "inside" and "outside." Jesus does not here claim any uniqueness for himself; he implicitly places himself as one among many other sons and daughters of God. Everyone is invited to become their complete self in a direct, unbroken, unmediated relationship of "sonship" or "daughtership" with the living and eternal Father; everyone, without exception, is invited to the birth, to the feast, to the marriage.

Characteristically, Jesus makes sure that his listeners understand the high stakes involved. "If you will not know yourselves," he says, "you dwell in poverty." Not to know the Kingdom "inside" and "outside" is to live in a blind darkness and confusion and misery and anxiety, which is "the poverty" of what Jesus is speaking about. It is to live not merely the unexamined but the unillumined life, and so hardly to be alive at all. The directness with which Jesus says, "And if you will not know yourself" makes it clear that, like all authentic mystical teachers, Jesus places the responsibility for the "real life" squarely on the shoulders of each human being: he does not claim to be the savior who will initiate everyone into this "abundant life": he is the sign that such a life is possible, but the work and sacrifice and passionate search for awakening have to be chosen and undertaken individually by each person. Each person has to will new life, and to go on and on choosing it to be transformed; every grace and divine help will be given, but the choice is always ours and ours alone. Divine love will not force anyone to enter or realize the Kingdom.

What Jesus is trying to wake us up to is the depth of our own individual responsibility to be a flame of the fire of the Kingdom. He ends by saying, "But if you will not know yourselves, you dwell in poverty, and it is you who are that poverty." If we do not choose to transform ourselves, then we will not simply live in misery and anxiety: we will "be" misery and anxiety, spreading their toxic destruction through all our thoughts and actions, and so actively preventing the wealth of the Kingdom from flaming out everywhere and healing the "poverty" of being.

As Jesus rails in the Book of Thomas the Contender:

Woe to you, godless ones, who have no hope, who rely on things
that will not happen!
Woe to you within the fire that burns in you, for it is insatiable!

Woe to you, because of the wheel that turns in your minds!
Your mind is deranged on account of the burning that is in you . . .
The darkness rose for you like the light because you surrendered
your freedom for servitude! You darkened your hearts and surrendered
your thoughts to folly, and you filled your thoughts with the smoke of
the fire that is in you.

Woe to you who dwell in error, heedless that the light of the sun
which judges and looks down upon the all will circle around all things
so as to enslave the enemies. You do not even notice the moon, how
by day and night it looks down, looking at the bodies of your
slaughters!

For Jesus, however, the "poverty" of the world and of the consciousness
of most of the people in it—the "godless ones who have no hope"—is not a
fixed absolute, not an irremediable consequence of some original disaster.
Jesus, in fact, never speaks, either in the Gospels or in the Gnostic fragments
that have come down to us, of original sin; his teaching, contrary to the teachings that have been derived from him and used to manipulate frightened followers, has—for all its realism and sober awareness—nothing whatever to do
with a denigration of human nature. For Jesus, every human being, however
lost or destructive, is still innately divine, innately capable, through grace, of
being divinized; the Kingdom is the final reality, not sin, or inevitable evil and
failure. Everything depends on the choice of the individual soul as to whether
the Kingdom shall become manifest in it and in the whole being or not. This
relentless emphasis in Jesus' authentic teaching on individual choice is what
makes it demanding: the doctrine of "original sin," after all, can offer a kind
of depressive comfort to those too passive or too despairing or too lazy to invite and pursue awakening. Jesus, by telling us that the Kingdom is everywhere and that all human beings are given the chance to enter it if they work
hard enough to transform themselves and are prepared to undergo all the
necessary ordeals of initiation, implicitly derides every human comfort in de-
feat, every neurotic embrace of limitation, every philosophy, secular or religious, that in any way diminishes the potential glory of the fully awakened
divine human life.

Jesus is always aware of how improbable his vision must sound to those
who have no idea of the reality and power of the Spirit, and again and again
he tries, in teachings and parables, to help his listeners understand how what
seems impossible to the human mind or will on its own is possible, even easy,

when God's grace is invoked. To an all-loving God, whose one desire for humanity is to see it realize its divine identity and origin and transform itself and the world it lives in into a garden of divine love and justice, nothing is impossible; God's Kingdom has an astonishing hidden strength of self-propagation, once its existence has been embraced and its power accepted and unleashed. This Jesus tells us explicitly in the parable of the Mustard Seed (Mark 4:30–32):

"And Jesus said, With what can we compare the Kingdom of the God, or what parable shall we use for it? It is like a grain of mustard seed, which, when sown upon the ground, is the smallest of seeds on earth: yet when it is sown it grows up and becomes the greatest of all shrubs and puts forth large branches, so that the birds of the air can make nests in its shade."

As in all the authentic parables of Jesus, his language works in several, sometimes contradictory, dimensions at once. On the most obvious level, Jesus is speaking in this parable about the vast hidden power of the Spirit, of the "tiny seed" of Godhead within each of us, which, once "sown" (really claimed and begun to be made conscious through prayer and meditation and service), grows rapidly and becomes a large "tree" capable of sheltering and nurturing others. The reality of the world and of the worldly mind denies the reality of the Spirit, because it cannot be seen; but, invisibly, its effects grow very fast, until the whole of external reality also is transformed, and what seemed a tiny "seed" has become a large, vibrant, powerful "tree."

What makes the parable startling, however, is its subtext—one that would have been recognizable immediately to Jesus' listeners in first-century Palestine. In his *Natural History,* the Roman author Pliny the Elder wrote: "Mustard . . . with its pungent taste and fiery effect is extremely beneficent for the health. It grows entirely wild, though it is improved by being transplanted; but on the other hand, when it has once been sown, it is scarcely possible to get the place free of it, as the seed when it falls germinates at once." So, when Jesus uses the mustard seed as the symbol of the Kingdom, he is pointing also to the way in which opening to the realities and powers of the Kingdom can dissolve the structures and orders of "ordinary" reality. As Dominic Crossan tells us in *Jesus: A Revolutionary Biography:* "The mustard plant is dangerous even when domesticated in the garden and is deadly when growing wild in the grain fields. And those nesting birds, which might strike us as charming, represented to ancient farmers a permanent danger to the seed and grain. The point, in other words, is not just that the mustard plant starts as a proverbially small seed and grows into a shrub of three, four, or even more feet in height. It is that it tends to take over where it is not wanted, that it tends to get out of control where it is not wanted, and it tends to attract birds within cultivated areas, where they are not particularly desired. And that, Jesus said, was what the Kingdom was like. Like a pungent shrub with dangerous take-over properties."

In the same parable Jesus is at once celebrating the miraculous power of the Spirit to grow in reality from humble beginnings and also pointing out the potentially radical, even destructive, nature of that growth. Once the power of the Kingdom is unleashed in the world, all the world's tidy symmetries and con-trolling orders, all man-made barriers, demarcations, and socially convenient distinctions are menaced. The radiant anarchy of the Spirit, whose laws of growth are divine and follow the law of divine extravagance and abundance, cannot be contained within the anxiety-driven constructions of humanity; in-troduced into them, they will all be overturned, disrupted, and eventually transformed beyond recognition. Once the splendor and mystery of the real-ity of the Spirit have been acknowledged, once its law of love has been seen in all its glory, then the world's games start to seem absurd and all the world's passion for control and security begins to be undermined by the experience of a wild, original freedom, the freedom of the common-as-muck mustard seed.

It is part of Jesus' brilliance that he would use a wholly "unreligious" image like mustard seed to try to describe the mystical core of his vision. The Spirit is both more powerful and more raw and ordinary and robust than the fragile, vain concoctions of the world; its force is the force of authentic divine nature, of nature without human mask or control.

By using such imagery, Jesus makes it clear that the Kingdom is not in any sense and under any circumstance either an elitist concept or designed only for an elite; it is a "mustard seed," after all, and can be seen anywhere, if only our eyes are open and attuned. And the power of the Kingdom is not, Jesus is saying, a refined, abstract, "holy" removed power; it is as natural as mustard seed, as pungent and fiery and wild, and as impossible to contain within our tidy dogmas and plans. Its natural abundance—the abundance of that life that Jesus claimed in St. John's Gospel he had come to give—is a nat-ural glory, dangerous to all snobbish, elitist, "unnatural" ways of thinking and ordering reality.

This inherent subversiveness of the Kingdom and the Spirit is illus-trated by another parable, that of the Leaven (found in Matthew, Luke, and the Gospel of Thomas, and considered by nearly all scholars to be authentic). The version in Matthew 13:33 reads: "The Kingdom of heaven is like leaven which a woman took and hid in three measures of flour, till it was all leavened."

Judaism regarded leaven as a symbol of corruption, while unleavened bread stood for what is holy; Jesus is here reversing all the accepted values of his world. To make the Kingdom of heaven "leaven," which has to be hidden (and by a woman!), implicitly mocks all conventional notions of the "holy" and "unholy" as well as rooting the business of the Kingdom firmly in the most ordinary, even banal, activities. The work of the Spirit, Jesus is implying, is everywhere, in all things, and not merely in those things that men (and they usually were men) designated holy and valuable: it is a work that begins by being hidden and mysterious, like the work of leaven in bread, but in the end, as when the bread is leavened and edible, the invisible presence and power of God's grace becomes obvious.

Jesus is also implying, in the dramatic structure of the parable, that the Kingdom and its values have to be "smuggled" into reality; they are too extreme, and too challenging to be brought in directly. With the discretion and cunning of a woman, the Spirit must be hidden like leaven in the unleavened bread of ordinary life and left to work out its own purposes. The woman's work is to hide the leaven; divine grace and power will do the rest. The result will be a transformation of consciousness and reality into "risen bread"—the life, the bread, of the Kingdom. The startling language and imagery of the parable show that for Jesus such transformation takes place outside all conventional categories and systems of thought, all man-made beliefs about society or "purity" or "holiness," with the mysterious, unstoppable force of nature herself.

❖ ❖ ❖

Other great mystics have discovered the royal sublimity of the human soul, the splendor of the divine presence in reality, and the power of the Spirit that streams from the essence of God. What makes Jesus unique, as the best of modern scholarship is making more and more obvious, is the extent, radical nature, and fervor of his application of his vision of the Kingdom to the society of his time.

The Jesus that is emerging in the finest modern portraits of him is that most dangerous and exciting of beings—an awakened, empowered mystic and healer with immense personal powers and a revolutionary vision of how the Spirit translated itself in society and history, someone who wants, in the name of divine love and the Kingdom of God, a revisioning and rehaul of the whole of society of his time; and, by implication, of all time. It was to this actual transformation of existing conditions that Jesus dedicated all his skills and powers; it is this that made him lethal to the ruling political and religious powers of his day, and this that ensured his death.

☒ ☒ ☒

The spiritual reasoning behind Jesus' radicalism is clear. If the Kingdom is the essential reality, the truth of truths, and if all human beings are—as Jesus' great awakening made him aware they are—innately gifted with direct access to the all-transforming power of the Spirit, then the entire meaning of human life lies in living and enacting the laws of the Kingdom so that its birth into reality, into the structures of human society and politics and religion, into every area of human life, in fact, can be ever clearer, and more complete. For that birth to occur, and go on occurring, all the forces, inner and outer, that block it or could block it have to be exposed and faced as unshrinkingly as possible, and with as mordant and unillusioned an eye as possible.

The extent of what Jesus knew to be possible with God's help for the whole human race—the transformation of the world into a living Eden—was what gave his vision of everything that blocked this possible miracle a terrible (and sometimes hilarious) beady-eyed clarity. Jesus has a peasant's eye for all the nuances of hypocrisy and betrayal and self-interest in all forces of power. The result is a teaching and practice that critiques, as none other has done with such ferocious purity and passion, all forms of every kind of power—social, sexual, and political. The mercilessness of this vision is as blinding as the glory of what it is trying to open up for the race; everything false or shabby or incomplete or uncreative gets exposed by it. In the Gospel of Thomas, Jesus said, "Everyone who is near to me is near to the fire; everyone who is far from me is far from the Kingdom." To be near to Jesus is to be near the fire of the overwhelming love and equally overwhelming fiery clarity of his vision, to be driven by the authenticity of his teaching and practice to throw into that fire all the self-protective concepts and fantasies of a lifetime.

In every arena, Jesus' teaching and practice, as modern scholarship makes clear, overturns the conventional pieties of his (and any) time. In Luke 16:15, Jesus is reported as saying, "That which is highly esteemed among men is abomination in the eyes of God." What he knew of the Kingdom made it clear to him that the only divine human world was, in Crossan's words, "a community of radical and unbrokered equality in which individuals are in direct contact with one another and with God": such an unbrokered equality between all human beings and such direct access to the Spirit of God could only, Jesus knew, empower all beings with the powers of the Spirit and so transform reality.

What Jesus saw in the world around him was the negative image of this possibility; everywhere his fellow human beings were being blocked from experiencing the fire of divine love and the power of just action it releases into the world by conventional wisdom of every kind. His teaching and the example of his life were dedicated to exposing the cruelty of this conventional wisdom and in trying to set others free from its often invisible or traditionally sanctified prisons. For Jesus, liberation, or salvation, was the ability to live as he did—in true radical freedom from all constricting theories or norms that could prevent the blazing out of love in all aspects of life. Love, in its abandon of all boundaries, in its disregard of all categories that separated beings, in its extreme healing power that leapt over all social constrictions and definitions, was, Jesus knew and experienced in his own living of it, the most revolutionary power of all, because it was the power most attuned to the inmost nature of God. The divine power of love could transform all things, but only if all the hypocrisies and cruelties and nonsensical fantasies that hid behind conventional pieties were ruthlessly exposed and transcended. Nothing less than such an exposure of the falsities of an unillumined and partly evil world could inspire beings to that fundamental shift of perception and will that could make them instruments of the establishment of the Kingdom.

To see Jesus' life and teaching in the context of the society and religious practice of the Palestine of his time only emphasizes the radicalism of his message. In every way and in every arena, Jesus consistently and consciously challenged traditional values and conventional ways of behavior and thought; he knew that from the perspective of what St. Paul later called "the glorious liberty of the children of God," both tradition and convention were winding sheets for the soul and prisons for the heart, and that it is what people believe to be true about life and God from what they have been told that blocks them from the full experience of either. The transformation he knew was essential for the Kingdom to be "seen" and prepared for could only occur through a death—a death to all ordinary ways of thinking about the self, and about its relations to others in the world. Anything that kept the human being fearful of becoming that vast force of sacred love that was his or her true identity was to be exposed and discarded. All the games and pleasures and fantasies of the world and the false self that loved them had to be seen for what they were—pathetic diversions and temporal distractions from a truth that demanded their transcendence. As Jesus says in Matthew 7:14, "Straight is the gate, and narrow is the way, which leadeth unto life," and in Matthew 6:19: "Lay not up for yourselves treasures upon earth, where moth and rust doth corrupt, and where thieves break through and steal: But lay up for yourselves treasures in heaven, where neither moth nor rust doth corrupt, and where thieves do not break through nor steal: For where your treasure is, there will your heart be also."

Jesus then adds, "The light of the body is the eye: if therefore thine eye be single thy whole body shall be full of light. But if thine eye be evil, thy whole body shall be full of darkness. If therefore the light that is in thee be darkness, how great is that darkness!" The menace of the last phrase is characteristic of Jesus' understanding of the urgency of the necessity for change; since the Spirit in human beings is so strong, it is essential to be conscious of it and dedicate its power to good; otherwise, perverted and betrayed, its thwarted force will create vast harm, create, in fact, the cruel and unjust world he saw around him, and in which we still live.

For human beings to be instruments of holy change and not half-conscious purveyors of "great darkness," they had to undergo willingly a death—a death to the false self, its pride and vanity, and all the securities and "values" that kept it smug and blind. Without such a death, the glory of the soul and Kingdom could not be experienced; without such a death, the energies of the human being could not be consecrated to the enactment of the vision of the Kingdom, and the sacred force of love that was the truth of every human heart and soul could not be unleashed in the real.

The Kingdom could not be experienced or lived without a complete turning-about in the seat of consciousness, a symbolic or literal giving up of everything that one clings to for safety or false comfort. As Jesus says in Matthew 13:44, "The Kingdom of heaven is like unto treasure hid in a field; the which when a man hath found, he hideth, and for joy thereof goeth and selleth all that he hath, and buyeth that field." And again, "The Kingdom of heaven is like unto a merchant man seeking goodly pearls: who, when he had found one pearl of great price, went and sold all that he had, and bought it." The new life and knowledge of divine identity with God and the experience of the growth-in-God that only life in the Kingdom could bring was the "pearl of great price," the entire purpose of incarnation on the earth; the only way the merchant could purchase so valuable a "jewel" was by "selling all that he had." For the one real security, every false security had to be abandoned: for the one saving truth, all other so-called truths had to be surrendered; for the one authentic consciousness, Kingdom-consciousness, all lesser ways of knowing and seeing had to be transcended; to be able to see and grasp and enact the supremely valuable, everything of lesser, worldly value had to be seen to be what it is—only a temporary and fragile treasure. While Jesus knew that such a way of death was open to everyone, he also knew that it was hard and demanding, because in T. S. Eliot's words, it was "a condition of complete simplicity that costs not less than everything." But only in such simplicity could truth be known and lived; and only from such a radical simplicity could the transforming fire of the Kingdom be lit and spread.

The Kingdom of God is people under direct divine rule, and that, as an ideal, as a lived inner experience of ecstasy, union, and outflowing charity, transcends and judges all human rule. Jesus' teaching and practice brought that fierce, exalted clarity of vision to bear on every area and problem of his contemporary world.

It is essential to see just how uncompromising, even extreme, Jesus' views often were. The icon must be allowed to turn back into the iconoclast; the distant, all-knowing savior-figure must be allowed to turn back into the inspired, ecstatic, and sometimes ferocious rebel, who fought all the accepted values and established powers of his time to try to realize his vision of a Kingdom of divine love on earth. If the historical Jesus is not allowed to return in the fullness of his fierce visionary presence and passion for justice, how can the Christ-path be restored and lived in its full truth and passionate, dangerous freedom?

Jesus and the Family

Jesus' ferocity is clearly seen in his scalding critique of the patriarchal family system that formed the core of society in his time.

Here are four different examples of Jesus' critique of the family system, which will be examined in some detail. The first and most startling one is from the Gospel of Thomas 55, the second from Mark 3:31–35, the third from the Gospel in Luke 11:27–28, and the last from the Gospel in Luke 12:51–53.

1. Jesus said, "Whoever does not hate his father and mother cannot be a follower of me, and whoever does not hate brothers and sisters . . . will not be worthy of me."

2. "Then his mother and his brothers came: and standing outside, they sent to him and called him . . . and he replied, Who are my mother and brothers? And looking at those who sat around him he said, Here are my mother and my brothers! Whoever does the will of God is my brother and sister and mother."

3. A woman from the crowd spoke up and said to him, How fortunate is the womb that bore you, and the breasts that you sucked!" But he said, How fortunate rather are those who listen to God's teaching and preserve it."

4. "Do you think that I have come to bring peace to the earth? No, I tell you, but rather division! From now on five in one household will be divided, three against two and two against three; they will be divided father against son and son against father, mother against daughter and daughter against mother, mother-in-law against daughter-in-law and daughter-in-law against mother-in-law."

No more radical "sayings" can be imagined, especially in the context of the universal family practice of Jesus' time, and in a Jewish setting where family and its laws were considered sacred. Jesus was aware, however, how limiting familial structures could be: how they could choke growing spiritual aspiration; how they could encourage precisely discrimination against others, contempt for people who disagreed or simply came from other families or groups of families, that destroyed the possibility of the free equality between all beings of the Kingdom from being established; how they could justify power games and social and even political wars that kept human beings divided from each other.

If the first two of the quotations I have selected are read "together," it can be seen that Jesus violently negates the closed group of the family in favor of another one that will be open to all who want to join it. "Whoever does not hate brothers and sisters," he says in Logion 55 of the Gospel of Thomas, "will not be worthy of me." To be "worthy" of Jesus means to see all beings as members of one vast fraternity and sorority. What Jesus is advocating is not, of course, anarchic isolationism, but the membership—through the awakening of divine love in the heart—of a universal family, where all beings are cherished and known as extensions and manifestations of God and of the divine inner self, and honored accordingly. Any personal addiction to family, to one's own "brothers and sisters," tends to prevent the very realization that is the foundation of the Kingdom, that every woman on earth is our sister, and every man our brother, and so blocks at its origin that explosion of universal charity that is the fuel for radical transformation of the actual. If, for Jesus, God's family has no walled gardens or rich and poor houses, just one vast open house—the earth—how, then, can the Kingdom begin to be created when old structures that destroy such openness at its root survive? How can the new wine of the vision of the Kingdom be poured into the old bottles of the patriarchal system of control that was the ancient Mediterranean family without splitting them apart?

In the second quotation Jesus makes this teaching even more poignant and explicit. His own mother and brothers are "standing outside" and want to talk to him: they make a special claim on his attention and "call" for him. Jesus refuses this ordinary act of definition for himself, and implicitly for all those who want to follow him: he asks, "Who are my mother and my brothers?" It is an outrageous question in the context of his, or any, time; he seems to be negating the most fundamental human way of being identified, the most fundamental human relationships. In a way he is but only, as the rest of the quotation shows, to establish a larger family, the family of the Kingdom; "Looking at those who sat around him, he said, *Here* [my italics] are my mother and my brothers! Whoever does the will of God is my brother and sister and mother."

The family that Jesus knows he belongs to and belongs to forever—and the family he wants everyone else to belong to—is the family of the lovers of God; it is this family that must spread all over the earth, and spread its warmth and charity and passionate concern for just conditions into every corner of human society if human life is to become divine. A simple-minded, unquestioned, or stubborn adherence to the family unit only blocks the creation of the real family of God. And in making—or implying—such a radical distinction between man-made families and the ultimate and universal God-created one—that of the brotherhood and sisterhood of the lovers of truth—Jesus is going against not only the conventional wisdom of Judaism and the Palestine of his time but against the inherited wisdom of almost every human religious tradition.

In the third quotation—from Luke 11:27-28—a woman declares Mary blessed because of Jesus. In typical Mediterranean fashion, she imagines that a woman's greatness stems from mothering such a famous and brilliant son. Jesus immediately challenges such patriarchal chauvinism by saying, "How fortunate rather are those who listen to God's teachings and observe it." Families can be united, after all, in greed, vice, crime, ignorance, or reactionary selfish politics; they can be grouped around holding onto and conserving possessions, property, land, power of every kind, and in such a way that excludes and even mutilates others. For Jesus, the authentic family is the one of those who "listen to God's teaching"—God's teaching about unconditional love and boundless charity toward all beings and who "observe it"—sometimes in ways that can only scandalize those addicted to narrow definitions of love. Just as there are two Kingdoms that co-exist—the Kingdom of this world and the real mystical Kingdom of love that is God's Kingdom—so there exist in Jesus' vision two kinds of family: the one that is man-made and is kept going by all kinds of invisible and limiting forms of social pressure, even coercion, and by the long inertia of conventional habit, and the family of the Kingdom, the family of the servants of the Kingdom, and of a love and truth that overflow all boundaries and definitions because they are inherently divine and so cannot be limited and contained by any human construction or tradition whatsoever.

In the fourth quotation—that from Luke 12:51-53—the thrust of Jesus' attack on the family becomes even clearer. The standard Mediterranean family, let us imagine, has five members: mother, father, married son with his wife, and one unmarried daughter. Jesus makes it clear that his vision will tear this tidy unit apart. One explanation of what Jesus is saying, the more or less traditional one, is that Jesus will bring "division" to the family because the force and power of his teaching will drive some to accept him, while others reject him. That is certainly part of what Jesus means. It is also important, however, to notice where and how the line of separation is drawn, between generations.

With the kind of precision that characterizes Jesus' statements about power of any kind, Jesus attacks here directly the Mediterranean family's axis of power, which sets father and mother over son, daughter, and daughter-in-law. He is implying that his teaching of the Kingdom will free those imprisoned in punitive family structures from being destroyed by them, will free them from age-old habits of patriarchal domination so as to be free to live in the world-family of love.

The concentration in this fourth quotation is on the divisions caused by power more than those caused by faith. And this attack on power gives us the clue as to why Jesus rails so vehemently against the conventional family. What is the family, after all, but society in miniature? It is the place where we first learn how to love, and to be loved; it is also the place where we learn how to abuse, or be abused. The family is not just an oasis of domestic serenity, a paradise of calm in an evil turbulent world; it also must involve power, and power of any kind invites the possibility of abuses of power that can deform and destroy human lives. All power is suspicious to Jesus, all power, that is, that is not directly derived from God. As historical scholar Dominic Crossan points out, "Jesus' ideal group, contrary to Mediterranean and indeed most human familial reality, is an open one equally as accessible to all under God. It is the Kingdom of God and it negates that terrible abuse of power that is power's dark scepter and lethal shadow" (*Jesus: A Revolutionary Biography*, p. 60).

Another reason for Jesus' attack on the conventional family can be adduced from Luke 4. After overcoming the temptations of the devil, Jesus' first act was to go straight to Nazareth—the place where he has been brought up—to announce (what he now knew to be) his extraordinary mission:

> And he came to Nazareth, where he had been brought up: and, as his custom was, he went into the synagogue on the sabbath day, and stood up for to read. And there was delivered unto him the book of the prophet Esaias. And when he had opened the book, he found the place where it was written, The spirit of the Lord is upon me, because he hath anointed me to preach the gospel to the poor; he hath sent me to heal the brokenhearted, to preach deliverance to the captives, and recovering of sight to the blind, to set at liberty them that are bruised. To preach the acceptable year of the Lord. And he closed the book and gave it again to the minister, and sat down. And the eyes of all them that were in the synagogue were fastened on him. And he began to say unto them, This day is this scripture fulfilled in your ears

> . . . And they said, Is not this Joseph's son? . . . And he said, Verily I
> say unto you, no prophet is accepted in his own country.

It is a terrible and poignant scene—Jesus choosing to go to his home-town of Nazareth to announce his discovery of the life of the Kingdom and of his role in bringing that life to birth, and being mocked and rejected. Later, in the narrative, the Nazarenes are so outraged by what they imagine to be Jesus' blasphemy that they attempt to kill him. As Luke writes in Chapter 4, v. 28, "And all they in the synagogue when they heard these things, were filled with wrath, and rose up and thrust him out of the city, and led him unto the brow of the hill whereon their city was built, that they might cast him down headlong. But he passing through the midst of them went his way."

Jesus experienced personally and in the most painful way just how conventional family and tribal values could not only block the life of the Kingdom but be actively dangerous to it. All the Nazarenes could do when presented with a Jesus on fire with his vision of a new world and his announcement of his role in the bringing here of the Kingdom was to react with scorn and contempt, and cling to what they imagined they knew about Jesus—that he was "Joseph's son," as if that defined in any way what had happened to him and what his consciousness now was. Trapped in their ignorance and its drastically narrow vision of human possibilities, they could not only not recognize Jesus' awakening and its significance; they explicitly denied it and found him blasphemous, and were driven by rage and jealousy to the extreme of even wanting to kill him.

In the life of nearly every major visionary, a break has to be made between him or her and the whole of his or her world; the new wine of mystical consciousness and intention cannot be contained in the old bottles of familial, banal "awareness"; while the family structure might provide exactly the kind of comfort and security that kept the world going, it can stifle or even kill any new adventure, especially one that threatens the very basis of that security and comfort, and all the distinctions and values they sustain.

In Matthew 23:9, Jesus says, when speaking to the multitude and to his disciples: "And call no man your father upon the earth: for one is your father, which is in heaven." This is perhaps his most startling statement of all concerning the family.

Jesus is speaking in a context in which he systematically and with vehement wit attacks all the honorific titles of patriarchal culture. He begins by painting a hilarious picture of the vanity and worldliness of the "scribes and

Pharisees"; he describes how "all their works they do for to be seen of men," and how they "love the uppermost rooms at feasts, and the chief seats in the synagogues, and greetings in the markets and to be called of men, Rabbi, Rabbi." Jesus then makes clear: "But be not ye called Rabbi." He adds, "And call no man your father." He finishes his comprehensive tirade against patriarchal hierarchy by saying, "Neither be ye called masters."

Rabbi, father, master are three of the highest, grandest titles that a male-dominated culture can award. Jesus, in the name of the Kingdom, derides them all; for Jesus, all hierarchy offends against the blazing egalitarianism and all-encompassing love of the Kingdom, and male vanity—the need to be adored and obeyed in ways that bolster social power and position—is one of the greatest enemies of the reality he knew was possible. It is one of Jesus' least appreciated but best "jokes" that in Matthew 23:9 he subverts the entire patriarchal order in the name of God the Father! In the Kingdom of the one authentic Father, all is one, and all are one, one heart, one will, one energy of brotherhood and sisterhood, for the Kingdom of the Father is the Kingdom of radical unity in the heart. In the Kingdom of the inauthentic, "social" father, everything is division, separation, fragmentation, the protection, by almost any means of the status quo. If the reign of the real Father—of Jesus' transfiguringly tender and forgiving "Abba"—is ever going to be established on earth, then the reign of the false patriarchal father had to be destroyed. Jesus did not simply condemn the family system outright: his first miracle at Cana was performed to sanctify a marriage. And he seems to have been especially close to the family of Lazarus, Mary, and Martha and to have raised Lazarus from the dead at least partly to heal his sisters' grief. But Jesus clearly saw that the patriarchal structure of the family of his time had to be transformed if the force of love needed to build the Kingdom on earth was to be released.

Jesus and Women

❖ ❖ ❖

Jesus' treatment of women was, if anything, even more radical in the context of his time. Despite some dissenting voices, the dominant voice of Judaism disenfranchised women. Women had few rights: they could not be witnesses in a court of law; they could not initiate divorce proceedings; they could not be taught the Torah. Both childbirth and menstruation were considered ritually impure. In public life, moreover, women were as separated from men as they still are in parts of the Arab world. Middle- and upper-class women did not go out of the house unescorted by a family member; adult women had to be veiled at all times when they were out in public. Meals outside the family were male-only occasions; if women were present, they were thought of as harlots or courtesans. A woman's identity in the world derived totally from her husband or father.

Also, as in all patriarchal cultures, women were the victims of male projections. In the Old Testament, it was Eve, not Adam, who was largely held responsible for the fall and the tragic suffering that consumed the human race because of it: it is to Eve that the "Lord God" of Genesis says the terrifying words (Genesis 3:16) that have been used to justify two millennia of crucifixion of the feminine: "I will greatly multiply thy sorrow and thy conception; in sorrow thou shalt bring forth children; and thy desire shall be to thy husband, and he shall rule over thee."

What possible connection could such socially and religiously sanctioned contempt and constriction of women have to do with what Jesus knew of the boundary-free love of the Kingdom? How could the Kingdom be anything but a world of *truth,* where all human beings of both sexes were treated—and treated each other—with divine tenderness and respect? This divine tenderness and respect characterizes all of Jesus' dealings with women, and is one of the most revolutionary and revealing aspects of his life and ministry.

Wherever and whenever he could—and sometimes in very "compromising" situations—Jesus stood up for the rights of women to be treated with dignity. Consider, for example, the account in John 8:3 of Jesus dealing with the woman taken in adultery:

And the scribes and Pharisees brought unto him a woman taken in adultery; and when they had set her in the midst, they said unto him, Master, this woman was taken in adultery, in the very act. Now Moses in the law commanded us, that such should be stoned: but what sayest thou? This they said, tempting him, that they might have to accuse him. But Jesus stooped down, and with his finger wrote on the ground, as though he heard them not. So when they continued asking him, he lifted up himself, and said unto them, He that is without sin among you, let him first cast a stone at her. And again he stooped down, and wrote on the ground. And they which heard it, being convicted by their own conscience, went out one by one, beginning at the eldest, even unto the last; and Jesus was left alone, and the woman standing in the midst. When Jesus had lifted up himself, and saw none but the woman, he said unto her, Woman, where are those thine accusers? hath no man condemned thee? She said, No man, Lord, and Jesus said unto her, Neither do I condemn thee: go and sin no more.

Here Jesus' teaching and actions reverse and expose the practice of an entire social and religious world, and what could have been a horrible but banal enactment of accepted "laws" becomes an initiation into the mystery of forgiveness through the beauty and wisdom of his presence.

From the beginning of the story, the woman is represented as harrowed and alone; after all, she is the one who has to bear all the blame for the adultery, not the man she was caught with. It is she that the scribes and Pharisees drag to Jesus before the eyes of her whole world; it is she that Moses' law condemns to stoning. In patriarchal cultures, it is the woman's sexuality, not the man's, that is condemned. The entire situation is perverse, cruel, and unjust from the beginning, and Jesus knows it.

What is Jesus' initial response? He says nothing and writes something with his finger in the sand "as though he heard them not." Jesus is not listening to the narrow, prejudiced voices of his world, or of any other human world; his ear is attuned to the divine music of the Kingdom, to the word of the law of compassion. His writing in the sand symbolizes the temporariness and fragility of all human laws, even those supposedly inspired by God and ordained by prophets; they are no more, his action implies, than his own scribbling in the sand that a gust of wind can efface. To live by such perishable, transient laws is absurd, and to kill in their name is tragic.

Jesus does not *say* anything, however; he knows that the scribes and

Pharisees want to trap him into saying something that they could represent as blasphemous, and so condemn him. What he does is to make a statement that unmasks the injustice of the patriarchal law of Moses: "He that is without sin among you, let him first cast a stone at her." It is important to remember that his audience is largely, perhaps exclusively, male. Jesus is exposing the absurdity and obscenity of the patriarchal double standard about women, and implicitly calling all the men ranged before him to examine the nature of their violent projections onto women of sexual impurity. Are men not also lustful? Do they not also have adulterous thoughts? Why then are women made to bear the brunt of so much denial? The sternness of the law—made by a man to be implemented by men against women—keeps men safe from self-knowledge; Jesus destroys that safety by making men acknowledge their own "sin."

The men "convicted by their own conscience" leave; the woman is left alone with Jesus. He treats her with exquisite respect and balance, restoring to her the dignity and choice that her society has wanted to deny her. "Hath no man condemned thee?" he asks. She replies, "No man, Lord." Jesus then says, "Neither do I condemn thee." Condemnation and moral self-righteousness belong to the law he has just symbolically "dissolved": his Kingdom is one of forgiveness and endless opportunity for transformation and growth. This is not to say that Jesus condones her adultery; he does not. He says to her, "Go and sin no more." What Jesus does do, with marvelous compassion, is separate the sinner from the sin; while condemning the sin, he does not condemn the sinner but empowers her by his acceptance of her to claim her own deepest self, to know the depth of her own goodness and so of her capacity for change. He demonstrates the Kingdom in action, preventing a murder, dissolving the ignorance and lack of self-knowledge that keep alive punitive patriarchal laws against women, and empowering the woman to change her life by his active compassion on her behalf, and by his belief in her.

Jesus' radical and unconditional embrace of women is shown even more clearly in the account of his meeting with the woman of Samaria at the well of Jacob in Sychar. Despite the fact that the woman comes from Samaria—Jews and Samarians were traditional enemies—and despite the fact, too, that the water of Samaria was described in certain traditional Jewish texts as being more impure than the urine of pigs, Jesus asks the woman to give him a drink, and goes on to teach her about the "living water" of the Kingdom and the nature of authentic worship of God. "God is a spirit: and they that worship him must worship him in spirit and in truth" (John 4:24). Whether John's account of Jesus announcing his Christhood to the woman of Samaria is authentic, what is amazing is that it is to *her* that he is announcing it; to a woman whom he knows has had five husbands and who is currently living with a man to whom she is not married. Jesus is reaching beyond all the racial and social and spiritual laws of his world to announce the great truths of the Kingdom—of the "living water" of love that always flows from its vision, of the truth of worship without boundaries—to a woman who was, at the very least, an outcast. No more powerful statement of his rejection of the rules of his world, and especially of them when they applied to women, could be imagined.

In fact, in all of his encounters with women in the four Gospels, Jesus breaks the rules of his world. He defended the woman who outraged an all-male banquet not only by entering it but also by washing his feet with her hair; he allowed himself to be hosted by two women, Mary and Martha, and took great trouble to affirm Mary's devotion to him and the holiness and worth of her choice (which in a world that barred women from serious religious education was almost scandalous). He broke all convention by openly traveling around with women (and for his pains he was mocked as a "companion of harlots and drunkards"); he let himself be persuaded by a Syro-Phoenician woman—seemingly against his will—to heal her daughter and complimented her on her wisdom and its role in her own daughter's healing (Mark 7:25–30). The Jesus movement itself was supported by some wealthy women, Joanna, wife of Chuza, Herod's steward, and Susanna among them. At the crucifixion, Jesus died in agony surrounded by mourning women (and a noticeable absence of the men who had supposedly supported him). The first person he appeared to after the resurrection was a woman—either Mary his mother (as in some of the apocryphal legends) or Mary Magdalene (as in the Gospel accounts).

Jesus' revolutionary honoring of women continued to be honored in the early church. In the early Gnostic churches, for example, women could teach, heal prophesy, baptize, and hold all ranks under bishop. The existing Christian churches' barring of women from ecclesiastical office and the general denigration of women's status and potential has nothing to do with Jesus himself, and represents one of the most damaging and saddest of all betrayals of his original message. The betrayal of Jesus in this, as in other matters, seems to have started quite early after his death: St. Paul can write, "In Christ there is neither Jew nor Gentile, slave nor free, male nor female," yet many of the letters ascribed to him (and written only twenty or thirty years after Christ's death) are stained by the banal misogyny of the contemporary Mediterranean world. Tragically, on this, as on many other issues, it was Paul's vision, not Christ's practice, that was to inform two millennia of church life.

The newly discovered Gnostic gospels (especially the Dialogue of the Savior, the Gospel of Philip, the Pistis Sophia, and the Gospel of Mary) are revealing an astonishing new aspect of Jesus' free and loving treatment of women and the extent and range of his relationship with Mary Magdalene. The tenderness and spiritual intimacy of Jesus' and the Magdalene's relationship irradiate those pages of St. John's Gospel that record the aftermath of the resurrection; the Gnostic gospels vastly extend what the canonical gospel tell us of this relationship and paint a picture of Mary Magdalene considerably at odds with the repentant whore of Christian legend.

The Magdalene they present has no parallel in biblical or New Testament literature; she is a woman with a brilliant, clear mind and a depth of mystic experience that makes her able to follow some of Christ's most abstruse and exalted teachings and to be the recipient of his deep secrets. In the Pistis Sophia, Jesus is reported as saying, "Mary Magdalene and John the Virgin will tower over all my disciples and over all men who shall receive the mysteries in the ineffable. And they will be on my right and on my left. And I am they, and they are I." The Gospel of Philip tells us "Jesus loved Mary Magdalene more than all the disciples and used to kiss her often on her (mouth). The rest of the disciples said to him, 'Why do you love her more than all of us?' The Savior answered and said to them, 'Why do I not love you like her?' " Jesus then goes on to compare Mary to one who is in the light while others are in darkness: "When the light comes, then he who sees will see the light, and he who is blind will remain in darkness."

In the Dialogue of the Savior, Mary Magdalene is said to ask Jesus, "Tell me Lord why have I come to this place—to profit or to forfeit?" Jesus is shown as not replying directly but as exclaiming to—and about—her, "You make clear the abundance of the revealer," astonishing praise from a teacher who rarely commends anyone, and the only praise of a disciple given in the Dialogue. Throughout the Dialogue of the Savior, Mary is shown as asking Jesus some far-reaching questions and eliciting from him some of his deepest teachings. Her passionate and noble character is clearly revealed by what she is recorded as saying: "I want to understand all things just as they are," and "There is one saying I will speak to the Lord concerning the mystery of truth; in this we have taken our stand and to the cosmic we are transparent."

It is Mary's "transparence" to the "cosmic" that the Gospel of Mary reveals. In it, Mary records an esoteric teaching of Christ about the nature of vision. She said, "I saw the Lord in a vision and I said to him, 'Lord I saw you today in a vision.' He answered and said to me, 'Blessed are you that you did not waver at the sight of me. For where the mind is there is the treasure.' I said to him, 'Lord, now does he who sees the vision see it through the soul or through the spirit?' The Savior answered and said, 'He does not see through the Spirit, but the mind which is between the two.' "

When Mary goes on to tell the disciples other teachings the Lord gave her concerning the evolution of the soul, Peter acts increasingly jealous. He questions his fellow disciples about the Savior: "Did he really speak with a woman without our knowledge and not openly? Are we to turn about and all listen to her? Did he prefer her to us?" Peter's jealousy wounds Mary Magdalene: "Then Mary wept and said to Peter 'My brother Peter, what do you think? Do you think that I thought this up in myself, or that I am lying about the Savior?'" At this, Levi springs to her defense: "Levi answered and said to Peter, 'Peter, you have always been hot tempered. Now I see you contending against the woman like the adversaries. But if the Savior made her worthy, who are you indeed to reject her? Surely the Savior knows her very well. That is why he loved her more than us.' "

Were Jesus and Mary mystic lovers as some feminist historians have suggested? Was there a special link of mystical transmission that came through Mary Magdalene directly into the general stream of Gnosticism and dealt with advanced esoteric teachings about the nature of the soul? We shall probably never know. But there is no doubt that Mary Magdalene played a far richer role in the growth of the early church at Jerusalem than has been understood, and that Jesus' love for her was known to be great and even, to some of his male disciples, deranging.

No other world-teacher honored women as profoundly as Jesus. What the Gnostic gospels suggest, too, is that it was to a woman (and to John "the beloved disciple") that Jesus gave the deepest of himself, in a way and to an extent unparalleled in the life of any other sage of the ancient world. It is a tragedy for the development of Christianity, and so for the evolution of Western society and the cause of freedom in the world, that Jesus and Mary Magdalene's relationship became edited out or ignored both in subsequent dogmatic developments in the churches and in the way in which the "canonical" gospels were put together. The restoration of its centrality to Jesus' life and teaching must effect a revolution in the core of Christianity, for it shows clearly that all patriarchal claims to exclusive male brokerage of religious power and exclusive male access to certain levels of mystical truth are social constructs, and nothing more, and have not only nothing to do with either the vision or the actual practice of Jesus but are directly antagonistic to them.

Jesus and the Rich

▨ ▨ ▨

Jesus did not confine his attacks on the social constructs of his time merely to his wariness about the nature of the family or his unprecedentedly open embrace of women and the feminine. In his many statements about the dangers and evils of wealth and the holiness of poverty and the poor, Jesus not only struck, again and again, at the heart of his contemporary society's belief that wealth was a sign of divine blessing, but implied, in his celebration of the simplicity, humility, and honesty of poverty, an alternative way of living. Here, as elsewhere, the vision of the historical Jesus is far more radical than that allowed by nearly all of the churches erected in his name.

No amount of special pleading or juggling with different texts can obscure Jesus' vehemence against wealth. "Ye cannot serve God and mammon," he says. There is no possible compromise and no possible way of combining the pursuit of money and power with the life of the Kingdom, which is based entirely on egalitarianism, serving others, and pouring out all one's skills and energies in love and charity. Wealth blinds, cossets, entangles, and makes ignorant and uncompassionate; Dives doesn't even notice the poor man Lazarus by his door, riddled with sores and begging for bread. The wealthy are prisoners of their money and of the confidence and sense of privilege and grace that it engenders, especially in a world where (as was the case in contemporary Palestine) their wealth was seen as a sign of divine approval. As Jesus says, "It is easier for a camel to go through the eye of the needle than for a rich man to enter the Kingdom of God."

Jesus' most profound reason for deriding wealth and its effects is shown most clearly in the parable of the Banquet (in the version in Luke 14:16–23):

> A man once gave a great banquet and invited many; and at the time of the banquet he sent his servant to say to those who had been invited, Come; for all is now ready, but they all alike began to make excuses. The first said to him, I have bought a field and I must go out and see it; I pray you, have me excused. And another said, I have bought five yoke of oxen, and I go to examine them: I pray you, have me excused. And another said, I have married a wife and therefore I cannot come. So the servant came and reported this to his master. Then the

householder in anger said to his servant, Go out quickly to the streets and lanes of the city and bring in the poor and maimed and blind and lame. And the servant said, Sir, what you commanded has been done, and still there is room. And the master said to the servant, Go out to the highways and hedges and compel people to come in, that my house may be filled.

This is clearly a parable about the Kingdom and its joyful free life; God has made a banquet for everyone. The rich, however, are too preoccupied with their own affairs—their fields and oxen and marriages—to notice or care for the feast that is offered to them, as it is offered to everyone. They simply cannot see, blinded as they are by their own transient power and importance, the glory of the banquet and the source of true wealth. There is an irony typical of Jesus' iconoclasm in this: the rich pretend to have the best of everything, believe they have (and are believed to have by a greedy and desperate world). In fact, however, they miss the true feast of life—the feast of the Kingdom—because their hearts are vain and their minds distracted by the necessities of staying powerful and in control. It is the "poor and maimed and blind and lame," the despised and rejected of the earth and of society who get to attend the feast and enter the Kingdom and fill the house of God; the glitter of possessions does not blind them to the need to share, and deprivation and loss have made their hearts humble enough to open to miracle.

Jesus does not simply honor the poor; he blesses them, and in a way that, implicitly and scathingly, condemns the games and power ploys of society. The radicalism of Jesus' vision was tamed early on in the evolution of Christianity. This can be clearly seen by looking at four different sayings about the blessedness of poverty, from the Gospel of Thomas, Logion 54, from the Gospel in Luke 6:20 and Matthew 5:3, and from James 2:5.

1. "Blessed are the poor, for yours is the Kingdom of heaven."
2. "Blessed are you who are poor, for yours is the Kingdom of God."
3. "Blessed are the poor in spirit, for theirs is the Kingdom of heaven."
4. "Has not God chosen those who are poor in the world to be rich in faith and heirs of the Kingdom which he has promised to those that love him?"

As Crossan caustically points out: "In the third example, Matthew's 'in spirit' diverts interpretation from economic to religious poverty, and James's emphasis on faith and love points toward a promised rather than a present

Kingdom of God. But the stark and startling conjunction of blessed poverty and divine Kingdom is still there for all to see in the first two versions."

This conjunction becomes even more "stark and startling" when it is realized that the Greek word that is being translated as poor here—*ptochos*—actually means "destitute." The usual Greek word for poor is *penes* and would have referred to a peasant family just scraping by year after year. Jesus is "blessing" those that are even poorer than that, who have no property at all, and who beg for a living. A more accurate version of what Jesus said would read, then, "Blessed are the destitute, for theirs is the Kingdom of God."

Such a statement overturns all accepted ideas about wealth and poverty and about who is "useful" in society and who isn't. In blessing the "destitute," Jesus is not indulging in a romantic dream about the charms of poverty; he is implicitly criticizing all societies and cultures in which wealth and power are not freely and equally distributed as they would be in the Kingdom (and were in some of the early Christian communities that sprang up after Jesus' death). As Crossan writes movingly: "In any situation of oppression, especially in those oblique, indirect and systemic ones where injustice wears a mask of normalcy or even of necessity, the only ones who are innocent or blessed are those squeezed out deliberately as human junk from the system's evil operations. A contemporary equivalent; only the homeless are innocent. That is a terrifying aphorism against society because . . . it focuses not just on personal or individual abuse of power but on such abuse in its systemic or structural possibilities—and there, in contrast to the former level, none of our hands are innocent or our consciences particularly clear." And cannot be, I would add, until the truth of the Kingdom lives not only in our hearts but also in our laws and in our cultural, economic, and political practices on every level and in every arena of society. Until that time, Jesus is saying, we are all guilty of perpetuating systems that thrive on degradation and treat millions of people as subhuman and worthless.

For Jesus, it is clear, poverty is not the problem; it is the solution. Until human beings learn to live in naked contact and direct simplicity and equality with each other, sharing all resources, there can be no solution to the misery of the human condition and no establishment of God's Kingdom.

Jesus' radical and paradoxical sense of who could and who could not enter the Kingdom is even more clearly illustrated by his famous praise of children in Mark 10:13–16:

"People were bringing little children to him in order that he might touch them: and the disciples spoke sternly to them. But when Jesus saw this, he was indignant and said to them, Let the children come to me; for it is to such as these that the Kingdom of God belongs. Truly I tell you, whoever does not receive the Kingdom of God as a little child will never enter it. And he took them up in his arms, laid his hands on them, and blessed them."

Jesus isn't simply extolling here the necessity of wonder, innocence, trust, and freshness of heart for seeing and entering the Kingdom: he is also speaking within a definite historical context in which children were treated as nobodies. Modern scholarship has pointed out that in the Mediterranean world a child—especially a girl-child—was literally a nobody unless her father "accepted it as a member of the family rather than exposing it in the gutter or rubbish dump to die of abandonment or to be taken up by another and reared as a slave" (Crossan, p. 75). Jesus, by touching, taking in his arms, blessing, and laying his hands on the children who came to him is acting like a symbolic spiritual father "designating a newly born infant for life rather than for death, for accepting it into his family rather than casting it out with the garbage" (Crossan, p. 65).

There may well have been a debate within the community that Mark came from about the status of abandoned infants; Mark shows Jesus as embracing them completely as he embraced the destitute and women even though the disciples try to prevent the children getting to him. In so doing, Jesus is showing that the Kingdom is a Kingdom of children, a Kingdom of nobodies, a Kingdom, in other words, of all those who are "useless" to the culture of the time, with its entirely man-made laws and needs, of all those, too, who cannot be assimilated within a hypocritical, power-obsessed, spiritually dead culture of the "blind leading the blind." It isn't the rich or powerful or conspicuously holy who are going to enter the Kingdom and be the family of God; it is the "nobodies," those whom culture cannot or does not want to embrace or define (except negatively).

Jesus is overturning the entire wisdom of so-called civilization in the name of the higher and more paradoxical wisdom of God for which, as St. Paul will say, "the wisdom of the world is foolishness." All that worldly social and religious wisdom can create is a divided, fragmented, unjust world, where women, children, and the powerless are treated with contempt. The family of God, rooted in the wisdom of unconditional compassion, embraces all beings without exception and honors precisely those the world despises. Jesus' indictment of his—and of any—social system rooted in differences could not be more chilling or more clear.

Jesus and Power

❋ ❋ ❋

Had Jesus merely traveled around Israel, healing, teaching, embracing women, children, and the destitute in the name of some nebulous "Kingdom of God," he would have been considered as little more than a harmless fanatic, just one more of the semi-crazy charismatic teachers that haunted first-century Palestine. What made Jesus dangerous, however, and eventually made it certain that he would be killed, is that he did not confine his iconoclasm to "marginal" issues; his teaching also criticized, devastatingly and blatantly, the religious and political establishment of his time.

A clue to what might be called the psychology of Jesus' "rebellion against power" in all its forms can be found in Logion 61 of the Gospel of Thomas. In this logion (of which only startling fragments survive), Salome asks Jesus, "Who are you that you have come up to my couch and eaten from my table?" Jesus replies, "I am he who exists from the undivided." That is how Jesus, here, characterizes Kingdom-consciousness: "existing from the undivided," living an "undivided" life, a life "undivided" into concepts, dogmas, categories, warring visions, and moralities and so part of the Father's boundless and perfect life. (Jesus goes on in the Logion to say, "I have been given some things of my Father.")

Jesus then goes on in the Logion to criticize implicitly those who choose the life of power in any of its forms. In the final fragment of Logion 61, Jesus remarks, "Therefore I say, if he is destroyed, he will be filled with light, but if he is divided, he will be filled with darkness." The "destruction" that Jesus celebrates is the death of the false self that his whole teaching is designed to effect, the death that he knows is the gateway to eternal life. The enemies of that saving destruction—which everyone must pass through to be part of the Kingdom of nobodies—are pride, vanity, and position, status of any and every kind.

What are games of power and control but ploys to shore up, cosset, and empower the very false self that keeps human beings from being "destroyed" into the all-embracing knowledge and compassion of God? To pursue them is to celebrate the death and darkness of that "divided" life that people are everywhere driven to lead. Jesus' condemnation of those who "choose division" is fierce and sad: "If he is divided, he will be filled with darkness." To be "divided," then, is not simply to be unable to enter the Kingdom of unity and wholeness and compassion; it is to be an active agent of darkness. Not to allow yourself to be "destroyed" into love and so to become an instrument of the Kingdom in reality is to invite being "filled with darkness" and so perpetuate the misery and squalor of that "divided" life that keeps human beings separate from God, each other, and their own divine identity. "That which exists from the undivided"—undivided mystical vision and the just, compassionate action that flows naturally from it—simply cannot manifest in a world where division is cannily kept alive and all inner and outer access to the undivided is blocked.

Jesus saw this with a more ruthless and agonized eye than any other world-teacher and fought against it in every word and action of his life. As he says in Logion 56, "Whoever has come to understand the world has found only a corpse, and whoever has found a corpse is superior to the world." What the various games of power make of the world is a "corpse," a dead, lifeless, monotonous horror of repetition; only by waking up to this (and transforming one's life accordingly) can one come out of the kingdom of death that is the search for power of any kind and be "superior to the world" and so free from its illusions to live in the Kingdom.

Jesus and Religion

▨ ▨ ▨

It is this vision and stark insight into the dividedness of the consciousness of those who seek power of any kind and the "darkness" it breeds that underlies Jesus' attacks on the scribes and Pharisees, the religious elite of his time. Jesus did not attack Judaism itself; he was brought up in the Jewish tradition and remained all his life a Jew who revered Jewish history, quoted the Scriptures accurately, loved and venerated Jerusalem the Holy City, and observed many, if not all, of the customs, even ritual purification (otherwise he would not have been invited to dine with the Pharisees). What Jesus was attacking was not the heart-core of Judaism, but betrayals of it through an obsession with purity and the law. And the way he attacked these had precedents within the Jewish tradition itself. As many scholars have pointed out, Jesus, in fact, stands squarely and magnificently within the Jewish prophetic tradition and carries on, with his unique incandescence, the prophets' legacy of indictment, warning of coming catastrophe, and calling for transformation in the name of God.

Like his great prophetic predecessors Isaiah, Jeremiah, Amos, and Joel, Jesus knew that he was risking everything by speaking out; Israel's prophets had always invited retaliation for their outspokenness. Jeremiah so angered the authorities of his day that he was beaten, put in the stocks, accused of treason, and finally lowered in a dark cistern to die. To honor the prophetic tradition, Jesus knew, was a dangerous business. But what else could someone who had seen the Kingdom and known the mercy of God do? Jesus had to call the attention of his time to the horrors and injustices that were being committed in the name of the God he loved; he, like his predecessors, had no choice.

Like the great prophets before him, Jesus' passion for God had led him to identify so completely with the divine that he not only knew the God of the Kingdom but also dared to be "invaded" by God's feelings, dared to feel not only the majesty and power of God but also the pathos of God-divine compassion for the victims of suffering, divine anger at the powerful, and oppressive, divine grief over the catastrophes that would destroy victim and victimizer alike if history was not transformed. Like the great prophets before him, Jesus became, in Rumi's great phrase, "a theatre of the divine emotions of God," a witness to what it is to live in the fire of the open heart and so feel the glory of God's compassion, the agony of God's intimate concern for every being in creation, the fury of God's rage at every form of injustice.

Matthew Fox has written: "The great contribution of the Jewish prophets to the human race is the sense of time as prophetic, urgent, unbound by cyclical inevitability: time is an occasion for divine breakthrough, the coming of new life, deeper justice, truer peace" (*The Coming of the Cosmic Christ*, p. 74). It is this "great contribution" that Jesus continues and takes to fresh heights of sacrifice and clarity; all of his life and teaching are dedicated to "divine breakthrough," the breakthrough of Kingdom-consciousness, the consciousness of the sacred open heart into the world, so that at last new life can be established and with "deeper justice and truer peace."

Like the prophets before him, Jesus saw that amongst the greatest enemies of the Kingdom and of God's rule on earth were precisely those who claimed to interpret, mediate, and represent it—the religious establishment. Selfish, hypocritical, time-serving, obsessed with honors and laws and rules that kept their power intact, they had no authentic mystical experience of the Kingdom: if they had, they would know that what they were doing and saying was a travesty of divine guardianship and divine justice. Yet by acting with such socially sanctioned authority—and in the name of God and the holiest aspects of the Tradition—they confused and diverted the authentic force of the Spirit, and kept vibrant systems of brokerage and division that not merely blocked the realization of the Kingdom in reality but were a kind of demonic shadow of it, its "living negation."

In Jesus' time, this "living negation" of the Kingdom's essence was most clear in contemporary Judaism's obsession with what Marcus Borg calls "the politics of holiness." The introduction of Roman rule had brought a crisis into every aspect of Jewish life, religious, political, social, and economic; in response to the threat produced by the Roman occupation, the Jewish social world had become dominated by the "politics of holiness."

Borg explains: "The politics of holiness was a continuation in intensified form of a cultural dynamic that had emerged in Judaism after the exile. It was expressed most succinctly in the 'holiness code,' whose central words affirmed 'you shall be holy as I the Lord your God am holy.' God was holy, and Israel was to be holy. That was to be her ethos, her way of life. Moreover, holiness was to be understood in a highly specific way, namely as separation. To be holy meant to be separate from everything that would defile holiness. The Jewish social world and its conventional wisdom became increasingly structured around the polarities of holiness as separation; clean and unclean, purity and defilement, sacred and profane, Jew and Gentile, righteous and sinner."

Borg goes on: "Holiness as the cultural dynamic shaping Israel had originated as a survival strategy during the exile and afterward as the Jewish people pondered their recent experience of destruction and suffering. They were determined to be faithful to God in order to avoid another outpouring of the divine judgment. Moreover, as a small social group—a conquered one at that, bereft of kingship and other national institutions—they were profoundly endangered by the possibility of assimilation into the surrounding cultures. Such has been the fate of most small social groups throughout history. The quest for holiness addressed both needs. It was the path of faithfulness and the path of social survival."

This "politics of holiness" was intensified by the Jewish renewal movements of first-century Palestine. The Jewish historian Josephus, who wrote during the last decades of the first century, spoke of four main "approaches" or "sects" within Palestinian Judaism: the Sadducees, who were a conservative, aristocratic group, not essentially a renewal movement; the Essenes, who believed that a life within society as it was, was impossible and withdrew into the wilderness; the Zealots, who took up active resistance against the "impure," "unholy" Romans; and, most importantly of all, that group against which Jesus most directed his derision, the Pharisees.

Like the Essenes, the Pharisees sought to subvert the threat to Jewish identity "by radicalizing the Torah in the direction of holiness. Unlike the Essenes, however, they sought to accomplish this within society by transforming the Jewish people into a 'Kingdom of priests.' To become a Pharisee meant to undertake the degree of holiness required of priests in the temple" (Borg).

What the Pharisees concentrated on were laws of purity and tithing. In Palestine, there was a double system of taxation—a political one, controlled by the Roman occupiers, and a religious one, rooted in the authority of the Torah. The Pharisees emphasized this authority and maintained that no one who had any desire to be holy (or to be thought holy) would eat untithed food: to be loyal to God was to be loyal to the Torah; to be loyal to the Torah was to pay tithes in full. The Pharisees had, of course, no police force or private army to enforce their demand, but they did wield religious and social power. For example, they boycotted the produce of nonobservant Jews and would give their tithes only to priests who observed their rules of purity.

The major weapon of the Pharisees, however, was social and religious ostracism. Those who did not observe what they considered to be the essential rules of purity and tithing were thought of as having lost all civil and religious rights; they could not sit on local councils, could not claim to be children of Abraham in the life to come, and became, in effect, foreigners, "gentiles." As several modern scholars have pointed out, the major vehicle and expression of social and religious ostracism was the refusal of table fellowship. Sharing a meal with someone showed that you accepted what they were and stood for; refusing to eat with them gave a clear, brutal signal that they were disapproved of, rejected, and even despised. No Pharisee would eat with the "impure" and the "unobservant."

The whole of Judaism—and most especially the pharisaic wing of it—was obsessed with questions of "purity." Holiness was understood to mean "separation from everything unclean," and the system of the politics of holiness equated holiness with purity. It created a purity system which established a spectrum of people that ranged from the "pure" down through differing degrees of "purity," to people on the outer margins of society who were radically and irredeemably impure. The righteous were those who followed the purity system, and "sinners" were those who did not. Certain professions, such as tax collectors and shepherds, were automatically impure; "sin" became not a matter for inner conscience, but of being "impure," and so "untouchable." The physically whole were "pure": the maimed, chronically sick, and lepers were not. Being rich did not of itself mean that one was "pure," but being abjectly poor almost inevitably made one "impure." This was partly due to the belief that wealth was a sign of divine blessing and partly because the desperately poor had no way to practice the purity laws. Men were not, of course, automatically pure nor were women automatically impure, but menstruation and childbirth, as I have already noted, were both considered sources of impurity, and these led, as in many other ancient cultures, to a general sense of the "impurity" of women. Being Jewish did not guarantee purity; but all gentiles were, by definition, impure.

The effect of this purity system, and of the "politics of holiness" that sustained it, was to create a world divided along rigid lines and divided by sharp, unbridgeable social boundaries; between the ritually pure and the ritually impure, between the physically whole and the physically damaged, between male and female, rich and poor, Jew and gentile. The entire system centered on and was controlled by the Temple and the priesthood, whose income and power depended on keeping the purity laws going, since they were derived from tithes, and the payment of tithes was one of the mainsprings of the purity system. Since the religious elite, in the form of the high priestly families, intermarried with the families of the economic and political elites, the "politics of purity" was, to a considerable extent, the ideology of all the dominant "cadres" of society, binding everyone in it together in a subtle web of definition, separation, and control.

In one of the most dramatic and pregnant of the logions of the Gospel of Thomas, Logion 37, the disciples ask Jesus, "When will you become revealed to us and when shall we see you?" Jesus answered, "When you disrobe without being ashamed and take up your garments, and place them under your feet like little children and tread on them, then you will see the son of the living one, and you will not be afraid."

What Jesus was making clear to his disciples was that until they have learned to "disrobe without being ashamed"—i.e., to strip themselves of all the social and religious concepts with which they have shored up their precarious sense of identity and with which they unconsciously protected themselves against the blazing demands of the Kingdom—and until they have taken up their "garments"—their notions, ideas, concepts of "shame" and "purity" and "holiness" and trampled on them with the abandon and vivid freedom of children—they will not be able to recognize who Jesus is, or what he is trying to birth in them. When they do learn, however, to live beyond all the traditional definitions of "purity," "shame," and "holiness" in the name of a love that transcends and obliterates all distinctions and drowns them in a burning ocean of communion, then they will see the "son of the living one" not merely in him, Jesus is implying, but also in themselves: freedom from the past and from all the dogmas and definitions of the past will disclose to them their own essential divine identity. The disciples will be revealed to themselves and will know themselves as him, as the divine consciousness, and know him in them, simply, naturally, and radically.

From the standpoint of such a vision of the freedom of divine consciousness from all man-made laws and concepts, it is easy to see why Jesus would have again and again fought vehemently against the politics of holiness and its punitive and separatist purity system. The abundant life that Jesus was and came to give and make possible could never be contained within the barriers of a man-made code. No dogmas or rules could contain its fabulous richness and vitality; authentic morality, in Jesus' living experience, flowed naturally and spontaneously from authentic and realized divine love, and could not be "imposed" from without, without withering the sources and secret origins of that love.

For Jesus, the entire creation and all the beings in it were light waves of a vast sea of light, of a vast ocean of fiery divine love. Every "level" of the creation was saturated and permeated by that light, the light of the divine consciousness and divine love. As Jesus tells us in the Gospel of Thomas, speaking in precise ecstasy from the core of his identification with this divine light-consciousness that is the truth of all things: "It is I who am the light which is above them all. It is I who am the all. From me did the all come forth. Split a piece of wood and I am there. Lift up the stone and you will find me there."

Jesus knew this transcendent immanence of the divine light-consciousness to be the truth of the universe and the truth of each human consciousness; he knew that its realization in human life brought with it a vibrant, boundary-shattering energy of love and wisdom and wild, pure freedom beyond all possible human categories. He knew that this love and wisdom-energy was the building force of the Kingdom, the force that had to be released into the real for the real to be transformed into the Kingdom. In his life and teaching, then, he sought to expose everything that masked this total vision and total possibility. And that meant exposing and overturning all the games of religious power.

Jesus' attack on the attitude and practice of the Pharisees could hardly be more ferocious. In Matthew 23:15, Jesus is reported as saying, "Woe unto you, scribes and Pharisees, hypocrites! for ye compass sea and land to make one proselyte, and when he is made, ye make him twofold more the child of hell than yourselves." For Jesus the very presence of the Pharisees is corrupting, because everything they represent betrays the truths of authentic religion. Jesus saw that the pharisaic religious elites (like all religious elites) used their authority not to ease the already terrible lives of the poverty-stricken and the weak and sick but to increase their difficulties and exploit them: "The scribes and Pharisees sit in Moses' seat . . . [and] bind heavy burdens and grievous to be borne, and lay them on men's shoulders; but they themselves will not move them with one of their fingers" (Matthew 23:2,4).

What obsesses the Pharisees is not the plight of the desperate or the truth of an authentic transmission of awareness of the Kingdom but their own honor and status; their "purity system" is a way of grabbing praise for themselves and of being honored by society and not in any way a worship of God: "But all their works they do to be seen of men: they make broad their phylacteries, and enlarge the borders of their garments, and love the uppermost rooms at feasts, and the chief seats in the synagogue" (Matthew 23:5–6).

Jesus describes the Pharisees scornfully as longing to be called "rabbi" and "master"; this betrays the egalitarian truth of the Kingdom and the paradox at the heart of the authentic divine human life; "But he that is greatest among you shall be your servant. And whosoever shall exalt himself shall be abased; and he that shall humble himself shall be exalted" (Matthew 23:11–12).

The false aping by the Pharisees of authentic divine life is not merely for Jesus a kind of blasphemy; it actively—and criminally—prevents the outbreak of the Kingdom in reality. If those who are supposed to be (and pretend to be) the arbiters of holiness, purity, and enlightenment in a culture are themselves worldly, spiritually bankrupt, and corrupt, they discourage and mislead all the beings of their world.

Jesus is reported as saying in Matthew 23:13: "But woe unto you, scribes and Pharisees, hypocrites! for ye shut up the Kingdom of heaven against men: for ye neither go in yourselves, neither suffer ye them that are entering to go in." Again and again in the Gospels, Jesus says that the worst sin of all is that against the Holy Spirit, for it is the Holy Spirit that carries to each being the inflaming message of God's compassion and of the secret divine identity of everyone. For Jesus, the Pharisees are worse sinners against the Holy Spirit than the Romans or their political flunkies, for in pretending to know God and in imposing the strict, narrow separatist rules of the "purity system," they are parodying the all-embracing nature of the Spirit and so "shutting up" the Kingdom of God against men—the ultimate betrayal in Jesus' eyes because it blinds and masks the astounding and transforming truths of the Kingdom from those who crave them.

It is important to note, I think, that Jesus does not in any way excuse the Pharisees for their "blindness or ignorance"; Jesus sees that there is a great deal of conscious and malign manipulation in what the Pharisees say and do "for ye neither go in [to the Kingdom] yourselves" (for they have neither the discipline nor the authentic mystical knowledge), "neither suffer ye that are entering to go in." Jesus is saying that anyone who is trying to live the life of the Kingdom will be derided, attacked, and sabotaged by the Pharisees "in the name of God," as he himself—and the prophets before him—had been. The malevolence and jealousy of the spiritually mediocre, Jesus knew from bitter experience, had no moral boundaries.

Jesus also denounced specifically the system of tithing that supported the Pharisees' power: "Woe unto you, scribes and Pharisees, hypocrites! for ye pay tithe of mint and anise and cumin, and have omitted the weightier matters of the law, judgment, mercy, and faith" (Matthew 23:23). Tithes on produce amounted to taxes paid to the priests and to the Temple; untithed produce was considered impure. In the name of the "purity system," then, the assiduous payment of taxes was insisted on; the authentic business of religion—"justice, mercy, and faith"—was abandoned. As a poor man himself, Jesus would have been aware of how much the poor peasant farmers who made up the majority of the society of Israel would have suffered from this system; some modern scholars believe that, with the Roman tax system and the religious tithing system, a farmer would have been paying up to thirty-five percent of his hard-earned income to the Romans and the priests. It was clear to Jesus—always a clairvoyant analyst of the games of power—that divine authority was being used to keep oppression in place. Jesus says in Matthew 23:25, "Woe unto you, scribes and Pharisees, hypocrites! for ye make clean the outside of the cup and of the platter, but within they are full of extortion and excess."

The brilliance of Jesus' analysis both of the "purity system" and the Pharisees' use of it is that he saw clearly how an obsession with purity could be used to "cover up" real "extortion and excess." As long as the pharisaic emphasis on external regulations, purifications, and requirements was kept vibrant, the actual inner practice of the Pharisees would not be scrutinized; a society terrorized into endless observances in order to "placate" God will not have time or energy or inclination to study the inner lives of its religious elite. The "purity system," then, by a brutal irony which Jesus was not slow to point out, became the "guardian" of dark inner impurity and outer injustice. In Matthew 23:27–28, Jesus rails, "Woe unto you, scribes and Pharisees! for ye are like unto whited sepulchers, which indeed appear beautiful outward but are within full of dead men's bones, and of all uncleanness. Even so ye also outwardly appear righteous unto men, but within ye are full of hypocrisy and iniquity."

Authentic purity for Jesus had nothing to do whatever with external observance. As he says in Mark 7:15, consciously subverting the entire religious system of his time, "There is nothing from without a man, that entering into him can defile him: but the things which come out of him, those are they that defile the man." When Jesus says in the Beatitudes, "Blessed are the pure in heart; for they shall see God," he is not talking about "ritual" purity but about something far harder to glimpse, let alone sustain: real purity of heart. And the reward that Jesus is offering for such "purity of heart" is not a sense of having "placated" God or obeyed some "divine" regulation but an actual mystical experience and "sight" of God. Obeying ritual regulations does not transform consciousness; struggling to achieve and sustain authentic purity of heart does, because it leads to the naked vision of God, and of the Kingdom.

A self-righteous obsession with "external" purity can, in fact, prevent that inner cultivation of purity of heart that leads to transparence to God and the "sight" of the Kingdom. It is easier, after all, to follow external regulations than to do the harsh, sometimes bloody and bitter, work of "guarding" the heart from defilement; this is humbling, pride-shattering labor that has always to be renewed and deepened.

And yet not to do such work is never to have the chance of a "sight" of God and so of one's own divine truth. Was it precisely to deny such a vision of God to people that the "purity system" was created? When Jesus says of the Pharisees, "For ye neither go in[to the Kingdom] yourselves neither suffer ye that are entering to go in," is he also implying that the whole pharisaic system is a subtle prison, a brilliant dark way of denying to human beings the taste of direct divine experience and the radical empowerment that must follow from it? A world terrorized by religious obligation will be easily policed in every way, after all; people compelled to spend their energies in external obedience will never devote them to the kind of inner discovery that could lead to knowledge of and entry into the Kingdom.

In Logion 70 of the Gospel of Thomas, Jesus says, "That which you have will save you if you bring it forth from yourselves. That which you do not have within you will kill you if you do not have it within you." But how can anyone trapped in a "purity system" ever hope to know how to "bring forth" "that which you have"? How can they ever enter into the full extravagance of divine love and of the secret of sonship and daughtership it reveals? Not to know what is "within you" leads, as the logion reveals, to death: the "purity system" and widespread spiritual death—the depression of a whole social world—are intimately connected.

For Jesus, true divine life is lived in and from an awakened "pure" heart in the sacred atmosphere of compassion for all beings. But how could such compassion be awoken in hearts deadened or scared by ritual obligations and categories? A society structured around the "purity system" and the "politics of holiness" was, in the deepest religious sense, both "impure" and "unholy" because it lacked the compassion that for Jesus is the one true sign of the divine life.

Jesus' parable of the Good Samaritan illustrates this lack of compassion. A man is beaten by robbers and left for dead by the side of the road; a priest and Levite see him, and see him bleeding, but do nothing, and pass him by.

By Jewish religious law, both priest and Levite were compelled to maintain a certain level of "purity"; one of the most contaminating of all sources of "impurity" was contact with death; the wounded man is described as "half-dead," suggesting "that one couldn't tell whether he was dead without coming close to incur impurity if he was" (Marcus Borg).

Because of their desire, then, to observe so-called "holy" laws of "purity," the priest (and supposed guardian of God's truth) and Levite pass by the bleeding man who needs help. The man who does help him is a Samaritan— not surprisingly, someone who is radically impure in the terms of religious law. The ones sanctified by law, Tradition, and religion do nothing to aid a dying man; the one whom Jewish law, Tradition, and religion condemn as a defiled outcast and outsider is the one who actually lives out the law of God.

Jesus did not confine his attacks on the scribes and Pharisees and their "politics of holiness" merely to his teachings; his actions also opposed and subverted the "purity system" and its hierarchies. Jesus healed many times on the Sabbath, contrary to established religious laws, saying, when the scribes and Pharisees objected, that "man was made for the Sabbath and not the Sabbath for man." He did not limit the use of the vast powers of healing graced to him merely to heal "good," "pure" Jews; he healed those who needed him and believed in him, whatever their class, previous life, or even nationality. (One of the most moving of all his miracles is that of the healing of the Roman centurion's daughter.)

The stories of his healings shatter all the boundaries of the purity system in his world. He dared to touch the ultimately unclean and impure—lepers and hemorrhaging women. He dared to go into a graveyard inhabited by a man possessed of a "legion" of unclean spirits, who lived near a herd of equally unclean pigs. In the manner in which he healed—freely, almost casually, normally—Jesus showed that access to divine power was possible outside of any established religious authorities; the grace of God and the power of the Kingdom were for every human being, and were poured out into the whole of reality and not just into those portions decreed "sacred" by the religious elite.

Unlike the scribes and Pharisees who chose carefully according to the "purity" laws those with whom they would eat, or not, Jesus kept an open table and practiced what Crossan has called "open commensality." To know what, where, how, when, and with whom people eat is to know the character of their society. In Jesus' world, the rules of "commensality" were very strict; Pharisees and others would not eat with anyone who was "impure," and no respectable person would dream of sharing a meal with an outcast. Table fellowship was, in Crossan's words, "a means of economic discrimination, social hierarchy, and political discrimination."

In his daily practice, Jesus rebelled calmly against the deepest rules of his world. He lived his own parable of the Banquet and the injunctions of the master in it: "Go therefore to the thoroughfare and invite to the marriage feast as many as you can find." In the parable, the master's servants "went out into the streets and gathered all whom they found," both bad and good, so the wedding hall was filled with guests. In his daily life, Jesus made a point of sitting down with every kind of person, even outcasts. Jesus' table had the freedom from man-made rules and concepts and differentiations of the Kingdom itself. Just as the table of the Pharisees was a mirror in miniature of the hierarchical world they lived in and strove to keep alive, so Jesus' table—where outcasts ate with unmarried women and tax collectors and apostles all together with Jesus himself—was a mirror of the all-embracing mercy and compassion of the Kingdom, a mirror, in fact, of the supreme feast and Sacred Marriage of matter and spirit, heart and body, heaven and earth to which God was always summoning the whole of humanity.

Very often, the meals Jesus shared with others were festive in nature. The Gospels reveal this in a small detail; they tell us that participants "reclined" at table. Ordinary meals were eaten seated; at feasts, guests reclined. In Judaic lore, reclining at a meal is also the sign of a free man. In a marvelous phrase, William Blake calls Jesus "the bright preacher of Life"; wherever he went, the Gospels tell us, he was accompanied by an atmosphere of joy and wonder (as well as by the opposition that his charisma and opinions excited). He called himself the "bridegroom"; the feasts that sprang up around him—in the open country or in private homes—were signs of the marriage of the divine and human that was taking place within his own heart and at the heart of the revolutionary teaching of transformation that he was giving the world. They were, in fact, living signs of the Kingdom, signs that it could exist, and did exist, when love was self-forgetful and all-tolerant enough.

Jesus' practice of "open commensality" aroused bitter controversy. In a world preoccupied as his was by the intricacies of ritual and status, the idea of eating together and living together without any differences, distinctions, discriminations, or hierarchies was irrational, absurd, and menacing to all the accepted notions of "purity" and "impurity," "sacred" and "profane." The religious elite might lecture about God's infinite love, but actually putting it into practice—and at the heart of social relations—was a radical act they could not understand or stomach.

The Gospels tell us that Jesus was accused of "eating with tax collectors and sinners" and charged with being "a glutton and a drunkard, a friend of tax collectors and sinners." Since women (and sometimes unmarried women) were often present, Jesus was also denounced as "eating with whores." In what scholars now call "the Jesus movement," all were embraced—women, untouchables, the poor, maimed, the marginalized. In a society ordered by a purity system, the inclusiveness of Jesus' table fellowship and movement embodied an alternative social vision, one whose radical egalitarianism reversed—and was intended to reverse—all the precedents of tradition.

Jesus and His Disciples

The way in which Jesus taught also overturned the accepted categories of "teaching" and the accepted traditional distance between "teacher" and "taught."

Jesus taught mostly in Aramaic—a rich, poetic language that does not draw sharp lines between means and ends, inner quality and outer action, and whose grammar, sentence structure, and way of moving, like Arabic, in webs of constellated meanings, enshrines a fluid and holistic view of the cosmos, in which the arbitrary boundaries in Greek or Latin between mind, body, and spirit fall away. In other words, the language itself that Jesus used—and used with such brilliance and spiritual beauty—emanated something of the consciousness of the Kingdom and involved those who listened to him naturally in an act of imaginative listening so much greater and more complex than any that can be conveyed by subsequent translations.

To study Aramaic and to read Jesus' sayings in the most ancient and probably most authentic version of all—the "Peshitta" Aramaic version of the Gospels—is to enter a non-moralistic, entirely numinous, and sacred field of energy, the energy of the Kingdom. In Aramaic, sayings that have been translated "definitely" in Greek, Latin, or English reveal multiple richness of meaning, all of which would have been accessible to his audience. Jesus spoke as "one having authority," but not usually in an "authoritarian" way; the language he used was, for the most part, not hectoring, linear, full of linear injunctions and stipulations but polyphonic, poetic, profoundly imaginative, designed not to "lay down the law" but to inspire and initiate.

To take just one example from the Peshitta version of the Gospels of one of the Beatitudes: "Tubwayhun layleyn dadkeyn b'lebhon d'hinnon nehzun alaha" is translated in the King James version as "Blessed are the pure in heart for they shall see God." As Neil Douglas-Klotz points out in his *Prayers of the Cosmos,* this beatitude can also simultaneously mean "Blessed are the consistent in heart; they shall contemplate the One"; "Healthy are those whose passion is electrified by deep, abiding purpose; they shall regard the power that moves and shows itself in all things"; "Aligned with the One are those whose lives radiate from a core of love; they shall see love everywhere";

"Healed are those who have the courage and audacity to feel abundant inside; they shall envision the furthest extent of life's wealth"; and "Resisting corruption are those whose natural reaction is sympathy and friendship; they shall be illuminated by a flash of lightning; the source of the soul's movement in all creatures."

According to the Hebrew scholar Fabre D'Olivet, the tragedy of biblical translation has been that expressions that were meant to resonate on many different levels of meaning—at least the intellectual, metaphorical, and universal—have been "whittled down to become wholly gross in their nature . . . restricted to material and particular expressions" (*The Hebrew Tongue Restored*, 1815). This tendency to divide and overliteralize was reflected in the whole modern scientific era. As Neil Douglas-Klotz points out, "A period that repressed mystical cosmology was also ill at ease with mystical translation."

This is especially disastrous in the case of Jesus, for overliteralized translation turns rich, transformative speech into moralistic "teaching," so betraying the essence of the imaginative participation and passionate intuitive listening and understanding that Jesus wanted and that is essential to his desire to bring the Kingdom alive on earth. Jesus, like another great mystical poet and teacher Rumi, was speaking out of the heart and under the inspiration of a supreme mystical understanding and vision; the way he spoke was designed not to "teach" the lessons of that understanding but to transmit mysteriously its presence and ecstasy, to bring, through imagery, humor, and constellated meaning, the electric richness of the Kingdom alive, to involve the listener in a heart-to-heart and soul-to-soul exchange of the deepest and richest "inner" truth, and not at all to promulgate a set of "laws" and "rules," which would merely carry on the kinds of "divided" awareness that blocked the Kingdom's truth.

Significantly, Jesus taught the truth of the Kingdom mainly in parables. Parables are an "invitational" form of speech, not an authoritarian one. They are evocative. They tease and stimulate the imagination into action; they suggest more than they say, and need for their full effect to be "completed" in the mind and heart of the listener. They are, in fact, invitations to a transformation in perception.

As an "invitational" form of speech, parables do not in any way invoke external authority. Unlike teaching that is done from specific texts or Torah commentaries, parables do not appeal to divine authority, as do the speech forms of divine lawgivers and prophets. They exist themselves and of themselves and their authority rests solely in their own effectiveness; they are innately egalitarian in the way they invite and respect the participation of the listener and open up meaning without narrowly defining them or insisting on any one set of interpretations.

The way in which Jesus used parables and stocked them with the images of daily life in Palestine suggested one of the essential truths of the Kingdom—that its presence is everywhere and in all things, not just in those activities and things deemed sacred by a religious elite. Jesus' teaching of the holiest and deepest truths in simple words and images drawn from ordinary life was not simply a marvelously effective way of interesting the people he talked to but a living sign and proof that God was everywhere, and that truth could flash out from and in all things and activities. It was a way of bringing the *nearness* of the Kingdom alive, and of *empowering* his listeners with the thrill and joy and responsibility of that nearness.

Jesus tried by all the spiritual and imaginative means at his disposal to limit the gap between him and his listeners, to awaken them not to a "vision" neatly set out in laws, dogmas, and "paradigms" but to the mysterious knowledge of divine truths that they already had within them, to reveal to them that the world they lived in and the lives they led were already instinct with divine possibilities. Just as at his table Jesus welcomed everyone, so, in his way of speaking, Jesus opened the arms of language to everyone, inviting all who listened to him to awaken to their own spiritual creativity and inherent wisdom.

Just as in the inclusiveness of his table fellowship and movement Jesus had manifested an alternative social order, so in the original and imaginative way in which he taught, Jesus manifested an alternative religious order, one in which a "son of man" spoke out of his passion for God to other "sons and daughters of man" without hiding behind authority, without the need for any external authority or justification, in simple, wonderfully rich natural images and stories that were available at one level or another to everyone but which also contained the highest truth. Just as everyone who sat with him at his table sat with the bridegroom at the marriage feast of the Kingdom, so everyone who listened to him participated in another kind of feast, prepared for them and served to them in love—a feast of insight, truth, belief, lavish, simple, and radiant as God himself, and as humble.

An iconoclastic humility characterizes Jesus' own presentation of himself and his mission. If Jesus had criticized the power struggles and hierarchies of his time (and by implication of all time) while pointing to himself continually as a "savior" or "guru" figure, he would merely have created another system of power and hierarchy with himself at the head of it; he would have perpetuated by other means exactly that need for adoration and exclusiveness that he castigated in the Pharisees and analyzed as lying at the heart of human misery. Jesus would, in fact, have been a hypocrite on an even more danger-ous, and more consciously demonic, scale than the false priests he derided, and no different from hordes of other charismatic healers and teachers—many with astonishing powers—who litter human history with their fantasy of "unique" divinity and their pretension to have discovered "new" ways of freedom, which are merely the old systems of slavery, updated and redeco-rated for changing circumstances.

Jesus went out of his way on many occasions to distance himself from the projections of "divinity" that his extraordinary gifts excited. He never claimed to be omniscient or omnipotent or enlightened or even completely good; he never claimed what the dogma of the Trinity, created three cen-turies after his death, claimed for him: that he was "one substance with the Father." In Matthew 19:16–17, for instance, we read: "And behold one came to him and said unto him, Good master, what good thing shall I do, that I may have eternal life?" Jesus' response is immediate: "Why callest thou me good? There is none good, but one, that is, God." He answered as the good Jew he was; only God can ever be completely good; the young man's vision of him as a "good master" is his own fantasy, not the reality.

In John 10:33—when he is accused of blasphemy by the Jews (precisely for claiming divinity)—Jesus quotes back at them (verse 34): "Is it not writ-ten in your law, I said, Ye are gods." Here Jesus is quoting from Psalm 82:

"God standeth in the congregation of the mighty; he judgeth among the gods. How long will ye judge unjustly, and accept the persons of the wicked? Selah. Defend the poor and fatherless; do justice to the afflicted and needy. Deliver the poor and needy: rid them out of the hand of the wicked. They know not, neither will they understand; they walk on in darkness; all the foundations of the earth are out of course. *I have said Ye are gods; and all of you are children of the most High* [italics mine]. But ye shall die like men, and fall like one of the princes. Arise, O God, judge the earth: for thou shall inherit all nations."

Here, Jesus is turning the accusation of blasphemy that the Pharisees are directing against him into an accusation of their ignorance of the depths of their own tradition. Didn't God say that all human beings were gods and children of the most high? Does this not mean that every human being has a secret divine identity and reality that must be realized? If it isn't realized, Jesus implies, the whole horror of oppression and injustice that characterizes human history will continue; the fatherless and the poor and the needy will continue to be ignored and dealt with unjustly; those who were meant to live in the Kingdom in an atmosphere of divine compassion as conscious divine human beings will "die like men, and fall like one of the princes."

Jesus is not claiming to be uniquely divine; what he is claiming is to have realized his divine identity and to be doing works in the power and with the effectiveness that such realization brings. He is implying that everyone who realized like him their "oneness with the Father" would also be able to perform miracles and inflame others to charity and justice. Later in the Gospel of John, Jesus makes the astounding prediction (John 14:12): "He that believeth on me, the works that I do shall he do also; and greater works than these shall he do."

Had Jesus wanted to be revered as a "unique" savior with "unique" powers he would never have made such a promise; the "belief" he is asking for in him is not as a "savior" but as a path-blazer, as one who has opened a path for others to follow and to come to live in exactly the same atmosphere of truth and empowerment. Like the historical Buddha, the historical Jesus presented his enlightenment as a sign of what was possible for all human beings if they gave, suffered, and struggled enough and realized the divine truth of their natures. As Jesus says in Luke 6:40: "The disciple is not above his master; but every one that is perfect shall be as his master." To become "perfect as his master," the disciple will have to take on the burden of realizing, as his "master" did, the truth of his divine identity; a far harder task than merely "adoring" the master or following superficially some of his or her injunctions.

As Jesus says in Luke 6:46: "And why call ye me, Lord, Lord, and do not the things which I say?" What Jesus clearly wanted was not even the most exalted kinds of lip service or celebration; he wanted to inspire everyone to become like him, their complete human divine self, and live consciously and actively in the holy fire and charity of the Kingdom. What else could change humanity?

Another set of dogmas or laws, even another "religion," would not change anything. Only a way of radical transformation—the way Jesus knew he was pioneering and representing—could alter the conditions of power on earth and reveal the mercy and splendor of the Kingdom to anyone who underwent its rigors with faith and sincerity.

Being called a "master," being set apart from others, would only unravel and destroy the core of his message to the world—that everyone would live in the divine glory of joy and power as he did; what Jesus wanted was a far more demanding intimacy of recognition. In the Gospel of Thomas, he is reported as saying, in Logion 2, "Let him who seeks continue seeking until he finds. When he finds he will be troubled. When he becomes troubled, he will be astonished and he will rule over the all." The "safety" of being a "follower" has to be abandoned for the "trouble" of discovering the vastness and majesty of one's own and everyone's divine identity, and for the "astonishment" that follows on such a discovery and such an effort (an astonishment that dissolves all previous categories of understanding and reveals the divinity of the universe). The safety of being a "seeker" has to be exchanged for the "trouble," "astonishment," and responsibility for rulership of being a "finder." Only then can the truth of what Jesus is and knows be recognized as the truth of all beings, and known not through worship but as he knows it himself in direct, suffering, astonishing, ecstatic knowledge.

As Jesus says in the Secret Book of James:

Become better than I; be like the son of the holy spirit! . . .

Be eager to be saved without being urged. Instead, become zealous on your own, and if possible, surpass even me. For that is how the Father will love you.

Don't let heaven's domain wither away. For it is like a date palm shoot whose fruit fell down around it. It put forth buds, and when they blossomed, its productivity was caused to dry up. So it is also with the fruit that came from this singular root: when it was picked, fruit was gathered by many. Truly, this was good. Isn't it possible to produce new growth now? Can't you discover how?

Jesus then is reported as saying, "Damn you who need an intercessor. Damn you who stand in need of grace. Congratulations on those who have spoken out fearlessly and obtain grace for themselves." Jesus himself had never needed an intercessor in his direct relationship with the divine; he himself had "spoken out fearlessly" and obtained grace. Those who followed him, then, followed him in the passion of his fight for justice and in the splendor of his independence, and would, like him, discover the life of fire in the Kingdom as their eternal reward.

The complete transformation of the being that Jesus wanted for everyone simply could not take place if Jesus himself were "externally" worshipped instead of being known and loved as the most intimate—and outrageous—of all possibilities. When Jesus says, then, "I am the way, the truth and the life," he is not speaking as a leader cajoling followers into accepting his authority (and his alone): he is speaking as the voice of the Kingdom within everyone, as the herald of that divine consciousness that is everyone's secret.

In the actual enacting of his mission, the historical Jesus seems to have taken enormous pains to avoid being deified or adored. After healing someone, he nearly always asks him or her to go to the Temple and offer up thanks for God; he does not claim the healing for himself. The way in which Jesus constantly moved—from village to village, district to district—showed how seriously he took his own vision of the Kingdom as a relationship between all beings and God of direct, unbrokered equality; to have stayed in any one place and built a "cult" around himself (which was the normal practice of charismatics in first-century Palestine and would have been very profitable for both Jesus and his family), would have been to privilege one place above others and to castrate the force of his message. Jesus wanted, during his brief ministry, to give away everything he knew and all the healing powers he had to as many people as could embrace them in as many different places and locations as possible; his vagrancy is an essential part of his message, since radical itinerancy is the "necessary concomitant, geographical equivalent, and symbolic demonstration of radical egalitarianism . . . the equal sharing of spiritual and material gifts, of miracle and table, cannot be centered in one place, because that very hierarchy of place, of here over there, symbolically destroys the radical egalitarianism it announces" (Crossan, p. 89).

In other ways, too, Jesus tried to destroy all forms of spiritual hierarchy. We are told in Matthew 20:21 that the mother of Zebedee's children came in and demanded of Jesus that her two sons should sit, "one on thy right hand, and the other on thy left, in thy kingdom." Jesus gently informs her that such a gift is not his to give, "but it shall be given to them for whom it is prepared of my Father" (verse 23). This small aside is revealing; Jesus is explicitly rejecting the creation of a hierarchy in his name; in fact, Jesus is saying he does not have the right to say who will sit on his left or right hand, for the power and the choice are always God's and always hidden in the mystery of God.

The other disciples then get angry with the sons of Zebedee; here Jesus takes the opportunity of their anger to give them an explicit teaching on what he wants for those who follow his path: "Jesus called them unto him and said, Ye know that the princes of the Gentiles exercise dominion over them, and they that are great exercise authority upon them. But it shall not be so among you; but whosoever will be great among you, let him be your minister;

and whosoever will be chief among you, let him be your servant. Even as the Son of man came not to be ministered unto, but to minister."

Jesus knew that in the love of the Kingdom all beings are equal and that any hierarchy would, however subtly, inevitably separate human beings from each other and from their own deepest selves. His experience had taught him not merely the beauty but the necessity of final humility; true "mastery," he had discovered, lay not in perpetuating all old forms of domination but in being the most abject servant of love.

The rules of the Kingdom of God were the reverse of all the rules that the false self projected and kept alive on earth. True divine mastery lay not in any kind of system of domination—that belonged to the princes of the gentiles, to the powerful of this world, the world created by insecurity and panic and inner desolation. It lay, rather, in the choice of service to others, in the deliberate effacing of oneself, and in the refusal of any human and therefore transient and imperfect authority for the eternal authority of love, which would always express itself in humbler and humbler "ministering" to others. He himself, Jesus tells them, has shown them this in the way in which he has been acting and giving of himself; the Son of Man has not come to be "ministered unto" but to minister.

In Matthew 23, Jesus returns to this theme: "He that is greatest among you shall be your servant. And whosoever shall exalt himself shall be abased; and he that shall humble himself shall be exalted." Jesus is suggesting that in the paradoxical world of the Kingdom, the very act of humbling oneself is an act of "exaltation," a "lowering" that is simultaneously an ascension to the threshold of divine consciousness. Sustained over a lifetime of service, such passionate self-annihilation before the needs and agonies of others ensures the continual conscious presence of God in all things and beings, the continual conscious living in the Kingdom. Nothing else for Jesus could be called divine life, and nothing less than the presence of this final humility could be a sign of holiness. Such was the life he lived, and such was the holiness he enacted, and wanted to transmit to those who followed him.

Jesus' own powers did not make him proud; he knew they came from the Father, and he wanted this humbling knowledge to be always present in the minds of those he was to send out to teach in his name. Jesus says in Luke 10:19: "Behold, I give unto you power to tread on serpents and scorpions, and over all the power of the enemy and nothing shall by any means hurt you. Notwithstanding in this rejoice not that the spirits are subject unto you, but rather rejoice because your names are written in heaven." Again, in Matthew

10, Jesus instructs the disciples he is sending out into the world: "Heal the sick, cleanse the lepers, raise the dead, cast out devils; freely ye have received, freely give." Everything the disciples knew or had, they had received from God *freely;* they should give it freely, and with a free mind and heart, without any thought of recompense or reward, and in the humility and joy of true love. For what were they to transmit but that humility and joy that were the foundations of all the powers invested in them? Transmitting those was part of the healing of the whole being that Jesus envisaged his followers being able to effect, and far more importantly necessary and difficult than teaching rules and dogmas. As Jesus says in the Gospel of Mary to his disciples: "Go then and preach the Gospel of the Kingdom. Do not lay down rules beyond which I appointed to you, and do not give a law, like the lawgiver [Moses] lest you be constrained by it." Nothing, nothing at all, was to be done in the "old way" and with the old hierarchical system in mind: the free and all-embracing nature of God's love and spirit was to be revered humbly and enacted in humble service.

Jesus also gave his disciples specific instruction as to how they should set about teaching and healing: "Provide neither gold, nor silver, nor brass in your purses, nor scrip for your journey, neither two coats, neither shoes . . . for the workman is worthy of his meat" (Matthew 10:9–10). His disciples were to go out as equals with those they were to help, sharing both spiritual healing powers and material resources with the world, dependent on good will. In doing so, they both symbolically and actually represented the loving, boundaryless, interdependent world of the Kingdom, a world in which all resources, since "freely given" by God, were to be freely shared, and without any special dignity or pride of any kind.

The earliest texts stress that Jesus wants the disciples to eat the food of those they help and to be sustained in this direct way. As Crossan writes: "Commensality was not, for Jesus, merely a strategy for supporting the mission. That could have been done by alms, wages, charges or fees of some sort. It could also have been done by simple begging. Commensality was, rather, a strategy for building or rebuilding peasant community on radically different principles from those of patronage and clientage." Jesus told his disciples also not to carry a knapsack or staff. Since commensality is not just a technique for support but itself a message, they were not to dress in such a way as to declare self-sufficiency or indeed authority of any kind; because they were apostles of the freedom and interdependence of the Kingdom, they would be signs of courage, total generosity, and total trust. They would combine, as Jesus did himself, itinerancy and dependence; they would do their work of healing, stay for a while, and then move on. No "center" would be created, no group of initiates would be left behind. Their task was to light the fire of the Kingdom and to move on, wherever they were called. Jesus never said anything about the founding of a church; nor is it likely, modern scholars now believe, that the original mission was confined to the twelve apostles. (This last belief is probably the addition of Mark.) The Jesus movement at its origin reflected the hierarchy-free and unbound vision of its founder.

That the refusal of all hierarchy was essential to Jesus' vision of the Kingdom and of his own role is illustrated by the account in St. John's Gospel of his washing of the disciples' feet at the Last Supper. In John 13:4–5 we read: "He riseth from supper, and laid aside his garments; and took a towel and girded himself. After that he poureth water into a basin, and began to wash the disciples' feet, and to wipe them with the towel wherewith he was girded."

In this extraordinary scene, which has no parallel that I am aware of in the life of any other world-teacher, Jesus strips himself of every rank and dignity. He takes on the role not merely of a servant but, as some modern commentators have pointed out, of a female servant (whose duty would be to wash her guests' feet), so putting himself absolutely outside all of his world's rules and social limits.

John's narrative continues: "Then cometh he to Simon Peter; and Peter saith unto him, Lord, dost thou wash my feet?" Jesus answered, "What I do thou knowest not now; but thou shalt know hereafter. Peter saith unto him, Thou shalt never wash my feet. Jesus answered him, If I wash thee not, thou hast no part with me."

What is significant in this passage is that it is Peter—Peter who would later be the "founder" of the hierarchical church—who, according to John, resisted Jesus' symbolic self-effacement; he simply cannot understand the profound mystical significance of what Jesus is doing, cannot understand or is too deranged by its reversal of his "beliefs" to dare to understand it. For Peter, it is a kind of blasphemy for the Lord to wash his disciples' feet; for Jesus it is a revelation of the essence of Kingdom-consciousness and of his own being. That is presumably what Jesus means when he replies, "What I do now thou knowest not but thou shalt know hereafter": he is telling Peter gently that he is not yet "awake" enough to comprehend the full importance of his gesture, but that he will be. Peter, with typical bull-headedness, resists this mysterious advice and seems to become angry: "Thou shalt never wash my feet." Unconsciously, Peter wishes to perpetuate the distance of reverence between him and Jesus, wishes to go on "adoring" Jesus and so living in subtle separation from him; it is just this subtle separation of "adoration" that Jesus' actions—and on such an important night—are trying to dissolve. Jesus then answers him: "If I wash thee not, thou hast no part in me." If Peter does not allow himself to be washed by Jesus, he will not allow himself to be "washed clean" by the true vision of the Kingdom, washed clean of all concepts and ideas of dignity, rank, and hierarchy, and so will never either understand the full divine madness of Jesus' love or come into the full divine madness of his own capacity for total self-donation; he will go on thinking he is serving Jesus' dignity by refusing to be washed by him but in fact will have "no part" in Jesus' authentic mission—the revelation of those laws of love of the Kingdom which destroy all barriers between all beings, and bring the whole of life into the conscious blaze of charity.

Jesus not only washes the feet of the disciples to dissolve the invisible barrier of adoration between him and them; he also does so specifically, on the last night that he will be with them in a human body, to try and destroy all rivalries and struggles for power within their ranks. As Jesus says in John 13:13–15: "Ye call me Master and Lord: and ye say well; for so I am. If I then, your Lord and Master, have washed your feet, ye also ought to wash one another's feet. For I have given you an example, that ye should do as I have done to you." The divine consciousness that Jesus is in—the consciousness of the Kingdom—cannot help serving others out of extreme love: no man-made separations or ranks or distinctions between "male" and "female" functions exist in it; it is not self-conscious at all, for there is no personal self to be conscious of. This is the one consciousness that can end the games of hierarchy and power that disfigure all human relations and release beings into their essential freedom. As Jesus says in verse 17, "If ye know these things, happy are ye if ye do them." In one ultimate, sublimely deranging act, Jesus tries for the last time to so shake the perceptions of his disciples that they can at last see who he is and who they could be, and who they must become if they are really to be in his—and the Kingdom's—true Sacred Heart.

It is not Jesus' fault if he was not understood and turned into precisely the savior and guru figure he never wanted to be. He did everything possible to avoid such a fate, knowing that the success of his real mission lay in avoiding it. In Logion 91 of the Gospel of Thomas we read: "They said to him, 'Tell us who you are so that we may believe in you.' Jesus said to them, 'You read the face of the sky and of the earth, but you have not recognized the one who is before you and you do not know how to read this moment.'" The one who was before them was the deepest secret of their own heart and soul made manifest, living out in front of their eyes their own richest life; if they had been able to "read this moment" and penetrate its present eternal depth, they would have known this. What they needed was not to be told anything or even to "believe"; being told and "believing" belongs to the old world that the living experience of the Kingdom supersedes. What they needed to do, Jesus tells them, is to recognize him, to see by the eye of the soul "who" he was (and is): not an external savior who needs to "tell who he is" and be "believed in," but the inmost mystery of themselves, and its consciousness of eternity and eternal love that sustain each moment in God's universe.

What his disciples recognized, Jesus knew, they would only recognize through their identity with it. Once the Spirit had opened their eyes, they would become, through the alchemy of grace, what they saw; then, as "readers of the present moment," they would live in the eternal present of the Kingdom, and be living fire-signs of its glory. Then, there would be no need to demand, "Tell us who you are so that we may believe"; they would be what they needed to know. And when they were what they needed to know, all distinctions between "master" and "disciple," "teacher" and "taught" would be forever destroyed.

Jesus as Political Revolutionary

Had Jesus merely been a social and religious radical, his message and vision might not have been so threatening to his time; but he was also—and in a unique way—a political revolutionary.

In Logion 10 of the Gospel of Thomas, Jesus is reported as saying, "I have cast fire upon the world and, see, I am guarding it until it blazes." The "fire" that Jesus cast upon the world is the fire of his burning ecstatic vision of the Kingdom, the light-fire that his great prophetic predecessor Isaiah saw and celebrated in his vision of a divinized world. "Violence shall no more be heard within thy land, wasting nor destruction within thy borders; but thou shalt call thy walls Salvation, and thy gates Praise. The sun shall be no more thy light by day; neither for brightness shall the moon give light unto thee: but the Lord shall be unto thee an everlasting light, and thy God thy glory. Thy sun shall no more go down; neither shall thy moon withdraw itself; for the Lord shall be thine everlasting light, and the days of thy mourning shall be ended" (Isaiah 60:18–20).

The fire that Jesus "cast upon the world" was his vision of the sun of justice and mercy, of Cosmic-consciousness, in and by whose light a wholly new and possible divine human world stood revealed—a world in which the will of Love would at last be done, and all hierarchies, all separations between beings, between male and female, black and white, rich and poor, would be obliterated in a blaze of mutual generosity and mystical recognition. This Cosmic consciousness with which Jesus wholly identified himself would "guard" the fire, keep its flame alive and active and brilliantly threatening to all forms of false power and false glory until it could install the only real power—that of divine authority—and the only authentic glory—that of the living fire-presence of divine love. And in the blaze of the one real power and the one authentic glory, all imitations of either in every arena of human life would be destroyed, and heaven and earth would at last, at long last, become one, one fire of God. The dream of the divine would at last be realized; the Kingdom would be birthed here on earth, in time, in matter, in the most intimate recess of every human relationship, in every cell of the transfigured body, "for the Lord shall be thine everlasting light, and the days of thy mourning shall be ended."

Such a vision threatens all political visions that do not have at their heart and deepest aim the establishment of the glory of God on earth; it burns down, in fact, all superficial divisions between "religious" and "social" and "political." In the blaze of the one fire, all such convenient separations seem absurd. To see and feel the compassion of God is inevitably to come to judge all human arrangements by the light of that compassion and to find them all wanting and to yearn and labor to see them all transformed; compassion cannot not be political, just as a vision of God's justice cannot not be a vision also of man's.

The vast mystical illumination that Jesus was possessed by and articulated with such clarity and consistency could not help but also be a political one, because by its light all the games and ploys of a power-seeking world were unmasked and the necessity for a total change in the way humanity performs all its tasks made clear. To someone who has not seen the Kingdom, the games of power can seem sad but unavoidable rituals in a mostly evil world that needs hierarchy and power elites not to crumble into chaos. But to someone to whom the Kingdom and its glory has been revealed—and to whom the glory of the human spirit and soul have also been revealed—no arrangement deserves to be fostered that does not constantly encourage and inspire the transformation of the human into the divine human and does not constantly invoke the potential splendor of a new world, one in which the glory of God and of the Spirit and of the love between them would not only be honored but actively reflected in every law, every transaction between beings, every concerted "social," "religious," and "political" action.

Far from splitting off "religion" from "politics," as so many Christian commentators from St. Augustine onwards have claimed (to the convenience of the Church whose own earthly power then would never be criticized), Jesus' radical act was to bring them together, to make them two halves of one enterprise—the revolutionary one of birthing the Kingdom on earth. All human powers, skills, feelings, and desires were to be concentrated in one constantly burning sacrificial flame of attention on this task; only through such a gathering together of all human faculties and all human ways of acting could the Kingdom be birthed. The undivided life of Cosmic-consciousness and divine love would create an undivided world.

Jesus knew that for this vast transformation to be possible, all ways of acting within the world would have to be changed. When he said "my Kingdom is not of this world," he did not mean that it belonged to some purely ethereal realm: he was not in any way an escapist. What Jesus meant was that the Kingdom had nothing to do with *this* world, the banal, violent world created by human greed, ignorance, and folly; the Kingdom was the hidden soul's reflection in reality and not the reflection of that blind false self that had—goaded on and inspired by evil forces—largely made human history. To make the hidden reflection of the soul "real" was the task of the life that Jesus came to "give more abundantly," of the new being he was trying to inspire into action, and of the living and very heteroclite community that sprang up around him.

The Jesus movement, as we have seen, embraced outcasts, celebrated the religious truth of women, praised, even venerated, the poor, and implicitly and explicitly critiqued all the ways in which religious power was mediated and transmitted by the Pharisees and priests. The magical power of Jesus' presence, healings, and teaching gathered around him the ragged beginnings of an alternative society dedicated to bringing into reality the beauty and compassion of the Kingdom. We can assume, I think, that the creation of this alternative society and world was wholly within Jesus' conscious intention; he did not want to engage the power of the world directly in any kind of display of military or even political power. His aim, as the parable of the Mustard Seed makes clear, was subversion by other means—an insemination of the body politic by the Holy Spirit that would result in a galvanic transformation from within, as more and more beings, awakened by love, came to yearn for and want to incarnate the Kingdom's laws of compassion, and so change all relations of power.

There are, however, signs of a radical social and political program within this larger vision of spiritual transformation. Consider, for example, Jesus' attitude to the poor. He may not simply have wanted to celebrate and honor the poor but also to transform their livelihood. According to the Gospel of Luke, Jesus used language traditionally clustered around the ancient Hebraic notion of the Jubilee year to announce his "good news to the poor." In Luke 4:18–19, Jesus announces his mission, as we have seen, by declaring, "The Spirit of the Lord is upon me, because he hath anointed me to preach the gospel to the poor." This includes, he goes on to say, "healing the broken hearted," "preaching deliverance to the captives," "recovering of sight to the blind," setting at liberty "those that are bruised," and—to culminate and sum up what he has been saying—to "preach the acceptable year of the Lord."

All these phrases, modern scholars have discovered, are tied to the Jubilee year, which is one of the most radical pieces of social legislation mentioned in the Old Testament. According to it, every fifty years land was to be redistributed to the poor, to all those who, since the last Jubilee, had lost their land. The legislation was designed to prevent the spreading of a dangerous, potentially miserable and subversive landless class; the law itself, of course, was so radical it was only rarely put into practice. What in effect the Jubilee year meant was the elimination of the worst kind of poverty, landless poverty, that had no honest means of gaining even a minimum wage.

In announcing his mission in these terms, Jesus may well have been calling for a wholesale redistribution of land as well as describing spiritual liberation; it would be like the Jesus we are coming to know to mingle the two and to show how authentic liberation was also radical justice and concern for the life of everyone equally—even of those traditionally despised and mistreated. The Jesus of the teachings and parables has, as we have seen, a very accurate eye for how abstract relations of power reflect themselves in actual situations and miseries. What would it mean, after all, to call the poor "blessed" without trying to help them feed themselves? The corrupt sentimentality of many churches who pay lip service to Jesus' honoring of the poor while supporting the regimes and systems that keep them wretched is very far from the example of Jesus himself, who always saw the connections between power and misery and exposed them.

Whether or not Jesus actually called for a redistribution of land explicitly, it is clear from the Gospels that he had fierce things to say about wealth and was anguished by the misery of the poor. He urged those who followed him to give generously to beggars, to lend money without expecting any repayment, and to give without anticipating any reward. The Jerusalem church after his death practiced a form of ownership-in-common, which may well reflect Jesus' own beliefs. A kind of mystical "communalism" may be the best analogy we have of what Jesus intended for a society that reflected the egalitarian compassion of the Kingdom. If everyone was equally welcome at the table of love, and love's healing resources were to be shared equally with everyone, why shouldn't wealth and land also be similarly equally distributed, so that no one need be poor and that everyone could have the chance at a decent life, and not at the expense of others but in admitted interdependence with them? It is at least probable, even likely, that Jesus' practical picture of the Kingdom on earth would have at its heart a vision of as equal as possible a distribution of wealth and property and access to, and control of, the sources of power. As the mystic realist he was, Jesus would have known that mystical inner-communion had to be reflected, as exhaustively as possible, in the actual day-to-day relations of society at every level, and that the holy equality of beings to the all-loving eye of God could not simply be "experienced" but had also to be implemented in the life of the world.

Such a vision menaces both of the predominant modern visions of political organization—the "socialist" and the "capitalist" theories of society. The socialist vision is "undermined" because the center of Jesus' ideal society remains God, Kingdom-consciousness, and the living experience of love through communion—and not the State or some vague feeling of "fraternity." Capitalism, both in its historical and contemporary "globalist" and "nationalist" forms, is questioned because its frank advocacy of competition and blatant celebration of power and wealth betray all of Jesus' beliefs about how human beings should live. Any political vision, in fact, that is not primarily a mystical vision of transformation betrays the fullness and majesty of what Jesus had in mind; any mystical vision of transformation which does not also attempt forcefully to be a political one also betrays his vision. As Jesus said to Salome in the Gospel of Thomas, "I exist from the undivided"; only those who are coming to exist in the undivided life can glimpse the glory of what Jesus is proposing or have the inner strength and clarity to carry it out in practice.

It is in this context of the "undivided life" and of the general mystical transformation of humankind that Jesus envisaged that his radical ideas about violence in politics should be understood. Nothing, in fact, separates Jesus more completely from nearly all other political visionaries than his adamant and consistent rejection of external violence in any circumstances. The Kingdom could not—and would never—be established in blood; how could the law of universal compassion that was its essence be defended by arms and killing? Only the Spirit—released on a massive scale by beings who had really and completely aligned themselves with God and chosen the path of humility, tolerance, purity of heart, and charity—could transform the existing conditions of the world. Any violence, even for "good" ends, would inevitably, by arousing hatred and the passion for revenge, be the source of more violence. As Jesus said to Peter in the garden of Gethsemane, "Those who live by the sword will die by the sword." How could the conditions of another world altogether—the world of the Kingdom—be established by using the crudest weapons of the very world they were intended to supersede and transfigure?

Jesus did not simply forbid violence; he insisted, as no other world-teacher has done with such passion, that we should not merely not hate our enemies but actively love them. God, after all, loved good and evil beings, rained on the just and unjust alike; to be perfect, a human being should mirror that all-embracing tenderness of the divine. Kingdom-consciousness did not merely obliterate the distinctions between rich and poor, black and white, male and female, Jew and gentile; it also destroyed all distinctions made in ordinary consciousness between "friend" and "enemy." "Ye have heard that it hath been said, Thou shalt love thy neighbor, and hate thine enemy but I say unto you, Love your enemies" (Matthew 5:43–44). The words Jesus quotes, "love thy neighbor," come from what we have called the "politics of holiness" and were taken by his contemporaries to mean "those who are within the covenant of Israel." Loving your enemy in the context of contemporary Palestine clearly meant not only those who were non-Israelite but also the Roman occupiers.

"I say unto you, love your enemies" is perhaps the hardest and most sublime of all Jesus' teachings; both Gandhi and Tolstoy thought it was the key to his vision of political transformation. Nothing could be done to bring the Kingdom on earth within the terms of the old consciousness of selfishness, self-protection, and possession. Only through an utter shedding of self-attachment could anyone rise to the trust and passionate belief in goodness necessary to enshrine and incarnate in every action the laws of the Kingdom. Really to love one's enemies entails the destruction of the ego; only someone who can exist in the pure atmosphere of love and forgiveness—whatever is done to them—can really love as Jesus wanted us to love. And to live always in that air is to be free of the false self and its wails and demands. Loving one's enemies is at once the revelation of the all-embracing truth of the compassion of God and the most effective journey toward that compassion.

Only such an unconditional love of all beings—the love that Jesus himself had—could make anyone transparent enough for the Spirit to blaze through them at all moments; only such an unconditional love of all beings could transform anyone into an instrument of the Kingdom in the real and give whoever practiced it the undivided consciousness and unshakable inner strength to fight peacefully for the establishment of the Kingdom without being exhausted by suffering or hatred. When philosophical and political commentators patronize Jesus' vision of forgiving one's enemies as "utopian," they do so from a far lower level of awareness than the one Jesus is trying to raise humanity to; they do not know what an awakened mystic like Jesus knows about the power of the Spirit to transform all things and so they imagine that their "bitter experience" is wisdom.

For Jesus, however, for one who has seen the Kingdom and known it as the only and final reality, the only ultimately "practical" politics must be one that changes definitively the consciousness of the human race; for only such a change can significantly alter the conditions of cyclical violence that entrap all societies and deform all eras of history. A political vision that accepts human evil and hatred in the name of "sober pragmatism" in fact keeps that evil and hatred alive.

Jesus' teaching of loving one's enemies is not the cry of a utopian dreamer; it is the announcement of a law of transformation, a law of mystical evolution that everyone needs to practice if the race is to have a chance to create those conditions of authentic peace and harmony in which the Kingdom can unveil itself. Jesus is always realistic; but his realism is that of the awakened heart; it is the realism of the highest dimension of reality and so the most astute and demanding realism imaginable.

In the context of his time, the mystical depth and intention of Jesus' teaching and its aim—the creation of the Kingdom on earth—made of the Jesus movement the contemporary "peace" party. It should never be forgotten that Jesus gave his adamant teachings on not resisting evil, on "turning the other cheek," and actively practicing nonviolence in the heart of a brutal and detested Roman occupation; Jesus was announcing the peaceful truths of the Kingdom from the center of a maelstrom of violence, pain, and hatred. When Jesus says, in Matthew 5:41, "And whosoever shall compel thee to go a mile, go with him twain," he is referring to the "right" of a Roman soldier to get a civilian to carry his equipment for one mile. Thus it is not hard to imagine how deranged such an injunction must have sounded to many of his listeners. When Jesus says in the Sermon on the Mount, "Blessed are the peacemakers, for they shall be called children of God," he is speaking among a crowd of humiliated and angry beings and is consciously distancing himself from the Jewish "resistance" movement, for whom practicing the code of holiness was synonymous with hatred of the Romans and resistance to them. For Jesus, the authentic "children of God" are not those who meet hatred with hatred, and violence with violence, but those who live in a dimension beyond the reach of either.

With the lucidity characteristic of him, Jesus must have seen that the "resistance" movement, for all its bravura, was in fact suicidal; it would inevitably arouse the Romans—far superior in numbers and force—to exactly that catastrophic violence that had already erupted in 43 B.C.E. when the inhabitants of the towns of Gophra, Emmaus, Lydda, and Thanma were all sold into slavery by Cassus, and in 4 B.C.E. (just before Jesus' birth) when Varus sacked the cities of Galilee and Samaria, including Sepphoris, and had two thousand protesters against Roman rule crucified. To Jews and Romans alike, then, Jesus was offering the way of peace, not the way of resistance and war.

It is in this connection that we should understand the famously ambiguous statement of Jesus, "Render unto Caesar what is Caesar's and to God the things that are God's." The setting of the saying is important. Some Pharisees asked Jesus a "trick" question: "Is it lawful to pay taxes to Caesar?" Had Jesus responded with a forthright "yes," he would have earned the contempt of many Jews who hated the tax; had he replied "no," he could have been arrested immediately on charges of resistance to the Roman law of occupation. Jesus therefore did not reply directly; he responded with a "trick" question of his own. He asked for a coin from his questioners. Then, he demanded, "Whose likeness and inscription are on the coin?" When they replied—as they had to—that the likeness and inscription were Caesar's, they offended those in the crowd who believed that it was disgraceful even to carry an image of Caesar. When Jesus then says, "Render to Caesar the things that are Caesar's and to God the things that are God's," he implicitly approved the paying of the tax to the Romans; this separated him from the resistance movement to whom the tax, as we have noted, was abhorrent.

Jesus' reply, however, did not make specific—as it has often been taken to do—the much vaster question of what belonged to Caesar and what was God's. To make his reply more inclusive than it is and to use it (as the church throughout history has done) as a justification for leaving the whole realm of politics to Caesar is absurd; everything that we know about Jesus and his teaching shows us that his message and vision were designed to transform all areas of human activity. Even more ironic has been the use of Jesus' statement as a justification for military service and the waging of one horrifying war after another, when it was precisely to prevent the use of military violence that the statement was made in the first place.

One of the many obscenities of church history has been the only barely comprehensible denial that Jesus' teaching about love of enemies had any kind of political validity. In text after text, theologians down the ages have tried to privatize Jesus' universal message, have tried to claim, for instance, that when Jesus was speaking of enemies, he was pointing to "personal" enemies and not "national" ones; some have even claimed that in advocating love of one's enemies Jesus was consciously promulgating an entirely impossible ideal so as to make us aware of how radically we fail it.

Such casuistry has contrived to blunt the passion of Jesus' teaching of nonviolence and so prevent the creation of the Kingdom. Had Jesus not taught nonviolence consistently, why would those closest to him in time have clearly believed he did? Why would the early church have been persistently pacifist through the most terrible situations of war and official persecution for the first three centuries? Jesus' teaching about nonviolence is at the heart of his teaching about the Kingdom and about the transformation of this world into its law; it cannot be ignored or glossed over without betraying everything that Jesus stood for. This is what, alas, Christian churches of all kinds have consistently done, either through ignorance of what Jesus teachings really are, or through cowardice and "enculturation."

One question remains: Why did the Roman authorities perceive Jesus as a threat when he preached and lived nonviolence? Unlike the Zealots (who were the main Jewish resistance party) and the many rebel bandit bands that roamed Judaea, Jesus explicitly and repeatedly urged his followers not to fight Rome but to embrace all beings in the spirit of God. Yet he was crucified as a political rebel.

The deepest answer is that, taken together, Jesus' teachings challenged the entire patriarchal order on which Roman power was based. To a world obsessed by power, Jesus offered a vision of the radiance of the powerlessness and powerful vulnerability of love; to a culture riddled with authoritarianism of every kind, he gave a vision of the holiness of inner and outer poverty and a critique of the vanity and horror of all forms of worldly achievement; to a society arranged at every level into different hierarchies, he presented in his own life, being, and daily practice a vision of a radical and all-embracing egalitarianism designed to end forever those dogmas and institutions that keep women enslaved, races separated from each other, the poor starving, and the rich rotting in prisons of selfish luxury. His extraordinary spiritual gifts and healing powers clearly convinced many people of the truth of his vision; whether he preached nonviolence was not as important to the Roman authorities as the fact that Jesus commanded respect and love wholly independent of them, had a large following, was preaching an alternative world that reversed the terms of their imperium in every way, and was declared by some of his followers on many occasions to be a "king" with his own "Kingdom."

Everything Jesus said or did was designed to bring into being the Kingdom of God, a Kingdom that had nothing whatever to do with the patriarchal system of power on which the Romans based their empire—nothing to do with its fierce rule of law, its vaunting of military power, its cynical disregard for all religious parties and institutions, or its myth of the divinity of the

Roman emperor. All the ideals that Jesus stressed—of humility, tenderness for life, embrace of the outcast and the abandoned—ran counter to the competitive and militaristic passions that fueled the growth of the Roman empire. At that moment when one of patriarchy's most powerful systems was to begin its long grim triumph, Jesus revealed and enacted a way of subverting all of its beliefs, practices, goals, and "truths." And he was killed for it.

Modern scholars believe that the picture painted in the Gospels of a vacillating, half-compassionate Pontius Pilate is unhistorical: they believe the Gospels were deliberately slanted against the Jewish religious elite so that they and not the Romans would bear the blame for Jesus' death. Such a bias would be understandable in the fearful and turbulent years of the early church, which lived constantly under the threat of annihilation by persecution. To present Pontius Pilate as almost innocent would mean that the Romans had nothing to fear from Christian revenge and would also send the Roman authorities the signal that the early church had no major quarrel with them.

While understandable, this "falsification" of the facts of Jesus' prosecution and death—organized, it now appears, both by the Romans and the religious authorities—diminishes the radicalism of Jesus' example, strips it of its extreme political significance in a way that later abetted the general political amnesia of the Christian churches, and provides the miserable "justification" for two millennia of anti-Semitism.

Jesus was killed by both the religious and political authorities of his time because his teachings and being aimed at creating a new form of life that would make both obsolescent. Jesus was killed because the glory of his vision of human equality in God and the sacredness of every individual implicitly subverted the entire order on which both religious and political society was based. Had Jesus simply been some kind of mystic healer with some vague "spiritual" ideas, he would have been left alone. Jesus' fatal gift was to see the cruelty of all man-made cultures and power systems, and to call for a unification of the world in the spirit of God's justice and mercy, and to show in his being, teaching, and practice that such a new fusion was real and possible. Had Jesus, like a modern archbishop or guru, combined a kind of "spiritual" ministry with acceptance of the status quo (dining with Herod, perhaps, on the shores of Tiberias, accepting the odd invitation to speak on abstruse theological matters with the Sanhedrin), he would have survived comfortably and now been totally forgotten.

But Jesus was the most dangerous kind of rebel—a rebel who had seen the Kingdom and knew it was the only reality. He was the most dangerous kind of rebel because he not merely talked about the Kingdom; he lived and manifested its splendor in the beauty of his presence, in the clarity and inner coherence of his teaching, in his fearlessness in the face of opposition. He was the most dangerous kind of rebel because he could not be swerved from his purpose by anything, and he could not be bought by any lure, not even that of being a "master" or a "god"; his integrity was terrible and final.

Jesus was the most dangerous kind of rebel, too, because the vision that guided and inspired him through everything flamed from a direct mystical knowledge of God and would give him the courage to die, if necessary, for what he believed; not even torture, humiliation, and death would destroy his spirit.

The End and the New Beginning

In the last week of his life Jesus went to Jerusalem at the time of Passover to make a final appeal to the Jewish people to transform themselves and prepare the Kingdom. Many details of the account in the Gospels that have been taken for granted for two millennia have now been questioned. It is unlikely that he entered Jerusalem on a donkey, for example; this was probably added later to suit an ancient prophesy about the Messiah in Zechariah. It is unlikely, too, that Jesus held a Last Supper, where he broke bread and offered wine in remembrance of him, anticipating and prefiguring the death that was waiting for him; there is no mention of such an event either in John or in the Gospel of Thomas or in the Q Gospel.

What is almost unanimously accepted, however, is that Jesus was making a symbolic and transformatory journey, and at a time—Passover—that celebrated the deliverance of the Jews from bondage in Egypt. He would have known that any public actions or teachings would be especially fiercely scrutinized; this was traditionally a time of unrest when the Roman authorities would be on the alert for anything that menaced their rule. Thousands of country-based Jews flooded into Jerusalem to honor their God, and celebrating a feast which commemorated the release from one set of imperial tyrants while living under another could obviously arouse bitter and rebellious memories; there had been a massacre at the Temple forty years before in 4 B.C.E. Yet if Jesus, as is likely, wanted to address as many of his fellow Jews as possible and at a time when their thoughts would be turned toward the divine and deliverance, then the choice of Passover was the only possible one. Jesus must have known, however, that in Jerusalem he would be surrounded by enemies and that the risks of being arrested or even killed if he spoke his truth were extremely high.

He did nothing to minimize them. Clearly, for reasons we can only now guess at, Jesus judged that the moment had come in his mission to risk everything in an attempt to educate his countrymen in the truths of the Kingdom. Did he see clearly that the politics of resistance would lead to catastrophic retaliation from the Romans, which would menace the very survival of Judaism? Did his prophetic gifts really give him, as the Gospels suggest, the vision of the fall of Jerusalem in 70 C.E.? Did he believe that the Jews had suffered enough to be ripe for his vision of a different way of being and living that would be the "deliverance from bondage" that they were longing for in a dimension they did not yet understand, but that it was his historical and spiritual mission to bring to them? We will never know for sure; the accounts of the Passion Week have been clearly doctored in all four Gospels to reflect the spiritual and ideological needs of early Christianity.

Of one thing, however, we can be reasonably certain: the event that precipitated Jesus' arrest and so his death was the turning over of the money changers' tables in the Temple. Everything that Jesus had preached on his journeys throughout Galilee—spiritual and economic egalitarianism, the need to exist in direct, unmediated relationship with God—exploded in one all-embracing act of holy indignation performed at the heart of religious and political power.

Jesus was not just "purifying" the Temple by overturning the tables; he was symbolically destroying it. His was a consciously iconoclastic act. This is brought out clearly in the earliest written account of the event, that of Mark, where the action is framed within the cursing of the fruitless fig tree in Mark 11:12–14 and its withering away, reported by Peter in 11:21. Jesus cursed the fruitless fig tree and it withered; his challenging of the "fruitless" Temple was also, symbolically, a destruction. Here is Mark's account of it:

> And they came to Jerusalem: and Jesus went into the temple, and began to cast out them that sold and bought in the temple, and overthrew the tables of the moneychangers, and the seats of them that sold doves; and would not suffer that any man should carry any vessel through the temple. And he taught saying unto them, Is it not written, My house shall be called of all nations the house of prayer? but ye have made it a den of thieves. And the scribes and chief priests heard it, and sought how they might destroy him: for they feared him, because all the people were astonished at his doctrine.

One small, often overlooked detail captures, I think, the comprehensiveness of Jesus' rage against the Temple and all that it had come to stand for: "He would not suffer that any man should carry any vessel through the temple." Jesus was trying to prevent even the sacrificial vessels from being carried to the Temple. He wasn't only attacking the commerce of holiness, he was attacking the entire paraphernalia of ritual also and questioning its necessity at all in a world where direct, unaffected contact with God is always possible.

It is important to note, too, that the Temple had always had money-changers and dove sellers. They were necessary to both its fiscal and its sacrificial life. There may also have been nothing particularly wrong with any of the money operations conducted in the outer courts of the Temple; they had always gone on and supported the priests and their families and those families that were linked to the priests. What was normal and accepted behavior for a whole religious culture was, however, an abomination for Jesus. In turning over the tables of the money-lenders and the "seats of them that sold doves," Jesus is striking at the financial heart of a religious empire; he is symbolically annihilating all the structures that uphold the world of the Temple, all its fiscal, liturgical, and sacrificial operations. He is, in fact, symbolically destroying a whole world, a whole accepted way of being and dealing in the name of the passionate interiority of the Kingdom.

Such an act, in the troubled atmosphere of Passover, amounted to direct provocation. Did Jesus want to be delivered to the authorities and martyred? Did he believe that such a martyrdom would inspire the repentance and transformation of his people? Did he expect his act of divine blasphemy to shock his contemporaries into a higher awareness, to be a kind of furious initiation into a new life? We cannot know. My own belief is that Jesus knew exactly what he was doing and what he was risking, and that his willingness to risk death did not reflect any lust for martyrdom or any self-conscious mystical desire to enact the part of the Messiah, but the holy desperation of someone who understands that in certain circumstances the only possible choice is one of open rebellion against injustice and oppression, whatever the results.

The time had come for Jesus to risk being a sacrifice for his revolutionary ideals. Conceivably, Jesus could have survived the hatred of the religious and political authorities that his teaching had aroused by hiding or continuing to teach in small villages or open country, but how could such a political withdrawal effect the kind of transformation of society he knew was essential? The passion of his vision of the Kingdom and the agony of tenderness for all beings that propelled it, propelled him to the moment when he crystallized all of his anger, hope, prayerfulness, and social and political ideals in one symbolic iconoclastic act that he knew would risk his life.

In the deepest sense, it was logical that Jesus would risk death in this way. He had risked death since the very beginning of his ministry; very early on in it, the scribes and Pharisees had started to plot actively against him, furious at what they perceived to be his blasphemy and jealous of his charisma. Only great canniness, the Gospels tell us again and again, had kept him alive. The inner logic of his teaching too—its radical and inflammatory fusion of the highest mystical awareness with the most astute and illusionless critique of power—made it inevitable that Jesus would have to try to swerve his world from the disaster he saw engulfing it by engaging in some kind of blatant— and therefore dangerous—public action. He would have known that it was precisely this kind of public display that his enemies were longing for; it would give them the opportunity they had long looked for to destroy him. How could he avoid it, however, if he wanted to remain true to his vision of the Kingdom? Jesus could not withdraw from the world and pray for deliverance on the fringes of catastrophe; he had to act, at the heart of the world, and with unambiguous majesty and full truth. He had to unveil Kingdom-consciousness at the heart of the world which denied its possibility, at the heart of the Temple; he had to release its sublime anarchic fire at the very center of the world which tried to contain or even wipe it out; he had to flame out with the wild and unbounded freedom of his—and everyone else's—innate divine identity at the heart of the place which tried to broker, mediate, or qualify the extremity of that truth. And if he risked being caught, tried, and killed for blasphemy and sedition, what did that matter? Had he not come to know, in the inmost core of his being, the truth of the great law: "Except a corn of wheat fall into the ground and die, it abideth alone; but if it die it bringeth forth much fruit"?

The time had come to risk everything and sacrifice everything for the Kingdom; to demonstrate in his own being and action the total fearlessness and boundless courage that divine love demanded of anyone who wanted to be an instrument of justice and mercy, to reveal the full majesty of that divine identity that could suffer and triumph over even the most terrible of ordeals.

And so, I believe, Jesus willingly and consciously precipitated the events that led to his capture, trial, and crucifixion. Whether or not he knew, in any human sense of "knowing," that his descent into the ultimate depths of humiliation and torment would utterly remake his being and the whole future of humanity we can never be sure; the account of the Gospels of the crucifixion and resurrection were written after the fact, and with certain clarities projected backwards.

I believe that Jesus did not know; that he risked his entire being in a final terrible adventure whose end was not certain. This better explains, I believe, his fear and fragility in the Garden of Gethsemane and the moments of doubt on the cross. He did not "know"; he loved and trusted and surrendered and went on loving and trusting and surrendering, more and more deeply, more and more abandonedly, as the storms of suffering that buffeted him became more and more atrocious. Everything that he had discovered and lived, every truth that he had taught, every passion for a new world that had awoken in him now had to coalesce into one overwhelming fire of love, which would test death itself and beat against the doors of that law of nature that had up to then kept heaven and earth separate, the living and dead in their different rooms.

In his life, Jesus had lived out the truths of the Kingdom on earth with extreme integrity; now in his dying he would subject that integrity to an even greater test—the test of annihilation. Had Jesus known that he would be reborn on the third day, some of the final work of that annihilation could not be done; the dying that led to the resurrection had to be a complete annihilation of everything, even of his belief in himself, in his mission, in his unfailing and infallible connection to God, perhaps even of his belief in the deathlessness of divine love itself. All certainties and forms of knowing and awareness had to be utterly annihilated in God for the new to be possible, the utterly unprecedented to be born.

No one, not even the greatest mystic, can know beforehand what such a stripping inevitably entails; its agony is too extreme for the mind to imagine and its torture reaches more deeply and finally into the ultimate recesses of being than any previous form of suffering. All that anyone who has come to this final place can do is what Jesus did—give up everything to the mystery of God, surrender totally. Such a surrender is a passing through zone after zone of loss, humiliation, and crushing, savage suffering; one of the many ways in which Jesus moves us to depths we hardly knew we possessed before we began to know him is that for him, too, such a surrender was dreadful and cost everything and had to be done in ever-more demanding stages of terror and weeping and deeper and deeper prayer. But a whole lifetime of the most passionate love and sacrifice had prepared Jesus to take this journey on behalf of the whole of humanity.

In his life and teaching, Jesus had shown the inner and outer truths of the Kingdom; he had been a living son of its fire. Now, in his dying, he would bring the realization of the Kingdom on earth even closer by sacrificing everything for it in extreme and final trust, abandon, and love. Through such an extreme gift of himself he was not "simply" redeeming the sins of humanity; that is too small a description of so vast an enterprise. He wasn't "just" redeeming the past of humanity but revealing the limitlessness of the powers entrusted by God to the human soul, and so revealing a wholly new possible future. By suffering horrible evil without hatred and in the spirit of forgiveness of the Kingdom, he put into ultimate practice his teaching of loving nonviolence on the deepest possible level, and showed that such love could birth a soul-force capable of carrying him—and anyone who truly believed and trusted it—not only through death but into the dimension of the deathless, where the King-dom's dream of fusing matter and spirit in one glory permanently would be re-alized, as it was realized in him "on the third day."

Jesus could not know, as some omniscient divine "savior" figure, that such a consummation would naturally be; such a belief demeans the actual extremity of his love and courage. It was as the "Son of Man" and for other po-tentially divine human beings like himself that Jesus undertook the journey that opened onto the splendor of resurrection. Like any other divine human being who wants to become one with the Kingdom beyond time and invoke its transfiguring power into the heart of reality and so into the heart of every thought, action, belief, and every cell of living matter, Jesus had to trust in the darkness, surrender to death after death, risk everything and suffer every-thing again and again.

Knowing this—and daring to face this—is what makes Jesus' achieve-ment devastating to all of our comfortable sense of human "fallibility" and "limits"; if Jesus is a divine human being like ourselves, what is to stop us from joining him in the undying but our cowardice, laziness, incapacity for sur-rendering, and unbelief? And with Jesus alive in every atom of the universe in eternal light and one with the highest aspiration of every soul and one with the divine now forever—but also turned toward us always as supreme friend, brother, lover, most generous, humble, and least authoritarian guide—what excuse do we have not to take our journey also through Gethsemane and Golgotha to the body ablaze with light outside the empty tomb?

It must be clear by now that I accept the resurrection as a mystical fact; this is where I part company from many of the modern historical scholars whose work I have learned so much from and whose scholarship I admire. The deepest learning and the wisest mind can never understand the mystery of the resurrection; it cannot, in fact, be "understood," only *known* and *experienced,* beyond words, dogmas, all possible theological formulations by the humbled and mystically awoken heart and through direct divine grace. Until all Chris-tians dare to accept this, there will be endless empty tragicomic "discussion" and "argument." But accepting this means accepting the entire mystical dimension of Christ's life, teaching, and death and taking up his undying challenge to us all to realize in more and more daring and radical ways our divine identity.

Until we have begun to live directly and taste and inwardly experience our divine identity, the resurrected Cosmic Christ cannot be known; only by daring to try and "Christ" ourselves can the universal Christ be discovered inside and around us.

Our greatest guide in this journey will be the historical Christ, for it was the task of Jesus in time to birth the eternal Christ, who could help all other beings directly from the heart of divine power and divine grace. This means nothing less than adopting the historical Jesus' fierce, humble, illusionless radicalism in every way and in every arena; nothing less will cost enough or strip us enough or awaken us sufficiently to the extent of the evil, ignorance, and suffering that make the transformation of the world into the Kingdom not a mystic dream but the most urgent of necessities.

Just as Jesus did in his time, we will have to fight with all our powers for the triumph of divine clarity, mercy, and justice; just as Jesus did, we will have to be prepared to excite and suffer derision, persecution, betrayal, abandonment; just as Jesus did, we will have to learn to pass through zone after zone of death and surrender; just as Jesus did, we will have to dedicate everything we learn and all we have and are to a deeper and ever-humbler service of all beings in the spirit of the all-encompassing compassion of Kingdom; just as Jesus did, we will have to be prepared to rest nowhere, and be ready always to dare to go deeper and deeper into the furnace of divine love, until we become, as Jesus has, one with its fire in all possible dimensions, now and forever.

We will, however, have one advantage that Jesus did not have: we will have Jesus himself, as the Cosmic Christ, to be our brother, lover, friend, divine and tender guide; we will have the Christ-force that streams forth from the heart of God toward humanity to inspire us; we will have the sign of his resurrection to give us the certainty that the impossible is possible; we will have the truth of his splendor in life and death and beyond continually to remind us of ours.

All those who risk Christing themselves know the truth of these words. Throughout Christian history, and often despite the church, the challenge to follow Jesus to and beyond the end has been taken up by beings who staked their lives not merely on following some version of Christ's teaching but on submitting themselves to the same, almost intolerable, recognitions, pressures, vicissitudes, and passions as he had so as to be "Christed" into the Kingdom with him. For them, Christ was far more than a teacher or sage or even divine icon; he was the pioneer of a wholly new kind of human being, one who wanted above all to become one with the glory of love and to be its selfless revolutionary in the night of history. Brave and loving enough—and constantly inspired by divine grace—these heroic men and women took up Christ's challenge—the challenge above all of the cross—and allowed themselves like him to be crucified into resurrection, killed into an eternal life dedicated utterly to love and the service of others, and to the birthing of the Kingdom in reality.

Slowly, over the centuries, these great lovers and brothers and sisters of Jesus discovered, with the help of the Cosmic Christ and divine grace, an ever-more accurate "map" of how the transformation into Christhood could be accomplished. This map—which will be detailed in "The Mystical Christ," the second part of this book—should be known by every Christian and, in fact, by every spiritual seeker, for it reveals just how the Christ-force can be unleashed at the heart of reality and how the human being can be transformed to stand its demands and incarnate its divine passion with ever-increasing, and ever-more radical, effectiveness. As Jesus said in Logion 106 of the Gospel of Thomas: "When you make the two one, you will become the sons of man, and when you say, 'Mountain, move away,' it will move." And in Logion 111: "The heavens and earth will be rolled up in your presence. And the one who lives from the living one shall not see death."

Part Two

The Mystical Christ

Introduction

This second part of *Son of Man* is devoted to the mystical Christ. In the first section, "The Eight Thresholds and Mysteries," the mystical Christ himself describes one by one the stages of "Christing," and their ordeals, glories, and infinite possibilities as unfolded in the life of Jesus.

In the second section, "The Map," what we have learned from the mystical Christ of the "Eight Thresholds and Mysteries" of his journey into full Christhood is—with the help, too, of other Christian mystics—condensed into the four stages of the Christ-path: Purgation, Illumination, Union (or Sacred Marriage), and finally, Birthing. This "Map" is designed to give the seeker on the direct path to Christ an accurate, rigorous, and complete guide to what is required for the Christ to be "born" in him or her, and after being "born" to go on "giving birth" in sacred action in the world.

The Eight Thresholds and Mysteries

I am the real voice. I cry out in everyone.

THE TRIMORPHIC PROTENNOIA

I speak even as I hear.
I command even as I received the order.
I show everything I have found.

SECOND APOCALYPSE OF JAMES

I am the resurrection and the life.

JOHN 11:25

Jesus said to his disciples, "Compare me to someone and tell me who I am like."
Simon Peter said to him, "You are like a righteous angel."
Matthew said to him, "You are like a wise philosopher."
Thomas said to him, "Master, my mouth is wholly incapable of saying who you
are like."
Jesus said, "I am not your master. Because you have drunk, you have become in-
toxicated from the bubbling spring which I have measured out." And he took
him and withdrew and told him three things. When Thomas returned to his
companions they asked him, "What did Jesus say to you?" Thomas said to them,
"If I tell you one of the things which he told me you will pick up the stones and
throw them at me; a fire will come out of the stones and burn you up."

LOGION 13, GOSPEL OF THOMAS

He, the Christ, who has exalted man became like God, not in order that he
might bring God down to man, but that man might become like God.

TEACHINGS OF SYLVANUS

Everyone baptized into Christ should pass progressively through the stages of Christ's life.

GREGORY OF SINAI

If you would appropriate him, then you must follow his whole pattern.

JACOB BOEHME

The eye is not able to understand
His glorious transformations
And tongues of flame live in him
Who sent tongues of flame at his Ascension.

ST. EPHREM THE SYRIAN

Who can bear the glory of transfiguration, of man's discovery as transfigured? Because what Christ is, I am; one can only speak of it after being awoken from the dead.

HENRI LE SAUX

After praying a long time to the mystical Christ, I opened the *Imitation of Christ* of Thomas à Kempis at the beginning and read, as if for the first time, these words:

> He who follows me, says Christ our savior, walks not in darkness for he will have the light of life. These are the words of our Lord Jesus Christ, and by them we are admonished to follow his teachings and his manner of living, if we would truly be enlightened and delivered from all blindness of heart.
>
> Let all the study of our heart from now on be to have our meditation fixed wholly on the life of Christ, for his holy teachings are of more virtue and strength than all the words of all the angels and saints. And he who through grace has the inner eye of his soul opened to the true beholding of the Gospels of Christ will find in them hidden manna.

Summoning up all my courage and praying for humility, I asked Jesus Christ directly to reveal to me the laws of his Christing and the stages by which he reached and became the one.

And this is what, at my stage of understanding, I heard the Christ say within me:

Everything you need to become one with the life I am will be revealed to you if you meditate with all your heart and body and mind and soul on the life I led when I lived with you. I passed through all of the different thresholds and mysteries that you, too, must pass through to become one with the one.

Because there was in me from the beginning of my life on earth a clarity and a complete concentration on God which you do not have, your journey will be less swift, less sure, less perfectly clean and dynamic than mine. But this must not dishearten you, for what I am you are and what you are I am; I am in everything around you with my arms outstretched to help you. What I have done, you can do, if you do it in my name and in my spirit and with my passion and my humility and my surrender to the Father-Mother.

I did not come to found a religion and be worshiped. I came to embody and enact a path to a wholly new life, the life of divine love on earth; a life so profound and abundant that when tasted and known it must transform everything into the Kingdom. I came as the first sign of a new creation, the first brother-sister of a whole new race of brothers and sisters. I came to birth the divine Child on earth, the Child of the Father-Mother whose essence is wisdom and compassion and whose every action blazes with the truth of love. I came to unite in my own being, and in a blaze of unity, the "masculine" and the "feminine," heart and mind and body and soul, the clearest and most naked and just vision of this world, and to live the mystery of perfect love in action in time. I came to root the light in the core of earth-matter so it could blossom there perpetually and to heal in my own heart and body all the wounds of evil so that a new being could be birthed both in time and in eternity and so that all those who loved me could become me, through mystical union and the grace of the Father-Mother. I came to discover and forge the path to a new humanity which I first had to birth within myself so that now you, too, can birth it within you and within me. I came to waken everyone from the dead, and to bring all beings into the continually fertile life of the resurrected heart and body.

I have performed the entire human journey into the divine for all of you. Out of love for love, I burned myself away like a coal on the hearth of infinite love. My life is the record of that burning. All those who want to be one with me will live through what I lived and in the order that I lived it, for what my life has written in lines of flame is the diagram of sacred passion.

Many things can never be said and can only be lived. Many things must pass between you and me in holy silence. Listen to what I say not with your mind only but with the full power of your open Sacred Heart that is my Sacred Heart in you. Let me-in-you listen to me. Then what I will say will not only be an "instruction," it will also move you as a kind of memory. You will "remember" what I am saying, for what I am speaking of to you is your true story, the essential journey of your and everyone's sacred being. There is only one journey and only one traveler. Each being is a unique face of this traveler, each being takes the same journey in his or her own unique way and in the terms of his or her own unique temperament, but the stages that have to be gone through are always the same.

There are eight thresholds and mysteries which all those who long to become me must cross and endure and embody completely. In my life and teaching I both crossed these thresholds and embodied these mysteries and also, as I did so, showed others forever how they must be approached and lived.

These eight thresholds and mysteries are: first, the New Birth, represented in my Baptism; second, the Temptation that followed; third, the Transfiguration on Mount Tabor that revealed the divinity within my humanity; fourth, the Agony in Gethsemane; fifth, the Crucifixion; sixth, the Resurrection; seventh, the Ascension; and eighth, finally, my Descent in-flame at Pentecost, when, after my Resurrection and Ascension, I manifested the perpetual cosmic birthing-power I am by descending in tongues of flame to inspire my apostles in Jerusalem, tongues of flame that never cease descending from me, now and forever, throughout the creation.

I am calling you, my beloved, to the New Birth, and to the purification of the great Temptation, and onward to the embodiment through unstinting prayer and service and ever-increasing immersion in me of the divine in the human. I am calling you beyond even the glory of Tabor to the final dissolution of all understanding, hope, will, and human power on the cross so you can become the I AM that I AM and live in the love-body of the resurrection, matter and spirit one at last in the One. Even beyond that, I am calling you to becoming a birthing flame of the heart that engenders in boundless compassion all transforming action in the universe, to becoming one dancing, praising, eternally active Flame of the sea of birth-fire I poured out onto the world at Pentecost and go on pouring out forever. I am calling you to an infinite journey into infinite love.

This is the glory I am and you are.

This is the passion I am and you are.

This is the miracle I am and you are.

This is the supreme beauty I am and you are.

This is the bliss and wisdom and tireless just action I am and you are.

So listen to what I am about to reveal to you with amazement and trembling and remember always the rule of the Christing: "If any one will come after me, let him or her deny themselves, take up their cross and follow me. For whoever will save his life shall lose it and whoever will lose his life for my sake will find it." I am calling you to an endless dying in love into life, an endless growth, an endless metamorphosis in the fire of love. You can only enter this field of boundless transformation if you surrender to the law that governs the whole universe of change, the law of sacrifice that springs from abandoned humility before the majesty and love of God, and from an always more ardent desire to be useful to love's work.

This is the divine law: only to the humble can the truth be revealed, only to those lost in love can the identity be given, only to those able to die again and again out of love into love can the mysteries of transformation-in-love be unfolded in all their unending splendor. And this law will have to be understood in ever-deeper and ever-more demanding ways at every stage of the journey.

Until the final freedom of resurrection and the final ecstasy of perpetual birthing-in-flame, which is the deepest meaning of Pentecost, there will always be death, ordeal, necessary agony. For with each new growth of my life in you there will be a need for an even greater surrender, an even more stable and abandoned faith. To keep on growing into my full splendor, you will have to learn how to keep on dying, and only those who can deny the self out of love and in an ever-more radical humility of spirit can ever learn how to die in this way.

I know that such words shake your whole being, make you afraid, in pain, anxious to escape the demands of so fierce a work. Do not be ashamed of your fear. I was afraid. Do not be ashamed of your anguish. I was anguished. Do not be afraid of your desire to flee the terms of true change. In Gethsemane I, too, begged that the cup be taken from me. Those who pretend they are not afraid break easily; those who cannot admit the depth of their anguish cannot learn its dark mysterious truths nor be taken by its force to a deeper faith and surrender; those who do not confess their terror at the price of true change can never know the rapture of discovering that with the help of divine grace that is always given they can endure far more than they know, suffer far more richly and fecundly than they ever imagined.

Never imagine as you take the journey into me that there is any pain or bewilderment that you could suffer that I have not also suffered, sometimes even more dreadfully and completely than you can comprehend. So you never have to hide your heart and its terrors and pains from me, for I know them all, grieve for them all, cradle them all, am here beside and around you as you suffer them; I am in you always to call on for wisdom, clarity, revelation, inspiration, the strength to weep and the strength to go on. Don't you understand yet? I am the divine in the human and the human in the divine, their meeting, their intersection, their infinite point and their sum. Nothing can ever be foreign to me that is in you, for I am you, transfigured, as you will be, and I remember everything of the pain of the journey I am asking you to take. I am the journey and the traveler; I am present in every stage of the journey, every suffering, and every revelation.

Now let me describe to you clearly the meaning in my life and in everyone's of the eight thresholds and mysteries. And may they all be accomplished in you, so there can be no barrier at all between us, and our hearts can live as one with the heart of all things forever. Allow the Christ to be born in you now, in this terrible time, when you are needed in your complete power and humility and passion for service, in your Christhood, more than at any other. For only a vast humble army of Christing beings, beings who have consciously chosen the path into the Christ and its laws of sacrifice and dying and embrace of ever-greater ordeals in the name of ever-more complete transformations can effect the changes that are needed in every arena of life if the planet is to be saved.

Open your hearts, know that the divine is real and know that your deepest truth is of the soul that is one with God. Pray and meditate and serve others humbly and call on God to reveal the God in you again and again with total sincerity, and the great moment will come that begins the journey into me—the moment when, for you, the skies will part and the dove of blessing will descend and a voice will say, "This is my beloved son or daughter; in him or her I am well pleased."

This is the moment you have been waiting for all your life and from the beginning of your evolution—the moment when you know as I did when John baptized me that I was one with and beloved by the Father-Mother, that the whole universe was mine in him and her, that my inmost consciousness was one with the consciousness-fire that is manifesting all the worlds forever.

This is the first threshold and mystery: the New Birth. And with this Baptism into divine awareness begins a wholly new life—a life in which you try with all your powers of mind and heart and soul and with constant invocation of divine grace to integrate the laws and visions of the fire of love you know are now, with all you do, feel, and think.

The time, cost, and suffering of this initial massive integration of the divine and the human will vary in every individual, but everyone will come to the second threshold inevitably. Everyone will be tempted, as I was in the desert when I withdrew there to bring all the new powers I knew in me to coherence and purity. And as you come to this second threshold and mystery—that of the Temptation—you will begin to understand one of the great laws of the journey into me: that every advance is met by a corresponding ordeal. This ordeal can either derange you or, by compelling you to deeper self-awareness and a more complete calling down of the divine wisdom and grace, breed in you a more mature knowledge of your strength and a more fundamental knowledge of the necessity of humility.

The second threshold and mystery of the Temptation is where many, many of those who want to become me, are ruined. Drunk on the glory of what the Baptism has revealed to them and, it must be said, on the experience of new powers of every kind—mental and emotional—within themselves that are kindled by this glory, everyone is tempted, whether consciously or half-unconsciously, to use the benefits and truths of the divine consciousness not for God and not for the service of others but for themselves. The ego and false self is still present in everyone at this stage, although in some ways weakened and irradiated by my light. But the false self is wily and manipulative and can appropriate even the most glorious experiences of divine beauty and divine being for itself. If it does, it becomes not divine but demonic; it says "yes" in fact to what the dark one tried to get me to say "yes" to—to miracle-mongering and using God-given powers not to serve God but to dominate the world.

The Christ cannot be born fully in anyone who still wants anything for himself or herself and who does not want to give everything away to and for others. Any movement of any kind to appropriate the powers of the divine awakening for the false self will end in disaster. The final power of love will only be given to the one who has emptied himself or herself completely of any personal desire for power; it will only be given in its beauty and transforming radiance to the one who wants only to serve and help and inspire others and bring about the birth of the Kingdom in reality. To such a person, all forms of worldly and religious status will be pathetic, dangerous, and absurd.

To overcome and pass beyond the threshold and mystery of Temptation you will have to allow yourself to be purified drastically. You will have to submit your senses and being to a drastic analysis and reordering; you will have to confront and dissolve everything in you that wants to be "adored," or still wants power of any kind. This is distressing, terrible, dark work, and requires tremendous constancy and clarity, and a great, continually renewed commitment to be one with me.

If the purification is complete—the purification that is appropriate to this stage—your whole being will be opened as mine was to the wonder and power of pouring yourself out in reality to help others. The more you pour yourself out, the more the light of God will be revealed to you and in you; the purer and more passionate your hunger to become one with me becomes and is expressed in action, the more of you will be transformed into me until the third great threshold and mystery—that of the Transfiguration—is reached.

In the Transfiguration on Mount Tabor the divine glory in my humanity was revealed to Peter, James, and John. In your transfiguration, my presence in you will flame out and the whole universe will reveal itself as being on fire with me-in-you. Your whole body and mind and heart and soul will appear in time and space and matter as one flame of my fire and you will see and know your true face, and it will be seen and known by all things and in all things.

But, as before in the journey to me, a great revelation and wonder will be succeeded by a tremendous ordeal. And the ordeal that follows on the Transfiguration is the supreme ordeal, the one which many souls cannot endure.

Just as the new powers and faculties born in you after baptism had to be integrated with the real and with your daily actions and be made adamant by the confrontation of the dark one in the Temptation, so now the glory revealed in you in the Transfiguration has to be wedded at every level and in every dimension with the whole of reality by continual acts of deepening sacrifice, which culminates in a great death to all human notions of self and identity.

The stages beyond Transfiguration—beyond the revelation of the divine in the human in glory—can only be reached by an ever-deeper embrace of the suffering of others, in an ever-deeper passion to flood every recess of human life, every corner of human affairs with the truth of love. And this involves sacrifice after sacrifice, death after death, until love has strengthened and matured you to be able to die completely into eternal life.

In the first purification the journey into me brought you to—that of the Temptation—what was purified in you was your senses, your past, your memory, the direction of your intention. Now a far more drastic purification has to take place: now what has to be purified utterly, in the agony of Gethsemane and its succeeding threshold and mystery of the Crucifixion, is your entire sense of identity separate from God. Everything that is "you" in any limited, biographical, "egoic" sense has to be burned away now from your essential divine self so it can merge, cleansed of all egohood, into the fire of eternal life and live there forever as a pure flame of its all-consuming furnace of presence.

After the Transfiguration on Tabor, to prepare you for Gethsemane and the cross, you will be filled with the grief that I was filled with on earth, an immense cosmic grief at the pain of the world, at the horror of injustice in all its forms. Almost clear and pure, your heart will be able to see now and understand the full grief of things, and it will be broken again and again. Out of repeated heartbreak will be born an immense divine longing to go even further into love, to be an even more complete sacrifice to love, to suffer and endure for love ever-greater trials and ordeals.

This recognition of the horror and pain of life and this divine longing to sacrifice everything for its transformation is what will take you to your Gethsemane—that terrible place where you, like me, will cry out that God has abandoned you and where you will have to abandon, as I did, every idea of God or of yourself, every merely human hope. Like me, you will weep there tears of blood: everyone you believe true to you will mock or desert you. All your powers, even those which you have partly divinized and flooded with light, will fail. You will enter a zone of final, inconsolable and illusionless aloneness, beyond the reach of any human help. In this place of ultimate desolation, everything you have understood about the journey up to now will be of no use. All you will be able to do is surrender to the darkness of God.

The death of this surrender to the darkness of God will drag you to the next, fifth threshold—that of the cross. And on the cross your "I" will finally die. For everyone, the cross will be at once different and the same. Each one will come to the cross most suited to their own temperament, the disaster or set of disasters that love will send that will end and annihilate them. All possible human knowledge ends here, as does all "spiritual" knowledge. Every secret recess of the "I" will be uncovered, and destroyed with dark flame.

When the "I" is utterly annihilated, when the false self is tortured to death, and finally destroyed in this most terrible and supreme of all graces, "you" will have vanished and love will wear your face. You will be the self of the universe, and as I did you will carry your entire being—your body as well—into the light of this fire and be alive forever in the glory of Resurrection, the sixth mystery and threshold on the journey to Christhood.

Now, in the light of Resurrection, love's body at last is complete. Now at last, the full birth has taken place. The body has become love, the heart has become love, the soul burns in love for love. You are one flame of the fire that burns in and as all things, and you have fused in yourself all the paradoxes of the universe, all the "differences"—soul and body, mind with soul, "earth" and "heaven." No human words, born out of division, can express the simplicity of this highest life, its burning, eternal simplicity. In it, the promise of the Baptism—of the presence of the human within the divine—is realized with unimaginably glorious completeness, delicacy, refinement, bliss, and boundless power.

But even this splendor of living the life of Resurrection, of the totally transfigured heart-mind-body-soul, is not the end of the journey into me. Only a state of perpetually expanding, ever-more blissful creativity in love could be the "end" of the endless journey into love.

Only by becoming one with the infinite dynamic creative power of love can you wholly become me. Only by becoming a living, constantly self-transforming, self-conscious center in the life of God, a center able to exist as such, beyond all limitations of any kind whatsoever, will you be able to enter into the beginnings of your final glory.

And so after the victory of Resurrection you will be transported by Grace into the seventh stage and threshold: the mystery of Ascension. Purified even of your resurrected form, your essential being will be swept up into origin, the always-birthing void-light of the Father-Mother. Unimaginable divine powers will now be yours to manifest healing light-forms in all dimensions, to appear in, and influence, all forms of life in all the worlds for the good of God.

But even here in this glory that human words stutter as they attempt to describe, the journey into me as me is not an end. Ascension has made you one with the infinite, fiery life of origin. Now, as I did at Pentecost and do continually, you must descend in tongues of blessing and initiatory flame, and become, like a sun, the source of a boundlessly abundant flame-life, become in me, a sun-sea of fire, whose waves incessantly wash, infuse, and purify the cosmos. You will, in this eighth and ultimate stage, unfolded in those who love me utterly, my clearest saints and most abandoned lovers, be a perpetually outpouring Pentecost in me, a birth-giving glory of my glory, a life of my life birthing new life-in-me throughout my creation.

This is the promise I make to all my saints and those who can bear its splendor: you, too, after your Resurrection and Ascension into the One will become birthers of Pentecostal fire, perpetual, creative fire-agents in the real. In ways you cannot imagine now and would not believe me if I told you, you will pour out of my flame-heart into all the different corners of the world and of the universe, working for the transformation of all things into God with ever-greater passion and humility, ever-greater ecstasy of adoration, working with me and in me and as a part of me to gather the entire cosmos back into the pleroma, the final fullness, when all things will be consciously ablaze with my love. The consummation of all these eight mysteries and thresholds can only be known completely beyond human time and beyond the body. But even in the body you have now, love's body in its glory can appear, and the Resurrection be known and the birthing-in-flame be lived, not totally, but in a luminous shadowing-forth of its ultimate truth.

Just as I knew and lived them in my body, on the earth, in time, you, too, can know and live them.

What I have told you will destroy and resurrect you, kill you and make you a birth-giver.

I am in you always until the end of all worlds, and beyond, working and waiting for the completion of my design.

The Map

Those who say they will die first and then rise up are in error. If they do not first receive the resurrection while they live, when they die they will receive nothing.

GOSPEL OF PHILIP

Truly I say to you, "No one will ever enter heaven's domain if I bid him, but only because you yourselves are full."

JESUS, IN THE SECRET BOOK OF JAMES

Christ is all. He who does not possess all is unable to know Christ.

TEACHINGS OF SYLVANUS

Every person who has been renewed in the spirit and has preserved the gift will be transformed and embodied in Christ, experiencing inevitably the supernatural state of deification.

GREGORY OF SINAI

It is given to every person to become the child of God by adoption through grace.

MEISTER ECKHART

If the adept experiences his own self—the "true man"—in his work, he encounters the "true man"—the Christ—in a new and direct form and he recognizes in the transformation in which he is involved a counterpart to the passion and resurrection.

CARL JUNG

If you wish to arrive, never stop on the way,
You must from light to light forever forward strain.

ANGELUS SILESIUS

Nothing is more important for the seeker who wants to take the direct path into Christ than an accurate "Map" of the journey, one that encompasses, "condenses," and interprets, in a way at once precise and accessible, the different thresholds and mysteries of Christ's own Christing. An incomplete Map will result in an incomplete unfolding of the Christ-essence within the being, and block the full manifestation of the fire of the Sacred Heart in reality. Nothing could be more dangerous now—when what is needed is as complete, vibrant, and radical a vision as possible of the Christhood open to everyone who dares to embody it and calls continually for divine grace. I believe the future of the planet depends upon a release of the Christ-force on a massive, worldwide scale, and in a way that mirrors precisely the radical passion for transformation of society and all its works of the historical Jesus. What is needed is a Map of Christing that remains faithful both to everything that Jesus himself has revealed of the process, and to everything the Christian saints and mystics over two thousand years of the most arduous and passionate exploration have themselves discovered.

What is crucial is that this Map should be as comprehensive as possible and should shirk neither the rigor nor the suffering that is necessary for real transformation, nor the focus on the transformation of society and the world that is the authentic, radical outcome of it. A mysticism that is purely otherworldly, or that treats the world as "illusion" or "dream," has nothing to do with the historical Jesus or the mystic Christ birthed from him, nothing at all to do with the living experience of the love of God and the necessity for the transfiguration of all aspects of human life into the Kingdom that came from it. Jesus and the Christ are one force of revolution that aims at the birth of a wholly new creation, with beings in it who are free with the glorious liberty of the children of God, and thus dangerous, as Jesus himself was, to all established forms of power. What the authentic Christ-force creates in someone who subjects themselves to its fire is a person involved, as Jesus was, with every aspect of society, active within the world from a divinized, inner being, from a center of sometimes deranging and disturbing divine human life and divine human creativity.

When this "new creation" is seen and understood in something of its all-encompassing passion and force, all the separations that now exist in the human mind (and the human "religious mind") will have to be dissolved. As I have shown, the historical Jesus did not separate "politics" from "spirituality," the deepest inward mystical experience from the most focused, critical, transformatory action with society: both were aspects, for him, of the same radical awakening, the same all-devastating and all-transforming living experience of the glory and responsibility of divine love.

An extraordinarily demanding transformation is needed to create the fully Christed self. Everything has to be devoted, given, surrendered to the fire of the Sacred Heart; everything—every faculty of thought, emotion, will—has to be utterly penetrated by the fire of divine love and divinized. All satisfactions of spiritual power have to be renounced; all desire to hide in mystical awareness from the horror of the world and the urgent need to transform that horror have to be abandoned, as Jesus showed, for a sacrificial and sometimes dangerous service of the real within society and for the glory of the Kingdom.

Such a Christed being goes beyond all previous categories invented by the human imagination for either "activist" or "mystic": he or she is both at once and at a radically inspired intensity of power in both domains. The activist who is not a practicing mystic will burn out quickly in the horribly cynical and difficult atmosphere of our world; nothing but an established mystical awareness and a constantly renewed and deepened capacity for summoning and embodying divine grace can give anyone the energy, calm, and insight necessary to fight for justice in so dangerous a world. On the other hand, a mystic who concentrates "only" on personal development and purification and a cultivation of the so-called "higher" mystical states cannot begin even to imagine, let alone embody, the fullness of the Christ-ideal, which demands at every stage—and increasingly at higher stages—an ever-more abandoned service of other beings and an ever-more critical, engaged, and transformatory commitment to justice and the words of love within the world. What Jesus in his life and the Christ-force in its power fuse together are two aspects of human activity normally (and conveniently) kept apart: the "contemplative" or religious and the active. This fusion shows, I would go so far as to say proves, that the aspects are not separate at all but two different facets of the same love, which cannot be fully embodied or rendered fully creative within the world without this fusion taking place at ever-greater levels of integrity and passion within the entire being, and so, increasingly, within the practice and daily choices of the whole race.

A true Map, then, of the Christing must reflect the deepest and highest insights of Jesus himself and all those who have followed him into the furnace of divine love. It cannot afford to miss any valuable information or to ignore any hint or revelation, for on such a dangerous and glorious journey every single insight is invaluable. It cannot gloss over the frightening necessity for suffering and ordeal at all but the highest stages of Christhood. It cannot rest in a vision of Christhood that is in any way passive, however radiantly; it must stress as its end and goal the active, fertile, life-giving ardent outpouring of love into reality through works that characterized Jesus' life and the lives of those who have most completely sacrificed themselves to embody the Christ. Moreover, it must not deny or domesticate or etherealize the radicalism and deranging unconventionality of the action that necessarily flows from the flowering of the Christ within. This action cannot but question, unnerve, expose, and threaten to transform—as Jesus' teaching and practice so clearly did—all the games and goals of all kinds of power; for it is fired by a fierce divine passion for justice that is permanently at odds with all worldly compromise.

The Map that I believe most convincingly represents all of these different aspects of the Christing process and depicts as comprehensively as possible the line of development of the eight thresholds and mysteries has four stages: Purgation, Illumination, Union (or Sacred Marriage), and finally Birthing.

The first three stages mirror almost exactly the "conventional" path of Christian mysticism, slowly developed over years of inner experimentation by the early Christians and Desert Fathers and Mothers, crystallized in the works of such medieval mystics as Hugh of St. Victor and Jean Gerson, and later refined by Teresa of Avila and St. John of the Cross.

The great advantage of this marvelous "system" lies in its sobriety and rigor. Unlike some "contemporary" versions of the Christ-path, this ancient one does not underestimate the immense power of evil, the terrible glamour and resourcefulness of the false self, or the necessity for sometimes harrowing and extreme ordeal. What characterizes its formulations is an awed humility before the achievements of Christ himself, and an unsparing, constantly humbling, and accurate awareness of the distinctions between Creator and creature, which have to be kept awake even in the highest reaches of mystical experience if the seeker is to avoid all pitfalls of pride or inflation.

The drawback of this system, it seems to me, is its insufficiently radical and active understanding of the final goal of Christhood. If union with the Christ is seen as the "end" and "goal" of all development, it is easy to see how a passive or wholly "enraptured" and ecstatic interpretation of such a state can occur. Here the actual practice and force of Christ himself and of the greatest of his lovers—St. Paul, St. Francis, Teresa of Avila, Catherine of Genoa, Ruysbroeck, Meister Eckhart—give us an invaluable clue. In them we can see clearly that "Union" or "Marriage" with the divine was not the end of development but the beginning of another "endless" development of a being-in-God that is at once absorbed in the bliss and joy of Godhead and fertile with its passion for transformation and justice in every area of life.

It is this "endless" stage of creativity and fecundity-in-God and for God and for realization of the Kingdom in time and on the earth that I call "Birthing." Just as the development of the Christ does not end with Resurrection or Ascension but flows on into the perpetual descent of fire that is Pentecost, so the development of the Christing-being does not end in "union," however multifaceted, inspiring, and glorious, but in a continual outpouring of the continually growing powers acquired in and from union into the world. It is essential to emphasize in the danger of our world the activism that such a stage implies, the commitment to working in and for the world.

Just as Jesus went on to become the Christ who descended and descends on the universe in a rain of fire that is still active everywhere, so we who follow him must become in him and for him flames of this fire, ceaselessly active with divine love, divine wisdom, and divine peace in the inferno of reality.

Stage 1: Purgation (or Awakening)

In the first stage of "purgation" (or awakening), the soul "awakens" to its divine nature, its inner Christhood, just as Jesus at his baptism received the news from heaven that he was "the son of God." So now the individual soul in an astonishing experience, or set of experiences, receives in rapture and wonder news of its own glory.

This wonderful awakening to the truth of God's presence in the core of one's being and consciousness begins the journey into Christ. In his spiritual autobiography *The Golden String,* twentieth-century Catholic monk and mystic Bede Griffiths writes:

An experience of this kind is probably not at all uncommon, especially in early youth. Something breaks suddenly into our lives and upsets their normal pattern and we have to begin to adjust ourselves to a new kind of existence.

This experience may come, as it came to me, through the nature of poetry or through art and music; or it may come through the adventure of flying or mountaineering, or of war; or it may come through simply falling in love, or through some apparent accident, an illness, the death of a friend, the sudden loss of fortune. Anything which breaks through the routine of daily life may be the bearer of this message to the soul. But however it may be, it is as though a veil has been lifted and we see for the first time behind the facade which the world has built around us. Suddenly we know we belong to another world, that there is another dimension of existence . . . We see our life for a moment in its true perspective in relation to eternity. We are freed from all the flux of time and see something of the eternal order that underlies it. We are no longer isolated individuals in conflict with our surroundings: we are parts of a whole, elements in a universal harmony.

Everyone is given experiences of this kind by God; what distinguishes those who take the path from those who do not is the depth of sincerity with which they greet such an experience and the disciplined intensity with which they set about arranging their whole life around it. As the great Flemish mystic Ruysbroeck wrote, "Grace touches everyone, for it is given by God but not everyone responds with a free conversion of his will and a purification of his conscience."

Just as Jesus after the glory of the Baptism had to enter the fire of the Temptation of the desert, so the soul, which has awoken in wonder and rapture to its divine nature and origin, has then to undergo severe purification of its entire being. It has to order its whole nature to reflect the glory of what it is coming to know of itself; all the senses have to be clarified and cleansed so that their innate spiritual essence can be revealed.

In this stage of the journey into Christ, the spirit has to be seen, known, and understood as being separate from the body and senses. Confused for so long in their workings and hardly known at all in its own authentic radiance, the spirit has to be ceaselessly invoked and loved, and everything opposed to its free action in the ego and in the life of the senses exposed. It is in this stage of the journey that it is essential to acquire as soon and as sincerely as possible a stable and disciplined spiritual practice of prayer, meditation, and contemplation: if this is not acquired, the awakening into divine origin will fade, the soul will not grow in adoration and self-knowledge, and the saddening revelations of the extent of greed and selfishness in the ego and psyche—revelations which are "designed" to annihilate all pride and vanity—will be unendurable.

In Logion 7 of the Gospel of Thomas, Jesus says, "Blessed is the lion which becomes man when consumed by man; and cursed is the man whom the lion consumes, and the lion becomes man." In the stage of awakening, the "lion"—the natural force within the being—has to be "consumed" by the spirit; all disordered appetites, fantasies, and longings have to be slowly and relentlessly transformed into their divine essence, or be renounced and even denied. This is bitter but crucial work, for if the "lion" of nature is not transformed into spirit in this way, the spirit and the soul can never become what they must become for the journey into Christhood to be possible—masters of the evolution under God, and not slaves servile to the haphazard rhythms of ignorance.

Without this initial stage of rigorous discipline and purification, and without the successful exposure of the workings of the false self that it makes possible, the soul cannot be known in its full splendor and freedom and cannot be released to become the power that transmutes all the other energies and powers of the being into ordered love. As the medieval mystic Richard of St. Victor writes in *The Mystical Ark:* "The soul that has not been practiced over a long time and educated fully in knowledge of self is not raised up to knowledge of God. In vain he raises the eye of the heart to see God when he is not yet prepared to see himself. Let a person first learn to see his own invisible things before he presumes he is able to grasp at invisible divine things."

Authentic self-knowledge—the kind of illusionless self-awareness that arises inevitably when the clarities of the soul's true life start to illumine the ploys and desolate games of the old self—wounds the core of that self-pride that keeps the ego going and cannot but breed an increasingly radical humility. As Jesus says in Logion 69 of the Gospel of Thomas, "Blessed are they who have been persecuted within themselves. It is they who truly come to know the Father." Blessed are they, in other words, who have allowed their falsity, vanity, cruelty, and ignorance to be exposed in all their futility and desperation to themselves and have suffered the inevitable "persecution" and inner war that ensues. Jesus says in Logion 58, "Blessed is the person who has suffered and found life."

Such inner persecution and wounding self-knowledge are essential on the path, too, because they give seekers all the information they will need to protect themselves on the journey from temptation, inflation, and self-destruction. As Jesus says in Logion 21 of the Gospel of Thomas, "Fortunate is the person who knows where the brigands will enter so that he may get up, muster his domain and arm himself before they invade." "Getting up," "mustering the domain," and "arming oneself" are the gifts of intense prayer, humble self-analysis, and sometimes painful renunciation of those habits acquired over many years of ignorance, which now block the true life of the soul. When Jesus is asked in the Gnostic Dialogue of the Savior, "How does the small join itself to the big?" he replies, "When you abandon the works which will not be able to follow you, then you will rest." Knowing which works can "follow" you—which works, in other words, can be taken into the new realm of love and charity which the soul recognizes as its divine truth—demands a total restructuring of the whole of one's life and aims. As Jesus says later in the same Dialogue, "Strive to see that which can follow you, and to seek it out, and to speak from within it, so that as you seek it, it can be in harmony with you."

This "saving of that which can follow you" demands total commitment to the new life that awakening has revealed and to a steady reordering of all the senses and energies of the old self to reflect the nature of God. As Catherine of Genoa has written in her *Treatise on Purgatory,* "God created the soul, pure, simple, clean from all stain of sin, and with a kind of instinct which draws it towards him as its beatific end . . . when a soul returns to its first purity and to the cleanness of its first creation, this instinct, which impels it towards God as to its beatific end, is awakened within it. Increasing every moment, this instinct reacts on the soul with terrifying impetuousness; and the fire of charity impresses it with an irresistible impulse towards its last end, so that it regards this feeling within it of an obstacle that stops this impulse towards God as an intolerable suffering; and the more light it receives, the more intense the torment."

Later in the *Treatise on Purgatory,* Catherine of Genoa writes: "The love of God does to the soul what fire does to material things: the longer it remains in this divine furnace, the purer it becomes. This fire, ever making it more pure, ends by annihilating it in all imperfection and all stain, leaving it wholly purified in God."

What the seeker has to acquire in the stage of awakening, then, is the heroism to stay in the furnace of divine love, whatever the suffering. This suffering will at times be—and has to be—intense. The "transition" that Jesus himself made so swiftly in the forty days' ascesis and temptation in the desert took St. Paul three years of fasting and solitude in Arabia and St. Teresa, by her own admission, over thirty years of struggle.

The most refined and accurate analysis of this necessary "purgation" in the "furnace" of divine love comes from St. John of the Cross in his *Living Flame of Love*: he compares the soul to a damp log that when initially placed in the fire of divine transformation spits, crackles, and exudes smoke:

> Before this divine fire of love is introduced into the substance of the soul, and is united with it, by means of a purity and purgation which is perfect and complete, this flame is wounding the soul and destroying it and consuming in it the imperfections of its evil habits; and this is the operation of the Holy Spirit, wherein he prepares for divine union and the transformation of its substance in God through us. For the same fire of love which afterwards is united with the soul and glorifies it is that which aforetime assailed it in order to purge it; even as the fire that penetrates the log of wood is the same that first attacked and wounded it with its flame, cleansing it and stripping it of all its accidents of ugliness, until by means of its heat, it had prepared it to such a degree that it could enter it and transform it into itself.

St. John of the Cross goes on to detail with chilling precision the sufferings of this necessary but terrible purification: "In this operation, the soul endures great suffering and experiences grievous affliction in its spirit which at times overflow into the senses, at which time this flame is very oppressive. For in this preparatory state of purgation the flame is not bright to it but dark. Neither is it sweet to it, but grievous; for although at times it kindles within it the heat of love, this is accompanied by torment and affliction. And it is not delectable to it, but arid; it brings it neither refreshment nor peace, but consumes and accuses it; neither is it glorious to it, but rather makes it miserable and bitter, by means of the spiritual light of self-knowledge which it sheds upon it, for God sends fire, as Jeremiah says, into its bones, and tries it by fire, as David says likewise."

St. John of the Cross continues: "And thus at this time the soul suffers great darkness in the understanding, many aridities and afflictions in the will and grievous knowledge of its miseries of memory, for the eye of its spiritual knowledge is very bright . . . Now, since this is the remedy and medicine which God gives to the soul for its many infirmities, that he may bring it health, the soul must needs suffer in the purgation and remedy . . . For here its heart is laid upon the coals so that every kind of evil spirit is driven away from it; and here its infirmities are continually brought to light and are laid bare before its eyes so it can feel them, and then they are cured . . . (In this way) God, who is all perfection, wars against all the imperfect habits of the soul, and purifying the soul with the heat of his flame, he uproots its habits from it, and prepares it so that at last he may enter it and be united in it by his sweet, peaceful and glorious love, as is the fire when it has entered the wood."

So devastating a process of purification would be unendurable were it not accompanied—as it always is—by many visionary initiations into divine truth and being and by a gradual revelation in the soul of the living presence of the divine light in all things. As the soul enters more and more abandonedly into the fire, or purgation, the mirror of the heart is cleansed and the light of God—the uncreated light of Christ-consciousness—starts, marvelously and with a kind of infinite tenderness and playfulness, to reveal itself in it. These inner experiences and their joy which are sometimes—as in the cases of Gertrude of Helfta, Hadewijch of Antwerp, Hildegard of Bingen, and Saint John of the Cross himself—accompanied by visions of Christ, give the seeker the strength, encouragement, and passionate stamina to go on subjecting herself to the fire of transformation.

In this stage, it is essential to go on incessantly cleansing the mirror of the heart by prayer and meditation and contemplation, and also by the steady, willed, humble, active practice of those Christ-virtues that slowly transform the old self—the virtues of the Beatitudes: humility, self-renunciation, purity and meekness of heart, "hungering and thirsting" after righteousness and justice, patience, and fortitude under inner and outer attack. This is what the Greek Orthodox mystic Nikitas Stithatos describes as "regulating our life according to the generosity of the spirit . . . and cleansing of the cup . . . so that it can be filled with the wine of the Logos that gladdens the heart of the purified and can be brought to the king of the celestial power for him to taste."

What ends the stage of Purgation and provides the seeker entry into the next stage of Illumination is an experience of the divine light in and as all things. All through the agony and ecstasy of Purgation, the seeker will have experienced sporadically the appearance of the uncreated light both in his or her own consciousness and in the "outer" world; slowly and marvelously the truth will have been revealed to the seeker that this light—the light of Christ-consciousness—is manifesting all things, is in, behind, and around all things, and saturates the entire creation with its calm glory, the glory of the mind and heart of God.

At the end of the stage of Purgation—when the seeker's senses have been purified, the mirror of the heart largely polished clean, and the seeker's life-energies reordered to a considerable extent around the Christ-virtues, the Christing self will be graced a vast experience of the divine light as the whole of the universe and as the innermost truth of his or her own soul, an experience that mirrors the third threshold and mystery of the Transfiguration on Mount Tabor. After this overwhelming experience, the seeker realizes his or her essential identity in this truth with all other beings, with the entire cosmos and the divine power emanating it. This realization, with its wonder and tremendous release of new energy and longing to help all beings, begins a wholly new life—a life where the whole nature of the seeker experiences increasing intensity, passion, delight, as it is continually and increasingly flooded by the fire-energies of the Holy Spirit.

Stage 2: Illumination

The continual calm "seeing" of the uncreated divine light, and the wholly new inflamed and inspired life it brings, start the seeker on the stage of "Illumination." In this stage, the seeker comes to experience his Transfiguration in the terms of his or her own awakened divine personality. As Nikitas Stithatos writes, "The illumination stage pertains to those who as a result of their struggles have attained the first level of dispassion. It is characterized by the spiritual knowledge of created beings, the contemplation of their inner essences and communion in the Holy Spirit." Stithatos goes on to be even more precise: "This stage involves the spiritual intellect's purification by divine fire, the noetic opening of the eyes of the heart, and the birth of the Logos, accompanied by sublime intellections of spiritual knowledge. Its final goal is the elucidation of the nature of created things by the Logos of Wisdom, insight into divine and human affairs, and the revelations of the mysteries of the Kingdom of heaven. He who has reached this point through the inner activity of the spiritual intellect rides, like another Elijah in a chariot of fire . . . and while still living, he is raised to the noetic realm and traverses the heavens . . ."

It is in this tremendously invigorated and empowered stage that the seeker often discovers his or her true life-vocation and pours out the gifts of the Spirit into it, just as Jesus after the Baptism, Temptation, and Transfiguration poured out his love in a many-faceted service of all beings. In this stage, the seeker, as Stithatos points out, will be instructed by the divine light itself as to the nature of divine reality; all the necessary inner mystical experiences will be given to the seeker to reveal all the different relationships of the divine to reality. The seeker will come to experience increasingly his or her own Christ-nature, and powers of healing, artistic creation, and prophesy may well be given. The whole of life will be increasingly revealed as the extraordinary theater of divine life and divine love. As the twentieth-century scholar and contemplative Evelyn Underhill writes of the mystic who has come into this stage of Christing, "He has got through preliminaries . . . The result is a new and solid certainty about God, and his own soul's relation to God; an 'enlightenment' in which he is adjusted to new standards of conduct and thought. In the traditional language of asceticism, he is 'proficient but not yet perfect.' He achieves a real vision and knowledge, a conscious harmony with the divine world of becoming; yet not yet self-loss in the Principle of Life . . . All pleasurable and exalted states of mystic consciousness in which the sense of I-hood persists, in which there is a loving and joyous relation between the Absolute as object and the self as subject fall under the heading of Illumination; which is really an enormous development of the intuitional life at high levels."

This stage of Illumination—in which the divine secrets of the universe are revealed to the seeker and in which she tastes the depths of the divine gifts and energies within her transformed self and pours them into reality—is not, however, as Underhill and the "story" of Jesus make clear, the end of the Christing journey. Another drastic and terrible purification has to occur, and always does, at the end of the stage of Illumination, to "kill" the human self entirely. As in the unfolding of the historical Jesus into the mystical Christ, this purification has two stages—the Agony and the Cross. All those who want to follow Jesus into the fire of life of the Resurrection, the oneness of the Ascension, and the boundless birth-giving fertility of Pentecost have to go through, of their own free will, the stripping and death of the Agony and the Cross.

In traditional Christian mystical writing, the first purification—that of the stage of awakening, which prepares the unfolding of the glories of Illumination—is the purification of the "senses." The purification which has to occur at the end of the stage of Illumination is a more drastic, disturbing, and devastating one, because it is a purification of the ground of the Spirit itself. The last irradiated traces of the "witness," "spectator," self-referential human "I" have now to die completely, for the unimaginable splendor of the divine I, the resurrected one, to be revealed, and this can only take place, as all those who have lived it from Jesus onwards have come to know, by a prolonged and agonizing "stripping" of the entire "created" self from the divine self. What the self "knows" and sometimes, marvelously, merges with in Illumination now has wholly to *become* in Union. From "knowing" and occasionally "merging with" the absolute to *becoming* one with it in love is a vast step, a step which all Christian mystics agree, the self on its own is totally unable to take. On its own, it cannot cross this abyss; it has to die before it and die willingly: only its willing "dying" on the cross, in what mystics know as the Dark Night, can allow divine grace to unveil the final revelations of Christhood. Jesus announces to Heinrich Suso: "None can come to the sublime heights of the divinity or taste its ineffable sweetness if at first they have not experienced utterly the bitterness and lowliness of my humanity." Experiencing utterly this "bitterness" and "lowliness" means undergoing Christ's passion in all its aspects—a terrible grace which permanently transforms the being. As Gregory of Sinai tells us, "Christ's passion is a life-quickening death to all those who have experienced all its phases, for by experiencing what he experienced we are glorified as he is . . . willingly to experience what Christ experienced is to crucify crucifixion and put death to death."

What happens then in the flowering of Illumination that is the Dark Night is a total annihilation of the self in God. At this stage, the seeker will experience, in the terms of his or her own temperament life and innermost being, all the torments of Gethsemane and Calvary, all the feelings of persecution, utter illusionless isolation, and sense of abandonment by God that afflicted Jesus himself and prepared him for the revelation of resurrection. Only supreme love and faith can take the seeker through this horrifying experience. The starved and tortured self has to learn to accept lovelessness for the sake of love, nothingness for the sake of the fullness in which all things rest; has to accept annihilation without the security of any sure promise of life. As Underhill writes, "So long as the subject still feels himself to be 'somewhat,' he has not yet annihilated selfhood and come to that ground where his being can be united with the being of God . . . Only when he learns to cease thinking of himself at all, in however deprecatory a sense, when he abolishes even such selfhood as lies in a desire for the sensible presence of God, will harmony be attained. This is the 'naughting of the soul' . . . Here, as in purgation, the condition of access to higher levels of vitality is a death; a deprivation, a detachment, a clearing of the ground. Poverty leaps to the Cross; and finds there an utter desolation without promise of spiritual reward. The satisfactions of the spirit must now go the same way as the satisfactions of the senses. Even the power of voluntary sacrifice and self-discipline is taken away. A dreadful ennui, a dull helplessness, takes its place. The mystic motto 'I am nothing, I have nothing, I desire nothing' must now express not only the detachment of the senses, but the whole being's surrender to the All."

In this state, the fourteenth-century German mystic John Tauler tells us, "Everything depends on a fathomless sinking in a fathomless nothingness . . . If a man were to say, 'Lord, who are you, that I must follow you through such deep, gloomy, miserable paths?' the Lord would reply, 'I am God and man and far more God.' If a person could answer then really consciously from the bottom of his heart, 'Then I am nothing and less than nothing,' all could be accomplished, for the Godhead has really no place to work in except where all has been annihilated. The schoolmen say that when a new form is to come into existence, the old must of necessity be destroyed . . . And so I say, 'If a person is to be clothed with New Being, all the forms must necessarily be destroyed that were ever received by him in all his powers—of perception, knowledge, will, work, of subjection, sensibility, and self-seeking."

St. John of the Cross tells us in detail of this "destruction": "God divests the faculties, affections, and senses, both spiritual and sensory, interior and exterior. He leaves the intellect in darkness, the will in aridity, the memory in emptiness, and the affections in supreme affliction, bitterness and anguish by depriving the soul of the feeling and satisfaction it previously obtained from spiritual blessings. For this deprivation is one of the conditions required that the spiritual form, which is the union of love, may be introduced in the spirit and united with it."

While the soul is, in fact, in closer and more naked contact with the divine light and the divine grace than ever before, it cannot "register" the brilliant mercy of this contact, and experiences it as a "Dark Night," an "extinction." As St. John of the Cross tells us, "This divine and dark light causes deep immersion of the mind in the knowledge of and feeling of one's own miseries and evils; it brings all these miseries into relief so that the soul sees clearly that of itself it will never possess anything else . . . Since the divine strikes in order to renew the soul and divinize the soul (by stripping it of the habitual affections and properties of the old man to which it is strongly united, attached, and conformed), it so disentangles and dissolves the spiritual substance, absorbing it in a profound darkness, that the soul at the sight of its miseries feels that it is melting away and being undone by a cruel spiritual death; it feels as if it were swallowed by a beast and being digested in its dark belly, and it suffers an anguish comparable to Jonah's when in the belly of the whale. It is fitting that the soul be in this sepulcher of dark death in order to attain the spiritual resurrection for which it hopes."

Nearly all contemporary mystical "diagrams"—including so-called Christian ones—play down the sacred necessity of the Dark Night. In doing so, they mislead the authentic seeker, denigrate the true glory of Christhood, and risk aborting the birth of the Christ-consciousness. "There is no way around the Cross," à Kempis cried, no way around the ultimate test of love that it represents, the ultimate test of selflessness that the self has to die to pass. Any version of the mystical journey, and especially one that endeavors to help the seeker enter into Christhood, that "plays down" or skimps this crucial stage—and does not attempt to describe its ordeals and terrors and desolations with as much objective accuracy as possible—betrays the seeker and the glory of the resurrected state. This is the abjection of New Age mysticism and the pseudo-Christian mysticism that have sprung from it; they delude people into believing that the self can be kept in serenity, fulfillment, and ecstasy forever and never have to go through any terminal stripping and annihilation. This is a refined and deadly form of narcissism, the final triumph, in fact, of the self that does not want to be destroyed in order to be wholly remade, that wants to call its minor mystic insights final enlightenment and its ecstasies "ultimate union," without paying the only price that could make its claims real—the price of real death. As Jesus says in the Apocryphon of James: "None will be saved unless they believe in my cross . . . Become seekers for death . . . When you examine death it will teach you election . . . the Kingdom belongs to those who put themselves to death."

Even the descriptions of so-called "ego death" that are given by many contemporary "transpersonal psychologists" seem ridiculously, even hilariously, tame compared with the Gospel's descriptions of Jesus' agony and Calvary and the descriptions in the Desert Fathers, the *Philokalia*, Catherine of Siena, St. John of the Cross, and Teresa of Avila of the real horror of the real process. One of the greatest dangers of the modern "spiritual renaissance" is that many seekers "mime" the highest truths without having an inkling of what they actually mean, describe as the Dark Night or "ego death" what are in fact minor crises of confidence or traumatic "transitions." The authentic Dark Night has little to do even with the most terrible crisis and traumatic events; its horrors, as Tauler and St. John of the Cross and Jesus himself make clear, are far subtler, more refined, and more terrifyingly *conscious* and *inescapable*. The old self not only does not survive them; it *cannot* survive them. Of those who have come through it, St. John of the Cross writes, soberly, and without any exaggeration, "These are the ones who go down into hell alive."

The Dark Night, the mystics tell us, tends to establish itself gradually; the powers and intuitions of the self are withdrawn one after another, until the "mystic death" in its full intensity is reached. So too when the "darkness" begins to dissolve before the advance of the new life, the life of the resurrection, the process is usually slow, though it may be punctuated by visions and ecstasies. Slowly, the agonies, terrors, and disharmonies of the Dark Night start to dissipate; affirmation usurps the rule of negation; rays of light begin to pierce, irradiate, and transfigure the desolation of the cross. These "rays of light" herald the birth of the sun of the divine resurrected self, the true Man, the Christ-sun. As Underhill tells us: "The act of complete surrender then, which is the term of the Dark Night, has given the self its footing in Eternity; its abandonment of the old centers of consciousness has permitted movement towards the new. In the misery and apparent stagnation of the Dark Night . . . work has been done; and the last great phase of the inward transmutation accomplished. The self which comes forth from the night is no separated self, conscious of the illumination of the Uncreated Light, but the new person, the transmuted humanity, whose life is one with the Absolute Life of God."

Stage 3: Union (or Sacred Marriage)

Now in Union, lover, beloved, and love are all known as one; the Christ-consciousness is born complete and the divine Child, radiant and eternal, appears at the core of awareness. All the powers of body, mind, heart, and soul are united in a fire of human divine love; the universe is experienced as a constant dance of supreme consciousness. Godhead streams normally from all beings and created things; the light of the resurrection reveals the sacred origin of matter at all moments; all emotions, all perception, every physical movement are lived in their divine truth, divine rhythm, and divine harmony. At last, the seeker enters into the "undivided" Edenic life of the Kingdom; the inner Christ that has been growing through all the ordeals and revelations of the journey now gazes consciously through the seeker's eyes, moves in the seeker's body, burns as divine love in all the cells of the seeker's heart.

The most complete statement that Jesus ever made about the nature of Union, and one of the key mystical clues to the transformation of the whole human being into a Christ, is found in Logion 22 of the Gospel of Thomas:

> Jesus saw some babies nursing. He said to his disciples, "These nursing babies are like those who enter the Kingdom." They said to him, "Then shall we enter the Kingdom as babies?"
> Jesus said to them, "When you make the two one, and when you make the inside like the outside and the outside like the inside and

the above like the below, and when you make the male and the female one and the same so that the male not be male and the female female; and when you fashion eyes in place of an eye, and a hand in place of a hand, a foot in place of a foot, and a likeness in place of a likeness, then you will enter the Kingdom."

Every detail of this logion is revelatory. It begins by Jesus seeing some babies nursing. Immediately, this image of total at-oneness, trust, and abandon arouses in Jesus' awakened mind the image of resurrected consciousness. The Kingdom-consciousness is divine Child-consciousness, a consciousness that is drinking the milk of divine joy, wisdom, strength, and protection at every moment. To become a Christ is to become a "nursing baby," one who experiences the universe as a Mother, who nourishes, feeds, sustains, provides, guides at all times, who knows, in fact, perfect intimacy while in time and in a body with what St. John of the Cross calls "the tenderness of the Life of God."

St. Catherine of Genoa describes the abandoned wonder and calm of this state: "When the soul is annihilated and transformed, of herself, she neither works nor speaks nor wills nor feels nor hears nor understands, neither has she of herself the feeling of outward or inward where she may move. And in all things it is God who rules and guides her without the mediation of any creature. And the state of this soul is the feeling of such utter peace and tranquility that it seems to her that her heart, and her bodily being, and all both within and without are immersed in an ocean of utmost peace; from where she shall never come forth from anything that can befall her in this life . . . It seems to her in her human and spiritual nature both within and without she can feel no other thing than sweetest peace."

After giving in the image of "nursing babies" a perfect sign of "unitive awareness," Jesus goes on in Logion 22 to define exactly what Kingdom-consciousness—divine Child-consciousness—is and how it is engendered; Jesus begins by saying: "When you make the two one." By this he means that when through intense prayer and meditation and increasingly all-inclusive mystical experience all separations between human and divine, heaven and earth, prayer and action are annihilated, the universe appears in the glory of unity. At this stage, as Jesus says next, "the inside" is seen and known as the "outside" and the "outside" like the "inside": all the distinctions of ordinary awareness are destroyed in the fire of non-dual knowledge.

When the state of non-duality is experienced—the state of "no separation" that is the truth of Union—then everything that normal awareness experiences as "inside" is seen as "outside" and the entire so-called external universe and all its created beings and things are known as "inner" manifestations of supreme consciousness: the whole cosmos and all its forms are revealed as creations of divine mind, as outstreamings of one heart-fire. All the separations that exist in undivinized awareness between what is "personal" and "impersonal," "inner" and "outer," are softly exploded, because the newborn Christ Child contains in perfect lucid self-consciousness the entire universe within the fire-circle of its own mind and heart. The miracle of this gnosis ends forever, as Christ goes on to tell us, all so-called religious distinctions between "above" and "below," between what has been previously defined as "sacred" and "profane," "pure" and "impure." Everything is revealed as divine and saturated with divinity. The transformed consciousness of the seeker knows what Jesus meant when in Logion 77 of the Gospel of Thomas he says: "I am the light that is above them all. I am the all. The all came forth from me, the all attained to me. Cleave a piece of wood, I am there. Lift up the stone and you will find me there."

In so complete a consciousness, naked at all moments to unity, even the most menial or trivial actions become blissful, actions of a divine self at home in its Mother-Father, the cosmos. This is the "glorious liberty of the children of God" that St. Paul talks of; in this state of final freedom the liberated being drinks joy, health, tenderness, and ecstasy from every thought, feeling, and movement in the resurrected body-mind. The earth and time and the body itself are revealed in the truth of unity as being infused at all moments, at all levels, and in all circumstances with divine force, meaning, and radiance; the divine Child lives at peace within the womb of the timeless-in-time, walks and breathes on earth in a heaven of divine love. All veils and masks that separated the seeker from God are now burned away so that God stares from every human face, shines under every stone, opens in every flower, speaks transparently in every event. What was once experienced as "above"—the light-world of divine love and knowledge—reveals itself as living in—and as—all things and beings. "Heaven" appears as a great eternal light-fire cradling all matter, all beings, nakedly visible now to the resurrected Child-self. At last, the seeker knows through identity exactly and completely what Jesus meant when he said in Logion 113, "The Kingdom of the Father is spread out upon the earth."

The Christing being now experiences in ever-expanding lucid wonder and bliss the precise truth of what Jesus proclaimed in Logion 111: "Heaven and earth will be rolled up in your presence. And the one who lives from the living one will not taste death." What he or she imagined as "heaven" and "earth" are "rolled up" in the glory of eternal "presence." The immortality of the soul's supreme consciousness blazes as a naked fact in all things.

In the rest of Logion 22, Jesus takes us even deeper into the truth of resurrected awareness. He tells us that a further condition for Union, or Sacred Marriage, is "when you make the male and the female one and the same, so that the male not be male nor the female female." In the knowledge of eternal unity—of being one with the ground of Godhead—that resurrection brings, all "male" and "female" powers of the being are fused in a oneness that contains but transcends both, as the universe itself, created by the interplay between "male" and "female," contains and transcends both in the divine unity. And through this "inner marriage"—and simultaneously with it—an ever-deepening "marriage" with reality in unity takes place.

Such an inner Sacred Marriage increasingly divinizes all the powers and qualities of the seeker's entire emotional, spiritual, and physical being. Something like, in fact, a nuclear fusion between the separated "male" and "female" powers takes place, and the resulting birth of Unity-consciousness in every dimension of being and every activity gives the whole nature of the seeker a vastly deepened purity, focus, intensity, passion, and strength unimaginable to anyone who lives a divided life. The undivided life of the divine Child, who has fused the "male" and "female" within, partakes directly, simply, and naturally of the divine bliss-energy and bliss-wisdom of divine love itself, and expresses itself on all levels and dimensions of the universe simultaneously with the "glorious liberty" of the resurrected Christ. This "glorious liberty" is what is called "Sahaja" in the Hindu tradition, "enlightenment" by the Mahayana Buddhists, and "living in the Tao" by the Taoist mystics.

Jesus goes on in Logion 22 to make clear that in this resurrected state the body too is transfigured: this is essential information, which a body-hating later tradition has often ignored. Christhood transforms not only the spirit, but also the flesh; the resurrection is not a "symbol" or "metaphor." The mystics who have entered its field tell us that the body too is "re-made," made infinitely suppler, more sensitive, tender, more refined, because it is now consciously alive in—and suffused with—eternal light, and refashioned—even, perhaps in its cellular structure—in the light-fire of divine love. Rebirthed now in origin and unity, all the senses become ways of entering into blissful contact with the one; the entire being becomes, in St. Macarius's words, "eyes that feast on divine presence." The "old" hand that touched in separation becomes a "hand" that knows it is touching an extension of itself; the foot that walked on alien ground now walks consciously in and on itself. The old "likeness"—the fallen likeness, the likeness of ignorance and illusion—becomes—and consciously—the likeness of the risen sacred one, the Father-Mother-Divine Child.

This oneness heals all divisions and fuses all "separate" powers and brings into the union of Sacred Marriage all the "male" and "female" powers of the self, unites and fuses intellect and divine love, imagination and ecstasy, the spirit and the body, the laws of the heart and the structures of mind, the light and every breath, gesture, thought, and emotion lived in its truth. What is born from this fusion, this Sacred Marriage of all the "separate" powers of heart, mind, body, and soul is the Sacred Androgyne, the one who in his or her being realizes the total interpenetration within the Christ of all normally "opposed" or "contradictory" qualities. This Sacred Androgyne—birthed in what early Gnostic writings such as the Gospel of Philip and the Acts of Thomas call again and again the "Bridal Chamber," the place of fusion between "male" and "female"—is a divinized human divine being free of all normal categories of "male" or "female" because it exists in a unity that contains, absorbs, "uses," and ecstatically transcends both. Empowered directly now with the "nuclear" divine energies of Christhood, this Sacred Androgyne divine Child consciously reclaims, lives in, and radiates the life of Eden, is the new Eve-Adam reuniting in his-her own being the Adam and Eve that were separated at the "Fall." In such a being, "heaven" lives on earth: through such a being the divine radiates divine grace and power directly.

The Gnostic Gospel of Philip takes us further into the mystery of androgynous birth in the Bridal Chamber: "There were three buildings specifically for sacrifice in Jerusalem. The one facing west was called 'the holy.' Another facing south was called the 'holy of the holy.' The third facing east was called the 'holy of the holies, the place where only the high priest enters.'" Baptism is the holy building; redemption is the "holy" of the holies; the "holy of the holies" is the Bridal Chamber.

The Gospel of Philip continues: "If the woman had not separated from the man, she should not die with the man. His separation became the beginning of death. Because of this, Christ came to repair the separation which was from the beginning and again unite the two to give life to those who died as a result of the separation and unite them. But the woman is united to her husband in the Bridal Chamber. Indeed, those who have united in the Bridal Chamber will no longer be separated. When Eve was still in Adam, death did not exist. When she was separated from him, death came into being. If he enters (the Bridal Chamber) again and attains his former self, then death will be no more."

In the Bridal Chamber, then, is born resurrected consciousness, the human divine awareness that lives in unity with the cosmos; in it the inner "Eve" and "Adam" meet in mutual honor, bliss, and communion; this perpetually renewed, always-transformatory inner meeting and fusion is the birth, the appearance of the divine Child, the consciousness of Sacred Androgyne. In the Bridal Chamber all women and all men are broken and remade in the Christ Man-Woman, the origin and core of all evolution, and its omega point, the point that simultaneously initiates, contains, and brings to consummation all creation.

As the Gospel of Philip tells us: "If anyone becomes a son of the Bridal Chamber, he will receive the light. If anyone does not receive it while he is here, he will not be able to receive it in the other place." It is here, in this body, on this earth, and in time that the Cosmic Christ longs for us to "enter the Kingdom."

The Gospel of Philip goes on to describe with wonderful clarity the splendor and freedom that the one who has united inner and outer, "sacred" and "profane," "heaven" and "earth," the "male" and the "female" in the glory of the Kingdom feels, lives, and knows: "He who will receive the light will not be seen, nor can he be detained and no one shall be able to torment a person like this even while he dwells in the world. And again when he leaves the world, he has already received the truth in the images. The world has become the eternal realm. For the eternal realm is fullness for him. This is the way it is: it is revealed to him alone, not hidden in the darkness and the night, but hidden in a perfect day and a holy light."

Jesus Christ's own example and the inner experience of the Christian mystics of Kingdom-consciousness reveal to us that it is not in any sense static. Once the divine Child, the Christ, has been born into the "eternal realm" that is "Fullness," it does not stay fixed in a divine trance of love: it enters a field of endless and boundless dynamic transformation which, we are told, never ends in any dimension or plane of the universe. Divine love is infinite and always ecstatically gathering up all things into ever-higher, ever-more refined union; what the Child born in Christ-consciousness into the Kingdom now begins is the endless life of love that will—and can—never end anywhere, in any dimension, because its potential for transformation is boundless.

No one has written of this boundless transformation more movingly or precisely than the fourth-century mystic Gregory of Nyssa: "In our constant participation in the blessed nature of God, the graces that we receive at every point are indeed great, but the path that lies beyond our immediate grasp is infinite. This will constantly happen to those who thus share in the divine Goodness, and they will always enjoy a greater and greater participation in grace in all eternity . . . In all the infinite eternity of centuries the being who runs towards you becomes greater as he rises higher, ever growing in proportion to his increase in grace. You, indeed, are the Most High, abiding forever and can never seem smaller to those who approach you, for you are always to the same degree higher and more elevated than the faculties of those who are rising . . . [So] for those who are rising in perfection, the limit of the good attained becomes the beginning of the discovery of higher goods. Thus they never stop rising, moving from one beginning to the next, and the beginning of ever greater graces is never limited of itself. For the desire of those who thus rise never rests in what they can already understand; but by an ever greater and greater desire, the soul keeps rising constantly to another which lies ahead, and thus makes its way through ever-higher regions towards the transcendent."

Stage 4: Birthing

Just as Jesus Christ himself did not "end" in the resurrection but went on to live the mystery of the ascension and then to "descend" again in an infinite and infinitely renewed rain of divine fire on earth (and throughout the cosmos), so the being that has been Christed enters the field of perpetual divine transformation, in which love and the ever-greater desire and adoration it awakens takes the Christed one into ever-more powerful forms of divine being and divine action.

This is why the traditional vision of the Christ-journey that "ends" with Union is inadequate. There is no "ending" in Union; Union is, in fact, the beginning of another unbounded and endless journey into ever-higher and ever-greater divine being. Dionysius the Areopagite tells us that the seraphim and cherubim transform themselves each second into higher and higher states of union through the always-expanding incandescence of their worship of the One; what a Christed Sacred Androgyne divine Child enters is this dimension of boundless transfiguration.

The clearest way of "imaging" this mystery is to say that the divine Child after being Christed becomes itself a Father-Mother, able to give birth also with the divine creativity, fecundity, and power in reality. As it is said in the Dialogue of the Savior: "There is the Son of Man and there is the Son of the Son of Man, the Lord is the Son of Man and the Son of the Son of Man is he who creates through the Son of Man. The Son of Man received from God the capacity to create. He also has the ability to 'beget' and so, by implication, has the one 'begotten' in and through him." The birthed one, then, comes ceaselessly to give birth in the birthing power of the divine itself; one with the Father-Mother, born into the Kingdom, infused with divine wisdom and divine love, the birthed one is flooded increasingly with the power in God to give birth in the real.

As the Gospel of Philip reminds us: "The heavenly man has many more sons than earthly man. If the sons of Adam are many, although they die, how much more are the sons of the perfect men, they who do not die but are always begotten." The Sacred Androgyne who has been born into Christhood is born into a field of "boundless begetting": birth for the Christed one is a perpetual and perpetually new, perpetually expanding experience: the one who is "always begotten" in this dimension is given God's own fertility ceaselessly to "beget." The Child of the Father-Mother becomes the Father-Mother of an endless and endlessly expanding stream of divine works, both before and long beyond what we call "death." Just as Jesus in Christing himself became a living self-conscious flame of the eternal creative fire of God, so all those Christed in him will become flames of the birth-giving fire, persons, like the Christ, wholly lit up with the love-wisdom of the supreme Person, one with that One in joy, gnosis, charity, and final creative bliss. As Meister Eckhart wrote: "All virtue of the just and every work of the just is nothing other than the Son—who is the new creation—being born from the Father. In the depths of our being where justice and work are home, we work one work and a new creation with God."

This mystery of becoming like Jesus Christ himself, a perpetual birth-giver, a worker of the "one work" of the new creation, is the final mystery of Christhood or, at least, the final mystery that can be expressed in human language. The only "door" into it is through total abandoned service of all beings and a humility as final, ruthless, and uncompromising as that of Jesus himself. Jesus Christed himself not for himself but for the entire human race, and for the whole universe: only those who constantly want to serve all beings everywhere with more and more selflessness and truth and with an ever-greater degree of effectiveness and clarity can enter this mystery, and go on living it for all eternity.

It is into this birth-giving dimension of eternal self-donation and divine fecundity that the very greatest Christian mystics—St. Francis, Catherine of Genoa, Teresa of Avila, the Cure of Ars—have entered while still on earth and in a body. What else could explain the extraordinary, more-than-human energy of their activity and still-transforming fertility of their influence? Birthed into Christhood, they, in total humility and selfless love, became Father-Mothers of fresh divine works. Therese of Lisieux revealed the truth of the aspiration that informs so boundlessly creative a life when in the agony of her deathbed she vowed to "spend all her time in heaven doing good on earth": she knew herself a flame of the divine fire of the Cosmic Christ and she knew that she would be graced in her lover some direct part of her lover's power to infuse and transform all things for the greater glory of God. In the humility of ecstatic surrender, she claimed and named this birth-giving power and, as all those who know the real help of the saints know, continues to birth miracle and grace in the souls and lives of those who turn to her. The life that the Christed one is invited to is nothing less than a part of the infinitely dynamic fertile, fecund, and transforming life of the Cosmic Christ himself.

Of all the Christian mystics who have tried to express in words this final mystery, Richard of St. Victor, in *The Four Degrees of Passionate Charity,* takes us deepest. In his marvelous treatise, the growth of divine love in the Spirit is charted with extreme precision. In the "third" degree of passionate charity (which corresponds to the third stage of the Map, "Sacred Marriage"), the soul achieves Union, entering into the unity of the Bridal Chamber. Richard of St. Victor makes certain that we understand that a further unfolding of truth and love is required; he tells us that the soul united to God in this third degree of Union has been reduced in the divine fire, softened to the very core, and entirely melted. "Now" he says, "nothing is wanted except that she should be shown what is God's goodwill, all-pleasing and perfect, even the form of perfect virtue to which she must be conformed. Just as metal workers when the metals are melted and the moulds set out, shape any form according to their will, and produce any vessel according to the manner and mould that has been planned, so the soul applies herself in this degree, to be ready at the summons of the Divine will; she adapts herself with spontaneous desire to every demand of God and adjusts her own will, as the divine pleasure requires. And as liquefied metal runs slowly down wherever a passage is opened, so the soul humbles herself spontaneously to be obedient in this way, and freely bows herself in all acts of humility according to the order of divine providence."

Richard of St. Victor continues to describe this "bowing" of love in "all acts of humility": "In this state the image of the will of Christ is set before the soul so that these words come to her, 'Let this mind be in you, which is also in Christ Jesus; who being in the form of God, thought it not robbery to be equal with God but emptied himself, and took upon himself the form of a servant and was made in the likeness of man. He humbled himself and became obedient unto death even the death of the Cross.' This is the form of humility to which every man must conform himself, who longs to attain to the highest degree of charity."

The "highest degree of charity," and so of Christhood, cannot be, Richard of St. Victor makes clear, a "resting" in the third degree of passionate charity, Union; only by imitating the Christ in all things and especially in a continual outpouring of all one's gifts and powers into the real, a continual action rooted in divine peace, love, and knowledge, can a person really live a Christ-life. This continual action entails a continual sacrifice of self. Richard of St. Victor continues: "For greater love has no man but this, that a man lay down his life for his friends. Those who are able to lay down their lives for their friends have reached the highest peak of charity . . . they can answer to the apostles' call: 'Be ye therefore followers of God, as dear children; and walk in love, as Christ has also loved us, and has given himself as an offering to God for our fragrant savior.'"

To become like Christ a "fragrant savior," the transformed seeker has to go beyond the rapture and identity of Union into a service and an action renewed by and birthed from the continuing experience of Union. In the third degree of passionate charity, Richard of St. Victor tells us, the being is glorified, tastes and knows Resurrection. In the fourth and ultimate state, however, she is "humbled for Christ's sake." "And though in the third she is in a way almost in the likeness of God, nevertheless in the fourth she starts to empty herself, taking the form of a servant. In the third degree of passionate charity, the soul is, as it were, put to death in God, in the fourth she is raised in Christ. He that is in the fourth degree can truly say, 'I live yet not I but Christ liveth in me.' He who ascends to this degree of charity is truly in that state of love that can say, 'I am made all things to all men that I, might save all.' . . . That which he hopes of God, that what he does for God and effects with God is more than merely human."

The great Flemish mystic Ruysbroeck also illumines this fourth and final stage of "birthing" sacred works in Christ as Christ. Union for Ruysbroeck means a full, conscious participation in the entire life of the Godhead, that "Trinitarian" life that is at once utterly and blissfully peaceful and completely dynamic, at once at rest and in perpetual and glorious action. As Ruysbroeck tells us in his *Spiritual Espousals:* "The divine persons who form one sole God are in the fecundity of their nature ever active; and in the simplicity of their essence they form the Godhead and eternal blessedness. Thus God according to the Persons is Eternal Work; but according to essence and its Perpetual stillness, he is Eternal rest. Now love and fruition live between this activity and this rest . . . the spirit of God himself breathes us out from himself that we may love, and may do good works, and again he draws us into himself that we may rest in fruition. And this is Eternal Life; even as our mortal life subsists in the indrawing and outgoing of our breath." Ruysbroeck continues: "Understand, God . . . demands of us both action and fruition, in such a way that the action never hinders the fruition, nor the fruition the action, but they strengthen one another. And this is why the interior man lives his life according to these two ways: that is to say, in rest and in work. And in each of them he is wholly and undividedly: for he dwells wholly in God in virtue of his restful fruition and wholly in himself in virtue of his active love. And God, in his communications, perpetually calls and urges him to renew both this rest and work."

This being breathed out and breathed in by the Godhead, as all the lives of the mystics who have achieved this state show, entails a life of superhuman dedication, passion, and loving action in every dimension of the real, of ceaseless "birthing" of the divine consciousness in action at every level. Ruysbroeck tells us further of this state that "the soul is active in all loving work, for it sees its rest . . . For love's sake (the soul) strives for victory, for it sees its crown. Consolation, peace, joy, victory and riches, all that can give delight, all this is shown to the mind illuminated in God, in spiritual similitudes and without measure. And through this vision love continues active. For such a just man has built up in his soul, in rest and in work, a veritable life which shall endure forever . . . Thus this man is just, and he goes towards God by inward love, in eternal work, he goes in God by his fruitive inclination in eternal rest. And he dwells in God and yet he goes out towards all creatures, in a spirit of love towards all things, in virtue and in works of righteousness. And this is the supreme summit of the inner life."

As Ruysbroeck says, this Christ-life, because it is one with the source itself, shall not end, even with death: "It is a veritable life which shall endure forever." What we call death, Ruysbroeck is implying, is only, for those who have already known the resurrection, a door into an even-wider field of loving and transforming action, the loving and transforming action on behalf of all beings everywhere of the saints, the angels, archangels, cherubim, and seraphim, and other divine agents of the fire of love whose names we cannot know and whose continuing eternal work we cannot, in our present state of knowledge, even imagine.

From Awakening and Baptism into divine awareness, the lover of Christ has dared all the stages of the Christ-journey—through Temptation and Transfiguration and the Agony and the Cross—and come into the Resurrection and Ascension and finally into the always life-giving fiery life of Pentecost, beyond space and time, in the eternal now that births all things perpetually afresh. "In the fourth degree of love," Evelyn Underhill writes, commenting on Richard of St. Victor, "the soul brings forth its children. It is the agent of a fresh outbirth of spiritual vitality . . . the helpmate of the transcendent order, the mother of a spiritual progeny. The great unitive mystics are each of them founders of spiritual families, centers from which radiates new life. The 'flowing lights' of the Godhead is focused in them, as in a lens, only that it may pass through them to spread out on every side . . ."

Such is the glory that Jesus Christ won for himself and for all of us; such is the glory the Christ pours into all those who turn to him; such is the glory of the endless life that he makes possible.

Part Three

Christ and the

Sacred Feminine

I am in the spirit and the truth of the Motherhood.

SECOND TREATISE OF SETH

Return, my son, to your first Father, God, and to wisdom your Mother.

TEACHINGS OF SYLVANUS

*Wise men of old gave the soul a feminine name. Indeed she is female in her
nature as well. She even has her womb.*

THE EXEGESIS OF THE SOUL

*I have cut off the works of the robbery: I have wakened that drop that was sent
from Sophia that it might bear much fruit through me and be perfected.*

THE SOPHIA OF JESUS CHRIST

*Jesus' teachings elevate "feminine" virtues from a secondary or supportive to a
primary and central position.*

RIANE EISLER, *"The Chalice and The Blade"*

Introduction

The complete meaning and significance of everything we have learned so far about the historical and mystical Christ and about the radical mission of Jesus and the different thresholds and mysteries of Christing will only become clear if the full nature of the relationship of the Christ-force with the Sacred Feminine is explored in all of its richness and radical passion.

The clue to the birth of the full authentic Christ-force on earth and in history lies in as complete an embrace as possible of the Sacred Feminine. Unless the practitioner of the Christ-path dives profoundly into an exploration of the Sacred Feminine and invokes it as intensely as possible into every aspect of his or her practice, the full Christ-birth in the soul and in reality will not be possible. Christ is as much the Child of the Mother as of the Father; the Christ-consciousness is born out of a profound realization of God's divine Motherhood as well as Fatherhood. It is because this divine Motherhood of God has been largely ignored—or even repressed—by the main Christian churches and mystical systems that the Christ-consciousness has not yet been born with its full revolutionary power, and history has not been transformed. The birth of the Kingdom in reality, then—the one birth that can now save humanity—depends on how richly, passionately, and radically we can imagine, invoke, and enact the laws and vision of the Sacred Feminine in every aspect of reality.

The goal of the Christ-path, as I hope I have made clear, is the birthing life of the Sacred Marriage, which depends upon a fusion at every level and in every dimension of the "masculine" and "feminine" powers of the soul in the Bridal Chamber. This cannot occur unless the Sacred Feminine—the divine Motherhood of God—is acknowledged in all of its wonder and beauty, and unless all the feminine powers of the soul are invoked and adored. There can be no Sacred Marriage without a bride, no birth of the full androgynous Christ-consciousness, no resurrection of the divine Child who exists in the mystery of a unity that at once transcends and contains in dynamic equilibrium both the "masculine" and "feminine" powers, unless the Sacred Feminine is entirely and consciously blessed, welcomed, and celebrated in all of its facets and powers.

The complete androgynous Christ cannot be born in a being who has not been through the purifying fire of the divine feminine, who has not allowed everything in his or her nature to be softened, refined, illumined, and made supple and constantly receptive in the truth of a "feminine" wisdom that reveals the glory of creation, the holiness of all matter, the sacredness of every cell in the body, the divine necessity to imitate the Motherhood of God by embracing all beings with love and pouring out the entire nature in works of compassion and justice. For the inner Sacred Marriage to take place at the intensity and with the explosive and transfiguring power with which the Christ intends it to, the bride—the "feminine" aspect of God—must be reinvoked, reimagined, and restored with all the powers of spiritual intelligence at our disposal, and with an all-transforming humility and urgency.

The restoration of the full Sacred Feminine, of the full—and "unedited"—majesty of the Motherhood of God to the center of Christian mysticism will effect that revolution that Christianity needs to go through if it is to be the authentic vehicle of the transforming passion of the Cosmic Christ. Such a restoration—at every level of Christian thought and in every area of Christian practice—is the only way of restoring to the world that electric balance between the highest transcendental contemplativeness and the most precise and prophetic commitment to cultural, political, and economic transformation that inspired the life and mission of the historical Jesus. This is the secret of the transforming force of the Cosmic Christ, a force that has never yet completely entered history, because it has been incompletely imagined, and its essential "feminine" aspect either suppressed altogether or defined in watered-down patriarchal ways that strangle its power.

The reinvocation of God-as-Mother as well as Father, of the full Sacred Feminine as a splendor of blessing of all embodied life, and an incessant demand for compassion, justice, and equality to be the laws that must govern all areas of life, will derange and transfigure all the existing forms of Christianity. It will undo the obscene misogyny, racism, and homophobia that have disgraced nearly all the churches and denominations created in Christ's name. It will dissolve the all-male hierarchies that exclude women and denigrate their holy passion, wisdom, and spiritual genius for bearing, cherishing, and furthering life in all its forms. It will explode with a great explosive laugh, the laugh of the resurrected Christ, all the sex and body hatred that has disfigured, warped, and sometimes wholly destroyed the inner lives of millions of Christians over the ages. It will, by revealing to everyone, whatever their color, status, caste, or sexuality, their natural unity and equality in the mother-ground of life, end the glamour of all forms of external authority, and so make possible at last the worldwide radical democracy of the Kingdom: it will arouse the awareness of all beings to the glory of creation, and the sanctity of all sentient beings, and so inspire whatever drastic and sacrificial actions might be necessary to preserve the environment and safeguard human divine life and evolution-in-God.

꘎ ꘎ ꘎

There are, I believe, four essential and interlinked ways of helping this complete restoration of the Sacred Feminine to Christianity. The first is to reassess the Sacred Feminine within the being, teaching, and mission of Jesus himself. To see, freed as far as possible from the distortions of "traditional" practice and ideology, how completely Jesus' life and teachings are saturated at every level with the sacred truths and revelations of the Sacred Feminine, to acknowledge that Jesus is as much the son of the Mother as of the Father, and that his journey is as much a journey into divine Motherhood as divine Fatherhood.

The second way to reimagine fully the Sacred Feminine in Christianity is to avail ourselves of the astonishing discovery in 1945 of several Gnostic Gospels in Nag Hammadi in the Egyptian desert and of their intricate and dazzlingly inventive speculations about the "feminine" divine in Jesus, the Christ, and in the nature of God. The suppression of Gnostic thought and practice by the "Orthodox" church in the second and third centuries was a tragedy in many ways that we are only beginning to understand: perhaps the most important of all the areas of Gnostic vision that need to be studied and reinvoked into the heart of Christian truth is the one that explores the Motherhood of God in all its implications.

The third essential way to revive the Sacred Feminine within Christianity to its full splendor is to honor in all of its mystic grandeur and power that tradition of devotion that began with Origen and the Desert Fathers and flowered a millennium later in Marguerite of Oingt, Guerric of Igny, Saint Bernard of Clairvaux, and most movingly and comprehensively in the *Revelations of Divine Love* of Julian of Norwich—the mystical tradition of adoring Jesus as "mother," as the incarnation of the all-embracing love of the Motherhood of the Trinity and of God.

This profoundly beautiful vision has caused boundless embarrassment to a church that persists in "masculinizing" Jesus for its own ends, but many modern mystics are beginning to see its importance as a powerful way of entering into the "feminine" mystery of the Christ-consciousness and into the transforming "maternal" force of the mystical love of Jesus.

The fourth and most radical and powerful way of all is to turn to face the full significance of the holy relationship between Jesus and his Mother; to face that his Mother is not merely "Mother of God" but an incarnation of the Motherhood of God: that Mary, in other words, is the divine Mother and that turning to Mary helps birth the Christ-consciousness with a direct effectiveness and urgency that no other devotion allows. It is this sacred revelation of the inextricable union between Mary and Jesus, divine Mother and divine Child, that is the great and potentially all-transforming mystical revelation of the last four hundred years. The deepest meaning of the "return" of Mary to the consciousness of the world in the hundreds of apparitions that have taken place over the last century and a half is a call to the birth of the complete Christ.

Just as Mary birthed Christ in time, so Mary is now returning to birth the Christ-consciousness in history, to redeem and transform the world afresh, making clear and inescapable the final connection between the divine Mother and her Child, the complete Sacred Feminine and the fullness of Christ-awareness. The Mary that is returning is the full Mother, and the Birth she is preparing is that of the full Christ, the second coming into millions of souls turned to her of the complete Christ-consciousness.

As more and more mystics are beginning to understand, the birth Mary the Mother is calling for and offering is one that will destroy and remake all structures of power throughout society, including all religious ones. The Mary of the apparitions of Guadalupe in Mexico, of La Salette, Lourdes, Fatima, and Banneux is not the passive girl of legend, but a passionate mystic social revolutionary, and the force of the divine Mother that she is now bringing into history is one that is engendering in all those who turn to it the complete and completely revolutionary Christ-consciousness, the full radical glory of the Sacred Androgyne.

Because the world is being destroyed by an unbalanced "masculine" vision and practice, the Mother is returning in total glory and power to restore the consciousness of the divinity of creation, the sacredness of the body, and the necessity of justice in every dimension as a last offering to all her children of the truth of human divine life. For a time of potentially complete catastrophe, the Motherhood of God is opening up to all of humanity a path of the most radical imaginable transformation: for the first time since shortly after Jesus' disappearance, the birth of the full Cosmic Christ, the Christ as one with all dimensions of reality, living in the resurrected body on earth and irradiating all dimensions of earth-life with its fire of transformation, is now possible.

As the eighteenth-century French mystic Louis Marie Grignion de Montfort wrote: "Mary is the dawn that precedes and reveals the sun of justice that is Jesus Christ . . . the difference between the first and second coming of Jesus will be that the first was secret and hidden, the second will be glorious and dazzling: both will be perfect, because both will come through Mary."

The age of the "second coming" that de Montfort prophesied has arrived in its full horror, agony, and potential for change. And, as de Montfort also prophesied, it is the age of Mary, of a "dawn" that must be seen and known and recognized and celebrated in its fullest and imaginable beauty, glory, clarity, and divine power if the Christ-birth it heralds, the "sun of justice" it births, is to be all-transforming before it is too late.

Jesus' Life, Teachings, Mission, and the Divine Feminine

■ ■ ■

Henry Suso, the medieval German mystic, once had a vision of the Cosmic Christ in splendor, a vision which transformed his soul. He saw Jesus surrounded by a bright transparent cloud and seated upon a throne of ivory. A radiance like the rays of the sun at noon streamed from his face. At one moment, the Christ appeared to Suso "like a young girl of incomparable beauty; at the next, like an equally beautiful young man." Sometimes, Suso writes, the Christ "looked wholly majestic," at other times his entire being was suffused with a "miraculous and melting tenderness." As the vision ended, Jesus turned to Henry Suso and said, "My son, give me your heart." Suso then threw himself at the Christ's feet and offered him his heart "for all eternity."

Three centuries later, Louis Marie Grignion de Montfort, attempting to describe the haunting and passionate beauty of Christ's presence both in history and in the experience of the soul, says of him that he "mingles the tenderness of a spouse with the kindliness of a friend." He adds: "If we consider Jesus in his origin, he is everything that is good and gentle . . . He was given out of love and fashioned by love. He is therefore all love, or rather the very love of the Father and the Holy Spirit." De Montfort celebrates this haunting and exquisite gentleness of Jesus as a "feminine" quality: "He was born of the tenderest and most beautiful of all mothers, Mary . . . Jesus is Mary's child: consequently there is no haughtiness, or harshness, or cruelty in him . . . He is the Eternal Wisdom and therefore pure gentleness and beauty . . . What does the name of Jesus signify to us if not ardent charity, infinite love, and engaging gentleness?" The eternal wisdom of whom, for de Montfort, Jesus is the perfect incarnation—"la sagesse éternelle"—is feminine in French, as it is in Hebrew (Hochmah) and in Greek (Sophia). The qualities ascribed to its operation—the quintessential qualities of the historical and mystical presence of Jesus—are ones of transforming "charity . . . love . . . and gentleness," the qualities, in other words, of the Motherhood of God.

Aesthetic and poetic representations of Jesus have, from earliest times, striven to capture his sacred androgyny and the sublime charm that radiates from it. From the iconic representations of him that are still visible in the Monastery of St. Catherine in Mount Sinai to the Christs of Memlinc, Donatello, and the early Michaelangelo, Jesus the man is depicted as fusing in his person masculine power with feminine grace, the clarity, dignity, and forceful majesty of the traditionally "masculine" with what de Montfort so subtly and beautifully calls the "tenderness of a spouse." In the great mystical music of the Christian church—from the early origins of chant in the Ambrosian codex through the long humble melismas of Gregorian monody, through the great flowering of mystical transmission in music—in the masses of Josquin and the motets of Thomas Tallis—the Christ-force is evoked in a sound that fuses lucid structure with an entirely "feminine" spontaneity, flow, and open-souled abundance. The Cosmic Christ, in the masterpieces of Western chant and polyphony, arrives in a music of divine androgyny—one that Octavio Paz describes as "fusing the sword and the flower," a music whose alchemical power is a result—as we have seen of the Christ-consciousness itself—of a fusion of "male" and "female," diamantine structure with boundless, unguarded tenderness. In its dogma and ecclesiastical and social practice, the church may have "masculinized" Christ—and with disastrous results. Yet in its aesthetic—and particularly its musical traditions—the ancient secret of Christ's androgyny not only lived on but flourished, and continued to "initiate" those sensitive to its power to truths of Christ's love beyond the reach of "conventional" dogmatic expression.

The greatest Christian art and all the rapt and wondering glory of the masses of Palestrina, Fayrfax, Ockeghem, and later Bach and Beethoven—as well as innumerable mystical testimonies to Christ's presence—could be an extended commentary on these words from de Montfort's *Love of Eternal Wisdom*: "The distinctive characteristic of Jesus, the Savior of the world, is to love and save men. No song is sweeter, no voice is more pleasing than Jesus, Son of God. How sweet the name of Jesus sounds to the ear and to the heart of a chosen soul! Sweet as honey to the lips, a marvelous melody to the ears, thrilling joy to the heart." St. John Chrysostom says of Jesus, "The beauty and majesty of his face were at once so sweet and so worthy of respect that those who knew him could not prevent themselves from loving him . . . How loving and gentle he is with men, and especially with poor sinners whom he came upon earth to seek out in a visible manner and whom he still seeks in an invisible manner every day." And this "invisible manner" as de Montfort (and all the other mystics who have known it) reassures us is in its resurrected form, if anything, even more gracious and sweet-hearted than that whose fragrance exalts and inebriates all those—men or women—who dare to open to it in the Gospels: "Do you think that Jesus, now that he is triumphant and glorious is any the less loving and condescending? On the contrary, his glory perfects his kindness. He wishes to appear forgiving rather than majestic, to show the riches of his mercy rather than the gold of his glory. Read the accounts of his apparitions and you will see that when Wisdom incarnate and glorified showed himself to his friends, he did not appear accompanied by thunder and lightning but in a kindly and gentle manner. He did not assume the majesty of a King or of the Lord of Hosts, but [and here is where de Montfort's magical definition of him appears for the first time] the tenderness of a spouse and the kindliness of a friend." If Jesus has haunted the soul-imagination of the world more completely and poignantly than any other figure, it is because of this complete combination of "feminine" and "masculine" powers, of mercy with justice, tenderness with force, authority with the radiance of tolerance and forgiveness.

Like de Montfort and many other mystics, we see this perfect androgynous balance in the life and example of the "historical" Jesus. I wrote at length in the first section of this part—on the life and mission of Jesus—about the uniqueness, range, and fervor of Jesus' honoring of women. That this formed one of the essential aspects of his teaching must now be obvious. What might not be quite so obvious is how profoundly this sacred love of women in Jesus must have expressed his own "femininity" and a sacred need to have his own "femininity" loved, honored, and sustained. In the Christian mystical tradition, it is often women who have recognized most acutely the feminine tenderness of Jesus. In so doing, a Julian of Norwich, Hildegard of Bingen, or Mechthild of Magdeburg are only extending through inner time a recognition that haunted the women around him and perfumed his encounters with the Samaritan woman, the woman taken in adultery, and, of course, the extraordinary and profound mystical love it now seems clear that he lived with Mary Magdalene. It is one of the most significant mystical facts about Jesus and his presence that he should have appeared after his resurrection first to a woman—either to Mary Magdalene, or, as some apocryphal sources allege, to the Virgin herself. Mohammed is said to have written toward the end of his life, "Paradise is at the feet of the Mothers"—a cryptic phrase which some Sufi mystics have ascribed to his meditation on the resurrection and its revelation of the sacred role of the feminine in recognizing authentic miracles and providing the womb of love and worship necessary for its holiest flowering.

If Jesus appeared in the glory of his resurrected body first to either Mary

Magdalene or Mary his Mother, it is because their all-accepting love for him had already shown itself brave enough to risk and embrace the seemingly impossible, just as the "feminine" strengths in his own temperament—those strengths of abandoned self-donation and capacity for extreme gentleness and suffering—had already opened him to the terrible transforming rigors of his own journey. It is the eyes of the bravest, purest, humblest lovers that are able to see the splendor of the resurrection; it is the "feminine" in every mystic that takes him or her into the final Bridal Chamber. As the great Hindu mystic Ramakrishna once remarked, "Knowledge the man can take you into the courtyard of the Majesty; Love the woman can take you into the bedroom." It was, perhaps, this "inner woman" in Jesus that the women who surrounded him with awe and adoration cherished and worshipped, and it is to this "inner woman"—the Mary Magdalene or Virgin in each of us—that the Man-Woman Jesus reveals himself in his complete glory.

It is, of course, not only in women or in women mystics that this "feminine" aspect of Jesus' spiritual genius is adored. The ancient tradition of Jesus' special love for John points to one of the subtlest truths about the enduring power of Jesus' presence—that it inebriates the "masculine" as well as the "feminine." Many commentators have pointed out the sublime and liberating homoeroticism of most of the great "male" mystical poetry about Christ. Unselfconsciously and with the rapture of tremendous inner freedom, nearly all the male mystics of Christianity have written of the Christ-presence in terms of blatant, all-embracing passion, and often from a "feminine" posture. Many of these mystics may have been what we now call "homosexual," and it may have been this "homosexuality" that gave them their peculiar sensitivity to the amazing beauty of the Sacred Androgyne in Jesus; but such speculations are dangerous, only because they limit the mystery of his androgynous appeal. The soul that dares to open to the sacred tender ecstasy of the Cosmic Christ discovers this androgyny both in its own inner nature and in the nature of the presence it is merging with, and lives the rapture of confused pronouns, genders, and identities that illumines, for example, the closing stanzas of the *Dark Night* of St. John of the Cross:

On my flowering breasts
Which I had saved for him alone,
He slept and I caressed
And fondled him with love
And cedars fanned the air above.

Wind from the castle wall
While my fingers played in his hair:
Its hand serenely fell
Wounding my neck, and there
My senses vanished in the air.

I lay, forgot my being,
And on my love I leaned my face.
All ceased. I left my being:
Leaving my cares to fade
Among the lilies far away.

It may be that male mystics who have accepted the homoerotic com-
ponent of their own psyches have access to this holy androgyne in Christ.
What is true is that in the innermost Christian mystical tradition, the full
Christ-experience can only flower in those souls and hearts that have allowed
themselves to become "Mary Magdalene" or "John," permeated and softened
by adoration for the one who in his-her being combines everything that allures
the beings of all sexes, and in the highest harmony, effortlessness, and intensity. One of the many tragedies of the Christian church's practice of homophobia is that it has drastically blocked this love of the "feminine" in Christ,
and so prevented the inner fusion of "feminine" and "masculine" energies
which, as we have seen, engenders the Sacred Marriage and the birthing that
streams from it.

It is time to see clearly that Jesus' entire teaching is everywhere saturated by the highest and most exalted and necessary truths of the Sacred
Feminine. What are the Beatitudes, after all, but the finest and most comprehensive statement in any mystical tradition of the wisdom of the divine
feminine? All of the qualities of soul and being celebrated with such precision
and force in them—"Blessed are the meek," "blessed are the pure in heart,"
"blessed are those who hunger and thirst after righteousness," "blessed are the
merciful," "blessed are the peacemakers"—run directly counter to the dominating patriarchal ethos of that (and our) time. Nietzsche's furious and con-
temptuous dismissal of Christian ethics as "the ethics of slave women"
registers both Nietzsche's own terror of vulnerability and a central truth about
the atmosphere of love that Jesus' teachings are intended to create and sustain—that it is an overwhelmingly "feminine" atmosphere and one which
menaces by implication all the so-called "masculine" patriarchal virtues of mil-

itary prowess, stoicism, authority, control, intellectual and social "categorization."

I have been in the bare chapel that now marks the place where Christ is said to have delivered the Sermon on the Mount, in Tabka, Israel. Its panoramic windows open onto the Sea of Galilee. Standing in that chapel and reading out to myself the Beatitudes in Latin that are printed on its walls, the revelation shook me that the landscape in which Christ delivered his quintessential message to the world is an intensely maternal landscape. The sea that stretches out its vast hand in a long low valley beyond the chapel is a glittering, pale, beautiful blue, very like the Mary-blue of the Sienese painters, of Duccio. The worn, warm, gold brown hills that cluster around it are like breasts caressed by Israel's pure light. Moses delivered the Ten Commandments against the striated, vertical, transcendent, utterly bare and naked desert landscape of Sinai; Jesus announces the rules of entry into the Kingdom in a landscape that breathes the gentleness and quiet strength of the Motherhood of God. For many miraculous moments in Tabka that day, it seemed that the Beatitudes were being "spoken" by nature itself, by that holy and gentle nature, by those hills like breasts, and by that softly glittering open sea, and by the unique light of Israel that renders all things it touches subtly and sweetly transparent.

Jesus, it is true, refers in the canonical Gospels to God as Father, but the side of the Father that he repeatedly emphasizes, as we have suggested, is the God of mercy and tenderness. Doesn't the father of the parable of the Prodigal Son behave as much like a Mother as a traditional father in his refusal to punish his wayward son? In parable after parable, Jesus goes out of his way to stress what must be called the maternal side of the Father, the side of the Godhead that protects, inspires, nurtures, encourages, sustains, gives with irrational, almost surreal, generosity, and above all, again and again, forgives.

"Jesus' Father has breasts," wrote Bernard of Clairvaux in a moment of ecstatic insight. In his loving and forgiving intimacy with the torments and possibilities of the human race, Jesus' "Abba"—Daddy, in Aramaic—has nothing whatever to do with the brutal maniac of Calvin or the apocalyptic and punitive psychotic of many, if not most, of the Christian traditions. The "Abba" of the Our Father gives "daily bread," forgives trespasses, protects from evil. As John Paul I announced, "God is our Father, but even more so, our Mother." The failure to see and follow the guidance of the Motherhood of God—and so of the core of the message of Jesus—has starved the mystic soul of all the churches, and abetted the growth of traditions and practices that not only do not represent Jesus or the Cosmic Christ but actively prevent the birth of Christ-consciousness.

It could be said, in fact, that the entire Christ-path is at least as much a "Mother" path as one of the "Father." As I tried to show in the first section, Christ did not choose the satisfactions and grandeur of transcendence that his illumination could have afforded him; he did not espouse the traditional vision of a Father God utterly beyond time and matter; he chose to work out his extraordinarily personal and dynamic vision of the Godhead not in a "flight" into sagedom but in the most vulnerable, risky, and abandoned imaginable embrace of time, of suffering, and eventually of death. This passion of "Descent," the fervid, uncompromising intensity of this embrace of the devastating conditions of working for compassion, equality, and justice within the world in an attempt to transform all its conditions, is the single most important and radical aspect of Jesus' journey. It demonstrates, I believe, how deeply his vision of the "maternal" side of the Godhead was, that aspect of God that nourishes all creation and serves it in extreme love and hungers like a Mother to see all God's children fed and housed and honored and treated as the potentially glorious human divine beings they are. The failure to see this "maternal" aspect of Jesus has also blinded Christians to the revolutionary nature of Jesus' message.

Modern scholars point out that Jesus consciously identified himself with the "feminine" aspect of Jewish tradition and identified himself on several crucial occasions with "Hochmah," divine Wisdom (feminine in Hebrew and translated by the feminine noun "Sophia" in Greek). This personification of the feminine aspect of God first appears in the opening chapter of Proverbs, is elaborated throughout the Book of Sirach, and comes to its richest expression in a book written just before Jesus was born, the Wisdom of Solomon.

It is in the Wisdom of Solomon that the divine qualities of Sophia are most developed. "Wisdom" is described as omnipresent. "She pervades and penetrates all things." She is described as a "breath of the power of God and a pure emanation of the glory of the Almighty and a reflection of eternal light." As in Proverbs, it is through Hochmah—eternal wisdom—that the creation was created: although she is one, she can do all things and while remaining in herself, she renews all things.

Hochmah-Sophia also enters into the creation and into sacred relationship with the creation; "In every generation she passes into holy souls." Sophia is the source of prophetic inspiration, and the force that makes people "friends of God and prophets": it is Sophia who is active in the history of Israel from the beginning of the Old Testament story. Sophia, not God, is described in the Wisdom of Solomon as leading the Israelites out of the horrible oppression of Egypt; "she brought them over the Red Sea and led them through deep waters; she drowned their enemies, and cast them up from the depth of the sea." In other words, it is clear that, as Borg points out, "Sophia is closely associated with God, at times becoming indistinguishable from God in the terms and functions ascribed to her, so that one might speak of a functional equivalency between Sophia and God . . . the language about Sophia is not simply personification of wisdom in a female form, but personification of God in female form." Sophia is a female image for God, a lens through which divine reality is imagined as a woman. "The first man knew her not perfectly; no more shall the last find her out. For her thoughts are more than the sea, and her counsels profounder than the great sea" (Sirach 24:28–29).

As Anne Baring and Jules Cashford write in *The Myth of the Goddess*, "In the old Testament, the figure of Sophia as the invisible, unnamed 'consort' of Yahweh is portrayed as the master craftswoman of creation, and in this sense transcendent. Yet she is also described in the language of immanence, for she walks in the streets of the city, crying out for people to listen to her. It is . . . in the later Kabbalistic image of the Shekhinah, that the imagery of immanence is completed, for then the 'dwelling place' of the Shekhinah, the bride of Yahweh, is in creation. Where are we to trace the origin of this idea if not to the goddess who was once Queen of Heaven and Earth, and united in her person those dimensions that, in Judaism, were separated in the name of Yahweh?"

Commenting on the glory of the poetry that adorns this ancient vision of the Sacred Feminine in Ben Sirach and the Book of Proverbs ("I also came out as a brook from a river/And as a conduit into a garden/I said I will water my best garden/And will water abundantly my garden bed"), Baring and Cashford write: "Echoes of Sumeria and Egypt play through the beauty of this poetry, particularly in its delight of the flowers, trees, fountains, rivers, hills, and fields of nature. If the meaning is transcendent, the poetic presence is irrefutably immanent. This feeling for the wondrous clothing of the earth recalls the fullness of the Goddess figure of early times, for the Sumerian image of the 'me' (the Laws of Wisdom) and the Egyptian Goddess of Wisdom, Maiat, contained within their meanings of wisdom many related ideas to which we now give separate names: truth, compassion, insight, knowledge, understanding, justice, divine law expressed in human institutions, and the whole ethical realm of human endeavor . . . so Hochmah-Sophia is judge (Enoch

91:10) and (Enoch 92:1) interceding to save her people, as Ishtar interceded to save humanity from the flood. She is transcendent, eternally one with the Godhead beyond creation, and immanent in the world as the presence of the divine within the forms of creation. She is the invisible spirit guiding human life, who may be discovered by the person who seeks her guidance and her help."

There are several passages in the Synoptic Gospels in which Jesus is associated consciously—or consciously associates himself—with the figure of Sophia. In Luke 11:49–50, Jesus is said to have announced, "Therefore also the Sophia of God said, I will send them prophets and emissaries, some of whom they will kill and persecute so that this generation may be charged with the blood of all the prophets shed since the foundation of the world." Jesus is described as being the incarnation of Sophia, Sophia in living flesh and speech.

In another verse, Jesus also speaks of himself as a child of Sophia. In Luke 7:33–35, Jesus says: "John the Baptizer has come eating no bread and drinking no wine and you say, He has a demon. The Son of Man has come eating and drinking; and you say, Behold a glutton and a drunkard, a friend of tax collectors and sinners. Yet Sophia is vindicated by her children."

In other ways, too, Jesus' teaching and practice are intimately tied to this "identification" with Sophia, the "female" aspect of God. Neil Douglas-Klotz, in his book *Prayers of the Cosmos,* has pointed out that the Aramaic for the words "Thy Kingdom come" in the Lord's Prayer—*teytey malkuthakh*—contain imagery redolent of that which surrounds Sophia in the Wisdom tradition. *Teytey* means "come," but embraces, as Douglas-Klotz writes, "images of mutual desire, definition of a goal, and in the old sense, a nuptial chamber—a place where mutual desire is fulfilled and birthing begins." As for *malkuthakh,* Douglas-Klotz tells us "it could justifiably be translated as either 'Kingdom' or 'Queendom.'" He goes on: "From the ancient roots, the word carries the image of a fruitful arm poised to create or a coiled spring that is ready to unwind with all the verdant, potential of the earth." He then adds, astonishingly, "The word malkatuh, based on the same root, was a name of the Great Mother in the Middle East thousands of years before Jesus." What Douglas-Klotz's groundbreaking work reveals is that Jesus' word for the Kingdom contains an immanent maternal "Sophianic" dimension as well as a transcendent one, is as rooted in nature, earth, and actual affairs as in the light of the transcendent, and brings in fact the "two" dimensions together in a blaze of unity.

Two other illustrations from the probable original Aramaic of the Beatitudes illustrate further this "Sophianic" dimension of Jesus' teaching. The

Aramaic for "Blessed are the meek; for they shall inherit the earth" is *tub-wayhun L'Makkikhe D'hinnon nertun arha*. Two of the translations that Douglas-Klotz offers of this crucial Beatitude are: "Healthy are those who have softened what is rigid within; they shall receive physical vigor and strength from the universe" and "integrated, resisting corruption are those who have dissolved heavy morality within; they shall be opened to receive the splendor of earth's fruits." Douglas-Klotz points out too that *L'Makkikhe* could also mean "gentle" or "humble," as well as "meek," and says: "Behind these root words, the old roots carry the meaning of one who has softened that which is unnaturally hard within." *Nertun,* he goes on to inform us, can mean "inherit," but in the "broad sense of receiving from the universal source of strength and reciprocity. In this case, softening the rigid places within leaves us more open to the real source of power—God acting through all of nature, all earthiness." In other words, the Aramaic Jesus used almost certainly in this Beatitude expresses both the "feminine" nature of receptivity and the natural, earthy, life-enriching rewards of such receptivity, both the necessity of a "feminine attitude" to the divine and its fruits of belonging and enduring strength.

One last example from the Aramaic of the Beatitudes carries this understanding of the feminine Sophianic depth of Jesus' teaching even further. The Aramaic for the Beatitude, "Blessed are the merciful, for they shall obtain mercy" is *tubwayhun lamrhmane dalyhun nehwun rahme.* Two of the suggestive translations that Douglas-Klotz offers are: "Blessed are those who, from their inner wombs, birth mercy; they shall feel its warm arms embrace them," and "Tuned to the Source are those who shine from the deepest place in their bodies. Upon them shall be the rays of universal love." Douglas-Klotz's commentary on the language of the Beatitude speaks for itself: "The key word 'lamrhmane' and 'rahme' both come from a root later translated as 'mercy' from the Greek. The ancient root means 'womb' or an inner motion extending from the center or depths of the body and radiating heat and ardor. The root may also mean 'pity,' 'love,' 'compassion,' a 'long drawn breath-extending grace' or 'an answer to prayer.' The association of womb and compassion leads to the image of 'birthing mercy.' As Meister Eckhart wrote, 'We are all meant to be Mothers of God.' "

Modern scholars have also pointed out that Jesus' love of feasts and banquets and frequent use of banquet imagery also evokes the tradition of Sophia. In Proverbs 9:1–5, for example, Hochmah (Sophia) is personified as inviting all beings to her banquet of bread and wine: "Sophia has built her a house, carved out her seven pillars, set her a table. She has sent out her servant girls and calls from the highest places in town, You that are simple, turn in here! To those without sense, she says, Come and eat of my bread and wine, drink of the wine I have mixed."

What else are Jesus' festive meals with outcasts but celebrations of the all-embracing love and divine human wisdom of Sophia, the "feminine" aspect of God? What else are they but the wisdom of divine love put into direct action? Jesus as Sophia welcomes all the disinherited and desperate, offering them all what Sophia the Mother offers—acceptance, healing, transforming wisdom, the "bread" and the "wine" of the conversion to dignity and love.

This identification of Jesus with Sophia was not unknown to his contemporaries. Indeed, scholars have shown that it is central to certain aspects of both Paul's and John's vision of Jesus. The language that Paul uses to describe Christ in Colossians 1:15–17, for example, "Christ is the image of the invisible God, the firstborn of all creation . . . all things have been created through him and for him. He himself is before all things, and in him all things hold together" is language used in the Jewish tradition about Sophia. The close parallel between what John says about the Logos in the opening prologue to his Gospel and what is said about Sophia in the Wisdom tradition has long been noted. If we were, in fact, to substitute "Sophia" for Logos in the prologue, we would see that it concluded "and Sophia became flesh and dwelt among us." For John, then, as Borg points out, Jesus can be said to be "the incarnation of Divine Sophia made flesh."

In other ways also, I believe, Jesus enacts the "feminine," "maternal" mystery of the Godhead. His terrible and transforming choice of a path of descent, of a path that embraced time and death, and the ordeals associated with fighting for the Kingdom, in reality shows, as I have said, a profound "feminine" understanding of the necessity of suffering to give birth to the new creation. This embrace of suffering in and with and for the creation is perhaps the deepest mystery of the Mother aspect of God and characterizes Jesus' personality and message.

Really to know Jesus in the truth of his suffering and really to open to the excesses of love that his terrifying and perpetual embrace of ordeal can awaken is to enter into the heart of the "feminine" mystery of the Christ and to risk the extremely demanding transformation that flows from it. To respond to so vast a love as Christ's invites, even compels, entails heartbreak, a fundamental shattering of all "safe" definitions of the divine, and the destruction of all "masculine" defenses of the ego and the spirit, and of all imaginable patriarchal ploys of authoritarian self-definition and control. The eternal scandal of Jesus is the eternal scandal of the love that streams from the Mother-hood of God—a love that will stop at nothing to express itself, that will always be ready to sacrifice itself for its children, and that embraces every kind of suf-fering and ordeal and horror and humiliation as the inevitable—and glori-ous—price of the King-Queendom it longs to create. To dare to respond to such a love—and its eery, all-deranging presence within the innermost psyche of every self—risks every kind of controlling self-understanding and entails in practice (and especially in mystical practice) a "feminine" surrender to the mysterious alchemy of a continual ordeal almost as demanding as the one that Jesus himself pursued.

In the fourteenth-century Latin poem the "Stabat Mater," the speaker prays to Mary in the following way: "Holy Mother, wellspring of all love, make me feel the force of Christ's suffering; make me capable of mourning with you . . . Make my heart burn to love Christ that with you I may be found pleasing to him . . . Holy Mother, please do this, fix the blows of the crucified one deeply in my heart . . . Make me truly weep with you . . . allow me to be united to you in your grieving . . . Make me feel wounded by the stripes, inebriated by this cross and the blood of the Son." This plea to the di-vine Feminine as Mary to initiate the speaker into the deepest mysteries of the Passion show that these mysteries are in a mystical sense the terrible and wonderful gift of the divine feminine: without being made "capable of mourn-ing," without weeping "truly," without permitting in herself the passive (and sometimes profoundly frightening) "marking" of her innermost psyche by the full meaning of the agony of Christ, the seeker cannot enter into the truth of Christ's divine love and its presence both in the nature of the Godhead and in the innermost core of her own soul.

One of the most disturbing of all the results of the traditional Christian suppression of the "feminine" aspect of God and of Christ has been to make this "piercing-through" by and for the sacred meaning of suffering hard to grasp, let alone imitate. The modern pseudo-mysticisms that play down the role of agony and horror in the unfolding of Christ-consciousness continue this tradition of repression, perpetuate the ignorance of the way of giving and suffering for love that Christ came to initiate the entire human race into, and make it almost impossible for the modern Christian to imagine, let alone ex-perience, the depths of the transforming ecstasy and gratitude that prompted St. Francis of Assisi to change his entire life to conform to that of the one he called "my crucified love."

Anyone who has ever had an authentic mystical experience of the Sacred Heart of Jesus—and so of their own Sacred Heart—knows that it can feel as if the whole body and heart are being torn apart, as if the entire being is being convulsed by an energy of extreme passionate love for the creation, which threatens to destroy the physical frame and annihilates what is normally known as "consciousness." The weeks or months that precede the "opening" of the mystical heart center can often be a time of acute discomfort in the body in general and especially in the area around the middle of the chest: it feels, in fact, as if the whole being is pregnant with a new creation to which it must give birth, but which will "kill" it if it is given birth. It is essential to endure this exacting period if the heart is to open—and impossible if the "feminine" virtues of trust, abandon, and surrender are not fully lived. Nothing real can be accomplished in the mystical journey to Christ without learning—and learning at ever-greater depth and with an ever-more acute and exacting fervor and sincerity—the "feminine" wisdom of surrendering in trust and with an abandon of love to the mystery of ordeal. There can be no living in the glory of the resurrection without undergoing—and allowing oneself to undergo fully—the crucifixion; this entails a commitment, especially during the period known as the Dark Night of the Soul, to a "feminine" passivity that is not only unendurable to the ego but meant to be annihilating of it. Only years of sustained adoration of the divine feminine can give the seeker the final courage to endure the terms of such a surrender.

The prayer the speaker of the "Stabat Mater" makes to Mary—"make it so I may carry Christ's death in my body; make it so I might share in the Passion and relive the blows"—is not, as so many modern Christian texts would have us believe, a form of sublime masochism or "moving poetry"; it is, in fact, a literal prayer, the literal prayer of every authentic Christ-mystic at a certain stage of evolution; the strength to go on and on praying such a prayer in the face of every kind of doubt and fear, and to endure the cost of both being answered. Both come through the grace of the divine feminine, of the Motherhood of God.

It should not surprise us by now to learn that the entire description, even in the Synoptic Gospels, of the mystery of the crucifixion and resurrection is saturated with lunar feminine imagery, as many scholars have pointed out. The cross itself is related to the Tree of Life in many legends, that Tree, which, as Anne Baring and Jules Cashford write in *The Myth of the Goddess,* was one of the primary images of the Goddess herself, in whose immanent presence all pairs of opposites are reconciled; Christ's descent into the underworld has parallels with the descent of Innana to rescue Ereshkigal; the "three days" between descent and ascent echo the three days of darkness when, in Baring and Cashford's words, "the moon is gone and Jesus has descended into hell, harrowing or ploughing the underworld dimension to release the life buried there—in lunar symbolism, to awaken the dormant light of the returning crescent." Mary's lament for her murdered son echoes the lament of all previous "Mothers" for their murdered son or daughter: Venus's for Adonis; Demeter's for Persephone; and the three Marys who ring the drama of the Passion recall the three visible phases of the moon, the trinity of the goddesses of Destiny. On Christ's return, he is greeted as the "gardener" by Mary who, as Baring and Cashford point out, "anoints him with precious balm before his death, as all the previous son-lovers had been anointed by the high priestess of the Goddess." Alan Watts, in his *Myth and Ritual in Christianity,* has made clear that "in the cycle of the Christian year the rites of the Incarnation are governed by the solar calendar, since they are connected with the Birth of the Sun, and so fall upon fixed dates. On the other hand, the rites of Atonement, of Christ's death, Resurrection and Ascension, are governed by the lunar calendar, for there is a figure of Death and Resurrection in the waning and waxing of the moon." The mysteries of the Mother, then, shadow in a final sense the crucial events of Christ's life and journey.

Such an exploration of the "feminine powers" of Christ and of the Sacred Feminine significance of his journey suggests a completely different answer to the question—why did the Christ-force appear on earth as a "man"?—than the one given by conventional Christianity. For almost two millennia, the main Christian churches have used Christ's "masculinity" as an excuse for giving exclusive ecclesiastical authority to men, for excluding women, and so the Sacred Feminine, from all real power or honor. In doing so, they have completely failed to see the true significance of Jesus "coming" as a "man"; or of the "feminine" mysteries and truths he entered and explored with such intensity.

Put bluntly, Jesus "came" to unleash a force of extreme love that would explode the patriarchy from within, that would undo and dissolve everything hard, violent, rigid, legalistic, obsessed with purely human order in the "masculine" psyche that ruled and governed the patriarchy. Everything in his life and practice shows us that he understood exactly where the values enshrined in patriarchal religion and authoritarian systems of control would take the whole human race—to the brink of unimaginable destruction of the whole of nature and the whole enterprise of humanity.

In his adoration of the values and mysteries of the Sacred Feminine, in his astoundingly complete absorption of the deepest feminine mysteries, Jesus tried to show in his own life and being the way out of the patriarchal nightmare, the way out of a disastrously imbalanced vision of the "masculine," which could only bring the world to ever-greater violence and horror. He showed, in fact, that the Sacred Masculine is whole and wholly itself only when it is fused at the greatest possible depth and intensity with the Sacred Feminine. In so fusing with its "opposite," the "masculine" would transform its tendency to alienation, half-psychotic detachment, and the pursuit of power at the expense of life, into a strong, majestic, and undauntable power of loving and brave action within the world and within society to transform them both. Jesus came as a man because the divine knew that the supreme danger to the human enterprise would come from the psychotic "masculine"; yet in Jesus, the world would be shown the real sacred man, the being who, while masculine, allowed the fullness and glory of the feminine to inform, inspire, and complete him. Perhaps the greatest tragedy of the historical development of Christianity has been the systematic destruction of this great truth, and, along with it, much of the transforming force of the authentic Christ-consciousness.

Perhaps the clearest example of the effects of this "suppression" of the Sacred Feminine aspect of Christ-consciousness can be seen in the way in which the mystery of the Eucharist—the central mystery of the Christian church—has been interpreted and performed. Unless it is realized that the Eucharist is above all a "feminine" mystery, much of its astounding mystical power is lost. Nothing could be more explicitly "maternal" than Christ's words over the bread and wine: "This is my Body and this is my Blood." As St. John Chrysostom writes in his *Catechisis,* "As a woman nourishes her child with her own blood and milk, so does Christ increasingly nourish with his own blood those to whom he has given life."

Just as a mother feeds the embryo within her by the forces and powers of her body and through her blood, so Jesus, through the intense earthiness and physicality of the symbols he uses for the highest mysteries of transmission, makes clear that for him his sacrifice, like a mother's for her child, is an absolute one involving the entire being, and so demanding the involvement of the "body" and "blood" of the one who receives the mystery. Just as he himself has, through suffering, sacrifice, and extreme love, utterly embraced the earth, time, and the necessity of death, so what he is transmitting through the rite of the Eucharist is the mystery of total donation within life to life. Christ the Mother is setting out the bread of his flesh and the blood of his extreme love for us to eat and drink, to take into the "body" and "blood" of our own deepest earthly being so as to birth us also into being sacred Mothers of the new creation, into becoming beings who have learned how to give extreme love like a mother and to live in a love that wants at all moments to give away everything so that the whole of life can become pregnant with divine creativity and power. Not to see how the Eucharist is in its depths a "feminine" mystery and how therefore the transmission it involves and makes possible is fundamentally connected to the Motherhood of God is to miss its true nature and divert its authentic power, and so cripple perhaps the most powerful mystical transmission ever given humankind.

Certain medieval mystics, as I will show later, make the truth of this mystery explicit when in their celebration of Jesus the Mother they picture the cross as a terrible childbed on which Jesus consents, like a woman giving birth, to be torn apart so as to engender the new humanity. This to me is not in any sense a "metaphorical" image; it brings to a consummation and a final intensity one of the central perceptions about Jesus—that his identification with the "feminine" went far beyond a merely philosophical or even mystical one; in some final, mysterious sense Jesus did give birth on the cross, through annihilation and dismemberment, to a new creation. A woman poet friend once astounded and illumined me by pointing out that when Christ was wounded in the side by the spear on the cross he acquired "a wound like the female genitalia." In the mystery of his destruction, then, Jesus acquired the living sign of fertility, of the power of cosmic birthing by an ultimately "feminine" act of total surrender to the darkness of love by opening in sacrificial love to every kind of humiliation and cruelty without hatred or any attempt to fight back. Christ "acquired" the ultimate "feminine" power, the power of the cosmic Motherhood of God, to give birth through his resurrection, ascension, and flowing out in Pentecost to the new creation. The path of Descent, in other words, ended in his becoming, in the most holy and final sense, a Mother, in fusing himself with the final "feminine" mystery of annihilation and creation, and so in becoming one with the Father-Mother in all things forever.

Gnostic Gospels and the Sacred Feminine

▨ ▨ ▨

The discovery of the Nag Hammadi scrolls in the Egyptian Desert in 1945 and the work of scholars in this century, in particular Elaine Pagels's *The Gnostic Gospels,* have revolutionized our knowledge of the Gnostic Christian groups that were systematically suppressed at the beginning of the third century. Thanks to Pagels (and to the work of her great predecessor G.W.M. Mead), we are no longer forced to rely on the condemnatory distortions of their philosophy by Orthodox theologians like Irenaeus of Lyons and Tertullian. We can now see that Gnostic Christianity—centered in Alexandria but flourishing all over the Hellenistic world and Asia Minor—was the fountainhead of an overwhelmingly varied, brilliant, and radical mystic exploration of the nature of God and of the Christ-consciousness, an exploration whose openness to the Sacred Feminine in particular contemporary Christian seekers urgently need to understand and learn from.

It is now clear that the main reasons for the suppression of the Gnostic Christian groups was that they encouraged direct access to the divine, without any need of mediation. They discouraged all forms of "fixed" and "inherited" religious hierarchy, in the name of Christ himself, and—just as we know Jesus had done—embraced the spiritual equality of women and celebrated them as prophets, healers, teachers, and priests. Such radical freedoms fundamentally threatened the philosophy and practice of those Christian groups that formed around the legacy of Peter and Paul. As these gained power, their vision of the necessity of hierarchy, of the exclusive claim of men to be priests and "mediators" of the divine, and of an overridingly "masculine" view of the Godhead—enshrined later in the "male" trinity of Father, Son, and Holy Spirit—gained ascendancy, until, in the early third century, the wonderful vitality and wisdom of Gnosticism was attacked from all sides as "heretical," the books of the Gnostic mystics, such as Valentinus and Marcion were burned, and their contribution to the understanding of the revolution of Christ obscured for almost two thousand years. With Gnostic vision and creativity silenced, God, in Christian practice, became exclusively male: Christ was "separated" from the human race and declared at the council of Chalcedon in 451 the "only" Son of God; women and the feminine were increasingly denounced and demonized, and the split between nature and spirit that Jesus had striven with all his powers to heal was celebrated as wisdom. The door of direct communion between the human soul and God that Jesus had given his life to open was slammed shut in the name of "mediation" and hierarchical control. In other words, all of the revolutionary aspects of Jesus' mission—and so of the Christ-consciousness that it engenders—were muted or distorted. Reclaiming the insights of Gnostic mysticism, especially those that explore and celebrate the Sacred Feminine, is essential for the future of Christian mysticism, and so to the "return" of the authentic mystic Christ.

In the large library of "lost" Gnostic Gospels restored to us at Nag Hammadi, we discover a very fecund and powerful vision of God as Mother as well as Father. Members of a group that claimed to have received a secret tradition from Jesus through James and through Mary Magdalene prayed openly to God as a dyad, who embraces both "masculine" and "feminine" elements. "From thee, Father, and through thee, Mother, the two immortal names, parents of the divine being, and thou, dweller in heaven, humanity, of the mighty name" (quoted in Hippolytus' *Refutation of All Heresies*). Pagels describes the Gnostic texts that we now possess as characterizing the Mother aspect of God in three ways: as "part" of an "original couple," as the Holy Spirit, and as the creative and endlessly fertile Wisdom-Sophia of God.

Of the Gnostic mystics that saw God as a Father-Mother, Valentinus was undoubtedly the greatest. Pagels writes of him: "Valentinus, the teacher, and poet, begins with the premise that God is essentially indescribable. But he suggests that the divine can be imagined as a dyad; consisting, in one part of the ineffable, the depth, the primal Father; and in the other of Grace, silence, the womb, and 'Mother of all.' " For Valentinus, "silence" is the "appropriate complement" of the Father, designating the former as feminine and the latter as masculine because of the grammatical gender of the Greek words. He describes how silence receives, as in a womb, the seed of the ineffable source; and how from this she brings forth all the emanations of divine being, ordered in harmonious pairs of masculine and feminine energies.

Valentinus was not the only Gnostic mystic who saw God in this way. Marcus the magician invokes the Mother as Grace (in Greek, the feminine "Charis"): "May she who is before all things, the incomprehensive and indescribable Grace, fill you within, and increase in you her own knowledge." And this is how the Great Announcement, a Gnostic text (also quoted by Hippolytus in his *Refutation of All Heresies*), describes the origins of the universe: "Out of the power of silence appeared a great power, the Mind of the

Universe which manages all things, and is a male . . . the other . . . is a great Intelligence . . . is a female which produces all things . . . There is one power divided above and below; generating itself, making itself grow, seeking itself, finding itself, being Mother of itself, Father of itself, sister of itself, spouse of itself, daughter of itself, son of itself—mother, father, unity, being a source of the entire circle of existence." Such a vision of the divine as both Mother and Father recalls the mystical systems of Egypt and India, both of which may well have influenced early Gnostic thought.

Another group of Gnostic mystics, as Pagels demonstrates, saw the Holy Spirit as feminine, as, in fact, the Mother aspect of God. One of the most astonishing revelations of the rediscovered Gnostic Gospels is that they show that Jesus himself spoke of the Holy Spirit in this way. In Logion 101 of the Gospel of Thomas, Jesus is reported as saying, "My true Mother gave me life." In Logion 105, Jesus goes even further, pointing to the potentially scandalous and radical knowledge of God as both Mother and Father: "He who knows the Father and the Mother will be called the son of a harlot." In the Dialogue of the Savior we are told: "The Lord said, 'When the Father established the cosmos for himself, he left much over for the Mother of the all. Therefore he speaks and he acts.' " In the Gospel of the Hebrews, Jesus is reported as saying, "My Mother, the Holy Spirit, even now took me by one of the hairs of my head and carried me to the great mountain Tabor." The Apocryphon of John relates how John, after the resurrection, had a mystical vision of the Trinity. Stricken with grief, John tells us that he saw "the heavens were opened and the whole creation . . . under heaven shone and (the world) trembled. (And I was afraid and I) saw in the light . . . likeness with multiple forms . . . and the likeness had three forms." When John questions this "likeness," it replies: "Why do you doubt, and why are you afraid. I am the One who (is with you) always. I am the Father; I am the Mother; I am the Son." Pagels comments, "This Gnostic description of God—as Father, Mother, and Son—may startle us at first, but on reflection, we can recognize it as another version of the Trinity."

In fact, during this early period of Christianity, the idea that the Holy Spirit was feminine was foreign only to Gentile (Hellenized) Christians. Professor Quispel, who discovered the Gospel of Thomas, writes, "Jewish Christians were entirely convinced that the Holy Spirit was a feminine hypostasis." This is an especially revealing piece of information in relation to the passages in the Gospels that describe the baptism of Jesus and the Holy Spirit descending on him in the likeness of a "dove." Doves, as modern scholars remind us, are sacred to the ancient Mother Goddess, to Ashtaroth and Venus in particular. In a fragment from the Jewish Christian Gospels, the Holy Spirit announces to Jesus at his baptism, "My Son, in all the prophets I was waiting for Thee." Quispel comments on this: "Here we come to a very simple realization; just as birth requires a mother, so rebirth requires a spiritual mother. Originally, the Christian term 'rebirth' must therefore have been associated with the concept of the Spirit as a feminine hypostasis."

Perhaps the richest expression of this vision of the Holy Spirit as the Mother of "rebirth" is found in the Odes of Solomon—Syriac mystical hymns of baptism written or recorded in the second century C.E.:

> As the wings of doves are over their nestlings
> And as the mouths of the nestlings are towards their mouths
> So also are the wings of the spirit over my heart.
> My heart continually refreshes itself and leaps for joy
> Like the babe who leaps for joy in his mother's womb.

Although the Orthodox version of the Trinity as entirely masculine triumphed doctrinally in the fourth century, traces of this earlier "maternal" knowledge of the Spirit can be found in the medieval mystics—in Peter Abelard, who images the Holy Spirit as a bird hatching an egg; in Hildegard of Bingen, who described the Spirit's power as "viriditas," a power of greening, of making all things alive and verdant (and feminine in Latin); and in the various philosophies and practices of alchemy whose overarching symbolic imagery is that of the Sacred Marriage between "King" and "Queen," "Sun" and "Moon," and whose inner realization engenders the "philosopher's stone" that integrates all opposites and brings about the birth into the Kingdom. It is not accidental that "maternal" imagery pervades Eckhart's vision of the "one birth" that takes "place in the being and in the ground and core of the soul." Eckhart writes, "Not only is the Son of the heavenly creator born in this darkness—but you too are born there as a child of the same heavenly Creator and none other. And the Creator extends this same power to you out of the divine maternity bed located in the godhead to eternally give birth." Official Christianity might banish all "feminine" symbolism from the Trinity, but authentic inner experience would always need to reclaim it.

The third way in which the Gnostic Christian groups imagined the Mother aspect of God was Wisdom. I have already shown, in the first part of this section, which dealt with the historical Jesus' relation to the feminine, that Jesus himself identified himself—and was identified—with Wisdom (Hochmah-Sophia). Gnostic mystics seized on this identification of Jesus himself with the Wisdom tradition of Judaism and discovered, or "uncovered," dazzling and sometimes bewilderingly intricate variations on it. The Apocalypse of Adam discovered at Nag Hammadi, for example, informs us of a feminine power that wanted to conceive by herself; Valentinus, in a famous myth, extends this vision and tells us of Wisdom withdrawing from the Father and engendering on her own the creation; since her desire to be sole creator violated the harmonious union of opposites innate in the nature of the one, what she produced was abortive and defective. From this, Valentinus claims, stem the terror and grief that deform human life. Valentinus goes on to claim further that the Creator God of Israel was created by this "unbalanced" feminine Wisdom as her agent.

Pagels informs us that "Wisdom" bears several connotations in Gnostic sources. Besides being the "first universal creator" who brings forth all creatures, she also enlightens human beings and makes them wise. Followers of Valentinus and Marcus therefore prayed to her the Mother as the "mystical eternal Silence" and to "Grace who is before all things" and as "Incorruptible Wisdom."

In another text, the Trimorphic Protennoia (literally translated "the triple-formed primal thought"), we find a glorification of such powers as Thought, Intelligence, and Foresight as "feminine." The text opens as a divine figure announces, "I am Protennoia, the Thought that dwells in the light . . . She who exists before the All . . . I move in every creature . . . I am the Invisible One within the All . . . I am perception and Knowledge, uttering a Voice by means of Thought. I am the real Voice." The second section, spoken by a second divine voice, explains, "I am androgynous. I am both Mother and Father, since I copulate with myself . . . I am the Womb that gives shape to the All . . . I am Meirothea, the glory of the Mother."

Even more astonishing and many-faceted in its evocation of Wisdom as divine Mother is the Gnostic poem known as "The Thunder, Perfect Mind." The text as we have it may well contain fragments of earlier texts now lost—perhaps even of a Mesopotamian incantation, which, as Anne Baring and Jules Cashford point out in *The Myth of the Goddess*, may have belonged to the same source as the verses spoken by Hochmah in Proverbs and in Ben Sirach:

> *I was sent from the power,*
> *And I have come to those who reflect upon me,*

And I have been found among those who seek after me.
Look upon me, you who reflect upon me . . .
Do not be ignorant of me anywhere or at any time . . .
For I am the first and the last,
I am the honored one and the scorned one,
I am the whore and the holy one,
I am the wife and the virgin.
I am the mother and the daughter.
I am the bride and the bridegroom
And it is my husband who begot me.
I am the mother of my father
And the sister of my husband
And he is my offspring . . .
I am the one whom they call Life
And you have called Death.
I am the one whom they call Law
And you have called lawlessness.
I am the one whom you have pursued
And I am the one you have seized.
I am the one you have scattered,
And you have gathered me together.

In this hymn all the powers of the Sacred Feminine—both in their "creative" and "destructive" aspects—are invoked and celebrated: as Baring and Cashford tell us, "It is clear that in this text . . . Sophia herself is speaking as Wisdom, as once Inanna spoke in Sumeria and Isis in Egypt."

In the nineteenth Ode of Solomon, Wisdom as Divine Mother is also richly and complexly celebrated and her relationship with Christ and the Holy Spirit (also seen as feminine) made clear:

A cup of milk was offered to me,
And I drank it in the sweetness of the Lord's kindness.
The Son is the cup, and the Mother is she who was milked;
And the Holy Spirit is the one who milked her;
Because her breasts were full.
And as it was undesirable that her milk should be released without purpose,
The Holy Spirit opened her bosom,
And mixed the milk of the two breasts of the Mother.

Then she gave the mixture to the generation without their knowing,
And those who have received it are in the perfection of the right hand.

In this, the author of the Odes of Solomon clearly envisages the Mother aspect of God and the Holy Spirit as at once "separate" and intimately related.
Both are feminine: the feminine Holy Spirit milks the "two" breasts of Divine
Sophia (her immanent and transcendent aspects); Christ-consciousness is
the "cup" from which the "milk" of the "two breasts" is drunk—in other words,
the "receptacle" of the full Gnosis of transcendence and immanence that
makes for the awakening, that "perfection of the right hand" that is clearly
thought of here as being the gift of the Mother-aspect of God.

Just as Gnostic mysticism explores with vitality, fertility of imagination,
and courage a variety of the aspects of the Motherhood of God, so in the mystical literature of this period—now available to us for the first time for serious study—we find, as we might expect, a correspondingly rich and varied
exploration of the nature of Christ-consciousness. The Son, who in the later
dogma of the Trinity is seen as the "product" exclusively of the Father, is
known in a plethora of Gnostic texts as the Son of the Divine Mother as well
as the Father, and as the sacred androgynous power engendered by their mystic union.

In The Wisdom of Jesus Christ, a Greek Gnostic text found in the Cop-
tic translation in what is known as the Akhim codex in 1896 (and quoted in
Mead's *Fragments of a Forgotten Faith*), it is the Mother-aspect of the divine
dyad that is explicitly described as being responsible for the "birthing" of the
Christ-consciousness: "The Father thinketh his image alone and beholdeth it
in the Water of pure Light which surrounded Him. And His thought energized
and revealed herself, and stood before Him in the light-spark; which is the
Power which existed before the All, which Power hath revealed itself . . . that
is the Perfect Power, the Barbelo, the Aeon perfect in glory—glorifying Him,
because She hath manifested herself in Him and thinketh Him . . . Barbelo
gazed into Him fixedly . . . and she gave birth to a blessed light-spark. Nor
doth it differ from her in greatness. Now the invisible Spirit rejoiced over the
Light, which had come into existence . . . in Barbelo. And he anointed him
with His goodness, that he might be made perfect."

Other more elaborate Gnostic myths that make clear another aspect of
the relationship between Christ and the Mother tell the story of Sophia, the
great Mother, who is the consort of the great Father (as in the nineteenth Ode
of Solomon) and that of their daughter, also called Sophia, and their son,

Christ. In this Gnostic cycle of myths, the earlier lunar images of the mother and daughter Goddess (Demeter and Persephone) are reanimated: Sophia, the mother, gives birth to a daughter, the soul-image of herself, also called Sophia, who loses contact with her heavenly origin, and in her anguish and distress brings the earth into being and roams the chaotic kingdom of darkness that lies beneath the kingdom of light—an "underworld" that was identified with the earth-dimension. A curtain or barrier falls between the worlds of light and darkness and makes it impossible for the daughter Sophia to return to her parents:

> *Sometimes she mourned and grieved,*
> *For she was left alone in darkness and the void.*
> *Sometimes she reached a thought of the light which had left her*
> *And she was cheered and laughed.*
> *Sometimes she feared.*
> *At other times she was perplexed and astonished.*

Sophia, in her desolation, whom Gnostics identify with the soul trapped in matter, cries out to Mother Sophia to rescue her. The Virgin Mother, in response to her daughter's agony, sends her son to rescue his sister. Her son is Christ, the embodiment of her light and wisdom; at his mother's instigation, he descends into the darkness of the Father-Mother's furthest and most ambiguous creation to awaken his sister Sophia, the soul, to remembrance of her true nature.

In other Gnostic texts, the relationship between Sophia and Christ is seen as one of mystical androgynous identity, and not of "brother" and "sister." In the Gnostic text known as The Sophia of Jesus Christ, the risen Jesus, teaching his disciples, describes himself as both male and female, "Son of God," and "Sophia, Mother of the Universe": "I desire that you understand that First Man is called begetter . . . He reflected with the great Sophia, his consort, and revealed his first-begotten, androgynous son. His male name is called 'First-Begetter Son of God': his female name is 'First Begettress Sophia, Mother of the Universe.' Some call her Love, her first begotten is called Christ."

Another variation on this theme of the intimate relation between the Christ-consciousness and Sophia is elucidated in the series of texts that celebrate awakening and the marriage of Christ and Sophia. A Syrian Gnostic text dating to the second century A.D., known as The Wedding Song of Wisdom (and which some modern scholars believe may be related to earlier pre-Christian texts celebrating the union of the Goddess Astarte and her son-lover), is addressed to Sophia, Light's daughter, and celebrates the wedding between the soul and her bridegroom, Christ, transcendent spirit:

> *The Maiden is Light's daughter;*
> *On her the King's a radiance resteth.*
> *Like unto spring flowers are her garments,*
> *From them streameth scent of sweet odour.*
> *On the Crown of her Head the King throneth*
> *With living food, feeding those beneath him . . .*
>
> *Her bridesmen are grouped around her,*
> *Seven in number, whom she hath invited.*
> *Her bridesmaids, too, are seven . . .*
> *And twelve are her Servants before her,*
> *Their gaze looking out for the Bridegroom*
> *That at his sight they may be filled with Light*
> *And then for ever more they may be filled with Light,*
> *And then for ever more shall they be with him*
> *In that eternal everlasting Joy;*
> *And share in that eternal Wedding-Feast . . .*

When we fuse all of these symbolic mystic approaches to God the Mother-Father and to Christ "brother," "bridegroom," or "inner twin of Sophia," it becomes obvious that in the literature of Gnostic mysticism we have a rich and comprehensive approach to the maternity of the Godhead and to the inextricable relation of the Christ-consciousness with the Sacred Feminine in a variety of aspects. This interconnected revelation, in turn, makes it obvious that the Orthodox description of God as "masculine"—and the hierarchical, patriarchal, male-dominated apparatus of authority that is justified by it—prevents the kind of sacred fusion between the Mother and Father that allows authentic Christ-consciousness to be born in all its unitive power.

How can we best use this inspiration from the Gnostic mystics? What must now be done, I believe, is that the dogma of the Trinity must be radically redescribed not as Father, Son, and Holy Spirit, but as Father-Mother-Divine Child. An alternative approach might be to expand the dogma within the existing "model" to embrace the Sacred Feminine in each of its powers, thus describing a source that is at once Father and Mother, a Spirit that is at once "masculine" and "feminine" in its origin, and a Sacred Androgyne-Man-Woman or Son-Daughter that is the Word of both in reality. Unless this revolutionary (but as we have seen far from unprecedented) restructuring of the metaphysical essence of the Christian message is undertaken, the full mystic force of Christ can be neither understood nor completely embodied, and the direct path to Christ cannot be as overwhelmingly transformatory as its founder intended—and still intends—it to be.

Jesus the Mother

In this urgent challenge to all the Christian churches to integrate the wisdom of the Sacred Feminine into every aspect of the message of Christ, another largely forgotten tradition within Christian mysticism—that which worshipped Jesus directly as the Mother—will be of immense inspiration. This tradition runs underground from the Greek fathers (who may have been surreptitiously inspired by Gnostic sources) to a group of Cistercian mystics of the twelfth and thirteenth centuries—Guerric of Igny, Bernard of Clairvaux, and Isaac of Stella—through to its consummate expression in the visions of women mystics such as Marguerite of Oingt, Mechthild of Magdeburg, and—especially—the wisest and greatest of all the "mother" mystics of Christianity, Julian of Norwich.

In this tradition of adoring Jesus as the Mother, the crucial Gnostic perception of the Sacred Androgyne of Christ-consciousness is preserved intact, and an effective and poignant way of describing the "maternal" nature both of Christ's life and of the Christ-consciousness it engendered is kept alive. The tradition never completely died out, despite ecclesiastical opposition and general theological embarrassment and derision. It inspired, for example, the life and practice of the Cure of Ars who, in the nineteenth century, wrote: "Our Lord is on the earth like a mother that carries his child in his arms. This child is naughty, kicks its mother, bites her, scratches her, but his mother doesn't only pay total attention to the child. He knows that if He leaves the child, the child will fall because he cannot walk alone. This is how our Lord is: he uses our dreadful treatment of him, and . . . he pities us despite everything we are and do."

The poignant, earthy tone of the Cure of Ars characterizes the writing of the whole tradition, in contrast to the grand metaphysical soarings of the Gnostics. In it, Jesus (and, by implication, the Christ-consciousness) is worshipped as Mother because of the sacrificial intensity and all-embracing generosity of his love. As Guerric of Igny wrote: "The bridegroom has breasts lest he should be lacking any one of all the duties and titles of love . . . He is a mother . . . in the tenderest of His affection and a nurse." St. Anselm of Canterbury asks, "Jesus, Good Lord, are You not also a Mother? Are you not like that mother who like a hen collects her children under her wings? Truly, Master, you are a mother. For what others have conceived and given birth to, they have received from you . . . You gather under Your wings your little ones, Your dead chicks seek refuge under Your wings. By Your gentleness, those who are hurt are comforted: by Your perfume, the despairing are reformed. Your warmth resuscitates the dead."

It is, however, a woman mystic—Marguerite of Oingt—who makes most movingly clear the "maternal" nature of Christ's path of Descent and sacrifice: "Are you not my mother and more than my mother? The mother who bore me labored in delivering me for one day or one night, but you, my sweet and lovely Lord, labored for me for more than thirty years. Ah . . . with what love you labored for me . . . But when the time came for you to be delivered, your labor pains were so great that your holy sweat was like great drops of blood that came out of your body and fell on the earth . . . and who ever saw a mother suffer such a birth? For when the hour of your delivery came you were placed on the hard bed of the Cross . . . and your nerves and all your veins were broken. And truly it is no surprise that your veins burst when in one day you gave birth to the whole world."

This is the frankest and most eloquent statement in the whole of Christian mystical literature of what might be called the "dark feminine" aspect of Christ's nature and mission, and so of Christ-consciousness. The Christ in history and in us is called upon to undertake the "labor" of "giving birth" to the "new creation"; such "labor" inevitably entails ordeal after ordeal, the embrace of horror, the commitment to extreme suffering without consolation. The Gnostic mystics introduce us to the high grandeurs of the Sacred Feminine; Marguerite of Oingt (and Mechthild of Magdeburg and Hadewijch of Antwerp after her) make us aware of the price these grandeurs demand when the call to incarnate and enact them in reality is attended to. As Hadewijch of Antwerp writes, expressing with unnerving sincerity the cost of such "maternal" commitment to the enacting of the highest love in the "flesh and blood" of the real: "What satisfies Love best of all is that we be wholly stripped of all repose . . . And this is a frightening life Love wants, that must do without the satisfaction of Love in order to satisfy Love. Those who are thus drawn and accepted by Love, and fettered by her, are the most indebted to Love, and consequently they must stand subject to the great power of her strong nature to content her. And that life is miserable beyond all that the human heart can bear." To embrace, then, as Jesus did, the "dark feminine" is to embrace its illusionless understanding of the price and demand of transformation, to know suffering as the condition of birth, and accepted agony as the continuing condition of the fertility of Motherhood.

The most integrated exploration of both the "sublime" and the "dark" aspects of the divine Motherhood of Jesus is to be found in the work of Julian of Norwich. As the Gnostic mystics had done, Julian discovers Motherhood at the heart of the mystic work of the Trinity: "As truly as God is our Father, so verily is God our Mother; and that showed He in all my revelations and especially in these sweet words where he says, 'I it am.' That is to say, 'I it am, the Might and the Goodness of the Fatherhood; I it am, the Wisdom of the Motherhood; I it am, the Light and Grace that is all blessed Love; I it am, the Trinity; I it am, the Unity.' "

For Julian, as for Marguerite of Oingt and Hadewijch, the enactment of the wisdom of Motherhood necessarily involves great suffering. Her evocation of the "divine Motherhood" of Christ integrates both the bliss and peace of the divine Feminine in the Godhead, with its commitment to sacrificial suffering in its incarnation. In doing so, Julian initiates us into one of the deepest mysteries of all in the "feminine" aspect of Christ-consciousness—into that awareness which paradoxically fuses extreme suffering and extreme joy in the unity of divine human love. Julian writes in her *Revelations of Divine Love*: "A mother's is the most intimate, willing and most dependable of all services, because it is the truest of all. None has ever been able to fulfill it properly but Christ. He alone can. We know that our own mother's bearing of us was a bearing to pain and death, but what does Jesus, our true Mother, do? Why, his love bids us to joy and to eternal life. Thus he carries us within Himself in love, and he is in labor until the time has fully come for him to suffer the sharpest pangs and most appalling pain possible and in the end he dies. Not even when this is over, and we ourselves have been born to eternal bliss, is his marvelous love completely satisfied. This he shows in that overwhelming word of love that he said to me [in one of the visions Julian received]: 'If I could possibly have suffered more, indeed I would have done so.' " In this complete vision of the divine Motherhood of God and the Christ-consciousness, Julian reveals to us that, in the depths of the Trinity, and so of the Christ-heart, extreme bliss and extreme suffering are not separate but one; that divine love entails and makes possible continuing—and painful—sacrifice, transmuting it, through the alchemy of surrender and grace, into the highest, noblest, and most mysterious form of joy.

The relevance of such a vision to the unfolding of the Christ-consciousness in our time should be obvious. Anyone who chooses to subject him- or herself to its demands and rigors in a time as vicious as ours will risk persecution, humiliation, and perhaps even death at the hands of those authorities and those "principalities and powers" that are dedicated to keeping the human race undivinized and enslaved. The supreme gift of the Motherhood of God to such a person will be in the end that fusion that Julian describes of bliss and suffering, ultimate calm and joy, both despite and in the core of necessary agony. Those whom the "maternal" love of the Trinity has initiated are at once, as Christ was, lifted above the horror of the world and plunged irrevocably into its worst and most fiery core, to live and work in both simultaneously, and so, as Christ did and does in all who turn to him, transform horror not from without but from within, in the final, and finally dangerous, alchemical intimacy of divine human love.

Only an initiation into the Motherhood of God can give this simultaneously transcendent and immanent relationship to reality; only an initiation into the Motherhood of God can arm the seeker on the Christ-path with the final love that alone can transform—with the help of divine grace—the horror and agony of time, death, and earthly reality into the glory of the Kingdom. What evil could discourage or outrage or dishearten the living Christ-Mother in us, who says still—as Jesus said to Julian—the "overwhelming word of love": "If I could possibly have suffered more, indeed I would have done so"? Such a being is beyond the reach of death or all the terrors of evil, one with the glory and always-outpouring, always self-sacrificing love of the Father-Mother.

It is to this terrifying and sublime height of love that Christ the Mother is summoning all who follow him on to—and beyond—the "childbed" of the cross. As Louis Marie Grignion de Montfort has Christ say to all of us in his "Letters to Friends of the Cross": "If anyone wants to follow me thus abased and crucified, he must glory, as I did . . . in the poverty, humiliations, and sufferings of my cross . . . let him take up his cross, the one that is his. Let that man [or woman] . . . take up his cross joyfully, embrace it lovingly, and carry it courageously on his shoulders, his own cross, and not that of another—his own cross which I have fashioned with my own hands . . . his own cross, which is the greatest gift I can bestow upon my chosen ones . . . his own cross, whose thickness is made up of the loss of one's possessions, humiliations, contempt, sufferings, illnesses and spiritual trials, which come to him daily till his death in accordance with my providence: his own cross, whose length consists of a certain period of days or months, enduring slander, or lying on a sick-bed, or being forced to beg, or suffering from temptations, dryness, desolation, and other interior trials: his own cross, whose breadth is made up of the most harsh and bitter circumstances brought about by relatives, friends, servants: his own cross, whose depths is made up of the hidden trials I shall inflict on him without his being able to find any comfort from other people . . . Let him carry his cross on his shoulders like our Lord, that it may become the source of his victories . . . Let him set it in his heart, where it may, like the burning bush of Moses, burn day and night, with the pure love of God being consumed!"

Jesus and Mary

❖ ❖ ❖

I must be the Virgin and give birth to God
should I ever be graced divine beatitude.

ANGELUS SILESIUS

O Woman, full and complete, pour your graces on this world and
make all creatures green again.

SAINT ANSELM

For your Kingdom to come, O Lord, may the Kingdom of Mary come!

LOUIS MARIE GRIGNION DE MONTFORT

One reason why so few souls arrive at the fullness of the age of Christ is that
Mary, who is as profoundly as always the mother of Jesus Christ and the fecund
wife of the Holy Spirit, has not been formed enough in their hearts.

BOURDON

The mother of God, since she gave her son the humanity of the second Adam, is
also the mother of universal humanity . . . in her, the creation is completely
divinized, and conceives, fosters, and bears God.

SERGEI BULGAKOV

I say that we are wound
With mercy round and round
As if with air: the same
Is Mary, more by name,
She, wild web, wondrous robe,
Mantles the guilty globe . . . And men are meant to share
Her life as life does air.

If I have understood,
She holds high motherhood
Towards all our ghostly good,
And plays in grace her part
About man's beating heart,
Laying like air's fine flood
The death-dance in his blood;
Yet no part but what will
Be Christ our Saviour still.
Of her flesh he took flesh:
He does take, fresh and fresh,
Through much the mystery how,
Not flesh but spirit now,
And wakes, O marvellous!
New Nazareths in us,
Where she shall yet conceive
him, morning, noon, and eve;
New Bethlems, and he born
There, evening, noon and morn . . .

— "THE BLESSED VIRGIN COMPARED TO THE AIR WE
BREATHE" — GERARD MANLEY HOPKINS

For many of the greatest mystics of the Christian tradition, the supreme mystical secret of the Christ-revelation is that the surest, fastest, most powerful, and most direct way to Jesus goes through an adoration and imitation of Mary his Mother. Summing up the wisdom of nearly two thousand years of mystical tradition, de Montfort put it this way in the early eighteenth century:

"The greatest means of all, and the most wonderful of all secrets for obtaining and preserving divine Wisdom is a loving and genuine devotion to the Blessed Virgin . . . Jesus is the fruit and product of Mary wherever he is present, be it in heaven, on earth, in our tabernacles, or in our hearts. So anyone who wishes to possess this wonderful fruit in his heart must first possess the tree that produces it; whoever wishes to possess Jesus must possess Mary.

"Mary is the surest, the easiest, the shortest, and the holiest of all the means of possessing Jesus Christ . . . She is like a holy magnet attracting Eternal Wisdom to herself with such power that he cannot resist. This magnet drew him down to earth to save mankind and continues to draw him every day into every person who possesses it.

"As Mary is everywhere the fruitful Virgin, she produces in the depths of the soul where she dwells a purity of heart and body, a singleness of intention and purpose, and a fruitfulness of good work . . . She causes Jesus to live continuously in the soul and that soul to live in continuous union with Jesus. If Jesus is equally the fruit of Mary for each individual soul as for all souls in general, he is even more especially her fruit and her masterpiece in the soul where she is present. God the Holy Spirit wishes to fashion his chosen ones in Mary. He tells her 'my well-beloved, my spouse, let all your virtues take root in my chosen ones, that they may grow from strength to strength and grace to grace . . . reproduce yourself in my chosen ones, so that I may have the joy of seeing in them the roots of your invincible faith, profound humility . . . sublime prayer, ardent charity, firm hope and all your virtues.'"

Devotion to the mystic Motherhood of Mary—and so to the role of the Sacred Feminine's "invincible faith, profound humility, sublime prayer, ardent charity, firm hope"—in the birthing of Christ-consciousness—began very early in the history of the Christian church as a necessary compensation, no doubt, for the exclusively masculine orthodox interpretation of Jesus and of the Godhead. By the second century, Gnostic Gospels describing Mary's birth, spiritual growth, and mission were being composed. By the third century, the transfiguring power of her Motherhood was being celebrated in the Syriac Odes of Solomon. By the fourth century, Mary was being adored as a fully divinized being in the hymns of Saint Ephrem the Syrian, the woman who redeemed the sin of Eve: "In her virginity, Eve put on leaves of shame. Your mother put on, in her virginity, the garment of glory that suffices for all!" In the fifth century, Mary is given the title, at the Council of Ephesus in 431, of "Theotokos," the God-bearer (or Birthgiver of God), and in 451, at the Council of Chalcedon, that of "Aeiparthenos," ever-virgin. Only a few decades later, in the Akathist hymn of Romanus Melodus, Mary is adorned with many of the cosmic powers of the goddesses and Motherhood of the ancient world:

> Hail to you, the throne of the King
> Hail, star that heralds the sun
> Hail, womb of divine incarnation
> Hail to you through whom the creation is reborn
> Hail to you through whom the Creator becomes a child

Hail to you who plant the planet of our life
Hail, table that bears a wealth of mercy!
Hail, Mother of lamb and shepherd . . .
Hail, key to the gates of paradise . . .
Hail, pillar of fire, leading those in darkness
Hail to you who bring opposites together . . .
Hail, inexhaustible treasure of life . . .
Hail, healing of my body
Hail, salvation of my soul . . .

As Anne Baring and Jules Cashford make clear in *The Myth of the Goddess,* "Mary appears infrequently in the Gospels, and then she plays a completely subordinate role to her son. Yet within five hundred years of her death, a pantheon of images enveloped her until she assumed the presence and stature of all the goddesses before her—Cybele, Aphrodite, Demeter, Astarte, Isis, Hathor, Inanna and Ishtar. Like them, she is both virgin and mother and, like many of them, she gives birth to a half-human, half-divine child who dies and is reborn." As Joseph Campbell wrote, "The entire ancient world, from Asia minor to the Nile and from Greece to the Indus valley, abounds in figurines of the naked female form, in various attitudes of the all-supporting, all-including Goddess . . . and so it came to pass that, in the end and to our day, Mary, Queen of martyrs, became the sole inheritor of all the names and forms, sorrows, joys and consolations of the Goddess-Mother in the Western world, seat of wisdom, vessel of honor, mystical rose, house of gold, gate of heaven, morning star, refuge of sinners, Queen of angels, Queen of peace."

As Mary's glory grew, both in the titles accorded to her and in the liturgies and hymns created for her, so her role—the role of the Mother—in the mystic transformation that the Christ came to bring became increasingly clearer. Already in the second century, Origen celebrates her unique significance for the Incarnation: "Elizabeth calls her who was yet a virgin, Mother, prophetically by her word anticipating the event, and names the fruit of her womb, because he was not to be from men but *from the Mother alone* [italics mine]." In the fifth century, St. Augustine hymns Mary as the "mold" into which all mystic souls should "cast" themselves in order to be re-made "in the living image of Christ." De Montfort says of St. Augustine's image, "Anyone who is cast into this divine mold is quickly shaped into Jesus and Jesus into him"; by the tenth century, Fulbert of Chartres is honoring "the Virgin Mother of God who will bear the Sun of Justice, the supreme King." And by the twelfth century, in the work of St. Bernard of Clairvaux, a complete vision of the mystic Motherhood of Mary was intact: "By you we have access to the Son, O blessed founder of grace, bearer of life, and mother of salvation, that we may receive him by thee, who through thee was given to us. With whom can we compare you, O mother of grace and beauty? You are the paradise of God. From you springs the fountain of living water that irrigates the whole earth." It is this tradition of Mary as "founder of grace, bearer of life, mother of salvation, paradise of God," and birther of Christ and Christ-consciousness, "the fountain of living water," that Dante takes to its consummation in the final cantos of the *Paradiso*. In canto 32, the transfigured Bernard of Clairvaux tells Dante:

> *Look now on her who most resembles Christ,*
> *For only the great glory of her shining*
> *Can purify your eyes to look on Christ.*

In canto 33, in his sublime prayer to the Virgin on Dante's behalf, St. Bernard makes it clear that the "final revelation," the gnosis that ends the *Divina Commedia,* of a love that "moves the sun and other stars," can be given only through her intercession and mystic power. It is the Virgin's power—and by implication her mystic virtues of humility, adoration, faith, and pure surrender—that prepares the soul for ultimate revelation, and the birth into Christhood:

> *Virgin Mother, daughter of thy son;*
> *Humble beyond all creatures and more exalted:*
> *Predestined turning point of God's intention:*
>
> *Thy merit so ennobled human nature*
> *That its divine Creator did not scorn*
> *To make himself the creature of his creature . . .*
>
> *Lady, thou art so near God's reckonings*
> *That who seeks grace and does not first seek thee*
> *Would have his wish fly upward without wings. . . .*
>
> *Now comes this man who from the final pit*
> *Of this universe up to this height has seen*
> *One by one, the three lives of the spirit.*
>
> *He prays to thee in fervent supplication*
> *For grace and strength, that he may raise his eyes*
> *To the all-healing final revelation.*

And I, who never more desired to see
The vision myself than I do that he may see it,
Add my own prayer, and pray that it may be

Enough to move you to dispel the trace
Of every mortal shadow by thy prayers
And let him see revealed the Sum of Grace.

The entire "journey" of Dante's soul in the *Divina Commedia* can be "read" as one that gives him, through repeated ordeal and "ascending" visions, the "eyes" to see the glory and power of the Sacred Feminine as incarnated first in Beatrice and finally in the one who, as the Akathist hymn tells us, "holds the keys to Paradise," the Virgin herself. Humbled, instructed, illumined, and transformed, through the grace of the divine feminine, Dante is changed to be able to see the "light supreme" and to be made "one with the eternal good." The divine smile of the Virgin's grace is seen, in retrospect, as illumining every step of his journey and every one of its agonies and revelations, through what St. Bernard calls "the glory of her shining." Dante is—in the closing stanzas of the poem—at last purified enough to "gaze on Christ," to know himself one with the Holy Trinity, and to be born into the beginning of Christ-consciousness:

Already I could feel my being turned
Instinct and intellect balanced equally
As in a wheel whose motion nothing jars
By the love that moves the Sun and other stars.

Dante's vision of the sacred and dynamic "balance of intellect and instinct" made possible, by the intercession of and exposure to the grace of the divine feminine brought to its most comprehensive expression, a millennium of mystical understanding of the role of the Mother in the birth of Christ in the soul.

There were—and are—other revelations to come. In one of its deepest, most surprising—and most radical—aspects, the inner history of Christian mysticism has been one of an ever-expanding awareness of the role of Mary in the birthing of Christ-consciousness. As this awareness has expanded to include, name, and celebrate more and more of the powers, strengths, and glories of that Sacred Feminine "rejected" by the patriarchal dogmas and practices of the dominant "male" tradition of Christianity, so too the awareness of the full nature, power, and mission of the Christ-consciousness to which it gives birth has expanded and grown until, in modern times, it has entirely transcended all traditional dogmatic interpretations. The return of the full and "unedited" divine Mother to the heart of Christian mysticism has transformed our understanding of her son and of the nature of his cosmic mission and force. A wholly new mystical Christianity is being born from this growth of awareness, one that simultaneously returns all those who practice it to the social radicalism of the original historical Christ and roots it, as the historical Jesus began to, in an all-transforming cosmic vision of the divine Motherhood of God. It is this new mystical understanding of Mary as complete and full divine Mother and of Christ as the Sacred Androgyne-Divine-Child, born of the total union of the complete Father and fully recognized and fully celebrated divine Mother, that is designed, I believe, to birth the Christ-consciousness in our time with a power and on a scale that has hitherto been unimaginable. The fusion that can now at last take place within the human religious imagination of the Father and Mother aspects of God is the equivalent in spiritual and mystical terms of the fusion that produced the atomic bomb: it unleashes an all-embracing, all-infusing power that could, if allowed to, transfigure the life of the world.

For this fusion of the Father-Mother within the psyche and in the living practice of every human being to occur, the all-essential adventure is to reimagine the role and figure and power of Mary. Until Mary is recognized as the divine Mother in all of her powers and attributes, the full nature of Christ cannot flame out and transform all things. Until the divine Motherhood of God in Mary is recognized in all of its mystical and radical revolutionary aspects, in all of the full meaning of its radical demand for transformation on every level, in every area of life and every dimension of our world-existence, then the full incandescence of the Christ-force, the Child of the transformed Father within the embodied Mother, cannot be completely imagined and so cannot be completely born.

Our great guides into this adventure that could transform life on earth will be, not surprisingly, Jesus and Mary themselves, and the mystics they choose to initiate completely into the meaning of their unfolding double dance in and through history. From her apparition at Tepeyac in 1531 in Mexico, through her revelations of herself and her role in the "Second Coming" to Louis Marie Grignion de Montfort at the beginning of the eighteenth century, and through the astounding proliferation of her apparitions all over the world in the last one hundred and fifty years, the Virgin herself has been making plain to everyone who can hear her that her power and force cannot be contained within the old dogmatic definitions and that she is returning as the force of the divine Mother in history, as the all-transforming power of the Mother's Immaculate Heart, and as the indispensable initiator into the Christ.

As de Montfort wrote in the *True Devotion to the Blessed Virgin*—a work that although written in the early eighteenth century was only rediscovered in 1842 (buried in northern France) just before the major Marian apparitions of the nineteenth century: "It is through the very Holy Virgin that Jesus Christ came into the world to begin with, and it is also through her that he will reign in the world . . . Until now, the Divine Mary has been unknown and this is one of the reasons why Jesus Christ is hardly known as he should be. If then—as is certain—the knowledge and reign of Jesus must arrive in the world (in the Second Coming), it will be a necessary consequence of the knowledge and reign of the very Holy Virgin, who birthed him into this world the first time and will make him burst out everywhere the second."

Through the increasing recognition, then, of "the Divine Mary," and the increasing restoration of Mary as the divine Mother in all of her powers and aspects to the heart of the Christian revelation, the Christ will come to be born in far greater power and fullness. Mary has said, in apparition after apparition, that the world will be destroyed in horror and terror unless humanity as a whole turns to the values of her Immaculate Heart—to its unity, love, faith, and peace of spirit. She has said again and again that she is coming to prepare in all human hearts for the birth of Christ, with whom her Immaculate Heart is one. All of her agonized warnings and every aspect of her teachings—on humility, mutual love, honoring of all forms of life, the necessity of serious transformation through service and prayer—are designed to birth the Christ through the agency and grace of the Motherhood of God.

Jesus himself, in apparition after apparition to serious and accredited mystic seekers and initiates throughout this century, has made Mary's mission and the mission of the divine Motherhood of God clear to anyone prepared to listen: to Berthe Petit, in 1915, Jesus said, "By confident consecration to my Mother, the devotion to my heart will be strengthened and as it were completed." To Marthe Robin, in 1918, Jesus said, "In place of the throne of the beast, two glorious thrones will arise, one of my Sacred Heart and the other of the Immaculate Heart of Mary." In 1929, Jesus said to Sister Lucia (one of the seers of Fatima) in the Convent of Jesus, "I want my entire church to know that it is through the Immaculate Heart of my Mother that this favor (of victory over evil) is obtained." In 1942, Jesus said to Berthe Petit, "Return to her heart united to mine will bring peace." To Rosa Quattrini, he said on April 5, 1968, "I will come in triumph. I will come to give light to lighten all souls. But it will be too late for those who do not understand the love of a mother." In 1986, he said to Sister Natalie in Hungary; "To save the world Mary needs power. Therefore we endow the Immaculate Mother of God with the powers of the Queen. Her title will be 'The victorious Queen of the World.'" To Gladys Quiroga, in Ecuador, Jesus said in 1987, "If this generation does not listen to my Mother, it will perish. I ask everyone to listen to her . . . Tell my children: to deny the Mother is to deny the Son." On November 1, 1987, Jesus told Gladys Quiroga, "My Mother must be accepted. My Mother must be heard in the totality of her messages. I want a renewal of the spirit, a detachment from death, and an attachment to life. I have chosen the heart of my Mother, so that what I ask will be achieved. Souls will come to me through the means of her Immaculate Heart." On December 30, 1989, Jesus made his message even clearer, if that were possible, when he said to Gladys Quiroga, "In the past, the world was saved by the ark of Noah. Today my Mother is the ark. It is through her that souls will be saved, because she will lead them to me." To Julia Kim, on May 16, 1991, in Korea, Jesus said, "Tell everyone that accepting my Mother's words is the same as accepting me and that holding her hands and following her is the shortcut to me . . . My Mother came into this world as the Heavenly Prophetess and my Helper who will lead you to my brilliant and glorious revelations. Follow her words."

Over the last hundred and fifty years, as if in partial recognition of the seriousness and splendor of the apparitions all over the world of Mary and Jesus, the Catholic Church has struggled to recognize the growing necessity of turning toward the Motherhood of God: in the declaration of the dogma of the Immaculate Conception in 1854; in its eventual recognition of the apparitions of La Salette, Lourdes, Fatima, Beauraing and Banneux; in its momentous declaration of the dogma of the Assumption in 1950; and in naming Mary as "Queen of Heaven" in 1954. And, as everyone knows, there are many influential powers within the church today that are pressing the Pope to declare Mary co-redemptrix, mediatrix, and advocate.

In many ways, however, even these recognitions of Mary do not go far enough. A church still mired in patriarchy on all levels—dogmatic, mystical, practical—cannot fully comprehend the "totality of my Mother's messages" and cannot even begin to enshrine their more radical implications. An absurd obsession with Mary's "virginity" continues. The 1954 papal encyclical, *Ad caeli reginam,* that declared Mary "Queen of Heaven," significantly glossed over the full meaning of her ancient title, "Queen of Earth," so perpetuating that "transcendentalising" of the force of the Sacred Feminine that has traditionally kept it from being embodied on earth in action. The vision of Mary that is still given by the church to its faithful is very much the "old" one of a patient, tender, grieving, essentially passive Mother who, while she is recognized as "divinized," is not in her own right divine; her separation from the Trinity and the Godhead remain subtly complete and so the full recognition of her role in manifesting the Divine Motherhood of God on earth cannot enter history to transform it. Within the church, Mary is still enclosed and confined within a golden cage of adoration, which defines her powers in largely patriarchal terms.

This cage must now be smashed so the full human and divine Mary and the full revelation of God's Motherhood can illumine the world. The mostly male Catholic theologians can go on dithering academically for decades on whether another Marian dogma can be admitted within the church; the world at large simply does not have time for a debate as to whether any new Latin title should be given to her. What must be done—and done fast if the Christ-consciousness is to be born on a sufficient scale before it is too late—is to reclaim as completely as possible all the powers of the divine Mother for Mary in living mystical practice and practical action. Meister Eckhart wrote, "We must be Mothers of God." On how richly and radically that Motherhood is interpreted depends the future.

Five Approaches to Mary's Mystic Motherhood

There are, I believe, five main new ways in which we can extend and enrich our understanding of the mystic Motherhood of Mary, which the rest of this section will explore in detail.

The first way is through a reevaluation of the historical Mary, and of her message in the Magnificat, the one "canonical" text we have attributed directly to her. The second way is to meditate in depth on the divine meaning of the Marian apparitions of the last four hundred years and accept them as revelations of a cosmic feminine force, the force of the Cosmic Mary, "the woman clothed with the sun" that appears in Revelation. The third is to explore the insights of the other main mystical traditions about the divine feminine so as to free our vision of the Motherhood of God from the prison of church dogma. The fourth is to reimagine Mary as what I call "the Queen of the Sacrament of Cana," the initiatrix into the mystical meaning of Sacred Marriage at the heart of human life and sexuality. The fifth way I propose is to explore the various mystical meanings of perhaps the most potent (and subversive) image of Mary the Mother in the Christian tradition—that of the Black Madonna.

Each of these five approaches reveals aspects of Mary's force and presence that have been "edited out" or muted by patriarchal tradition; each of them makes available to us, at this moment when we need as full a vision of the divine feminine as possible, a new range of insights, passions, and powers. Through linking the historical Mary of the Magnificat, "the woman clothed with the sun," the vision of the divine Mother in other mystical traditions, the "Queen of Cana," and all the rich and paradoxical meanings from the image of the Black Madonna, and interpenetrating and fusing all of these five approaches to her together, we can uncover in Mary the full glory of her divine Motherhood and so the full glory of the Christ-consciousness she gives birth to in all the beings who turn to her.

The Historical Mary and Her Message in the Magnificat

The Jewish "Miriam" was not in any sense a merely passive "absorber" of tragedy and agony as she is often represented in male theological fantasy and patriarchal tradition: she was a strong, passionate, powerful, prophetic woman of the poor, who withstood ordeal after ordeal—including the horrible crucifixion of her son—with extraordinary stamina, spiritual vitality, and courage. She was a woman who knew from terrible experience everything about social ostracism, poverty, and oppression in all its forms, and who did not accept them in the name of "purification" or of an "otherworldly" vision, but protested them vehemently and dedicated her whole life—as did her son—to enacting a way of life that would unravel the conditions that engendered them. This Mary, like her son, fused in her inmost being a gnosis of the Kingdom of love and justice of God, lucid knowledge of the viciousness of the actual power relations, and a revolutionary vision of how the world must be transformed.

In the one message we have from "Miriam," the Magnificat, we see clearly—if we dare to look—the limitations and hypocrisy of the predominant patriarchal interpretation of Mary. The Magnificat is not—or not only—a glowing interior hymn of mystical victory. It is also, as modern liberation theologians and feminist mystics have made clear, a prophetic call for an all-comprehensive and interlinked mystical, cultural, economic, and political revolution. As Mary says of the God who has given her, a poor, "despised" woman of the depressed and marginal classes, the honor of bearing the Messiah: "He hath shewed strength with his arm; he hath scattered the proud in the imagination of their hearts. He hath put down the mighty from their seats, and exalted them of low degree. He hath filled the hungry with good things; and the rich he hath sent empty away." The God that Mary invokes is not merely an all-holy transcendental power, but the Lord of justice, who intervenes passionately and directly in time and in the heart of history on the side of the poor and oppressed to "shew strength with his arm," to "scatter" the "imaginations" of the proud, to "put down" the mighty from their seats and fill the hungry "with good things."

The miracle of the new birth, the new consciousness, that Mary knows she is to bear into the world, is not, then, merely a religious or "mystical" miracle—it is one that is destined to transform the facts and relations of reality, as Mary tells us, in three linked and ascending stages. First, the new messianic consciousness will shatter all the "imaginations" of "pride" by revealing the truth of the "equality" and all-leveling love of the Kingdom. Then, it will undo all existing systems of power and control and "put down the mighty from their seats" and "exalt," in actual institutional terms, those of "low degree." Third, it will seal and make "practical" this revolution of the heart and of the relations of power by a radical redistribution of all forms of wealth, spiritual and physical, that will fill "the hungry with good things."

Mary has understood the deepest significance of the Messiah being sent to be born in her, a poor woman. She has understood that this birth will mean a reversal of all the terms that have governed and dictated history. As Leonardo Boff writes in the *Maternal Face of God,* "The backdrop of the Magnificat is the tragic character of a world that is unjustly ordered and therefore an obstacle to God's plan for society and human beings. However, God has resolved to intervene through the Messiah and to inaugurate new relations with all things . . . [in the birth of Christ] God has left the resplendent shadows of an inaccessible abode and now draws near the murky light of the human race. God enters the conflict; takes up the cause of the conquered and the marginalized against the mighty . . . The mercy of God takes historical forms, is made concrete in deeds that transform the interplay of forces. The proud, with the power in their hands, do not have the last word: they think they have, but the divine justice is already upon them in history itself . . . The reign of God is anything but the consecration of this world's law and order—the decree of the overambitious. The Reign of Justice is the reign of a different justice. God promised this new world to our ancestors, and this promise is our certitude."

The message of the historical Mary—and of the divine feminine through the historical Mary—is exactly that of the teachings and life of the historical Jesus. It is a message of the most complete imaginable revolution that menaces all forms of political and religious power and all existing human structures of oppression. It is easy to see why patriarchal churches should have muted or "etherealized" the full outrageousness of its challenge. The "taming" of Mary and the force of sublime outrage of the Sacred Feminine that streams through her song of victory has coincided with the "taming" of Jesus by a "distancing" of him from the human race as the unique Son of God. A domesticated and "etherealized" Mother has led to a "domesticated" and "etherealized" Son and the convenient castration of the radical force of Jesus' teachings. It is this castration that the restoration of Mary to her full dignity will make impossible.

The Woman Clothed with the Sun: Apparitions of the Cosmic Mary

And there appeared a great wonder in heaven, a woman clothed with the sun,
and the moon under her feet, and upon her head a crown of twelve stars: And
she being with child cried, travailing in birth, and pained to be delivered.

REVELATION 12:1–2

Just as we must now radically reconsider and re-envision the historical Mary, so, I believe, we must try with every strength of imagination to listen to the Cosmic Mary who has been appearing in apparition after apparition over the last four hundred years. The Mother, whose cry of revolution was muted in time and in the unfolding of the disastrous history of the church, is returning as "the woman clothed with the sun," in full splendor, majesty, agony, and power to give the human race one last chance to hear her message and so really to hear and implement the message of her son.

It is especially in the apparition of "the woman clothed with the sun" as the Virgin of Guadalupe at Tepeyac, near Mexico City, in 1531, that we can see the full—and radical—implications of this reappearance of the Mother at the heart of the Christian revelation.

The most complete vision of the significance of what happened at Tepeyac can be found in a text that is still far too little known—the *Nican Mopohua,* written in the 1560s in the Aztec language of Nahuatl, and translated in this century into Spanish and other European languages. This mystical "Gospel" of the Cosmic Mary, written by an aztec christian only a few decades after the events it describes, makes clear that the force appearing as the Virgin in early December 1531 at Tepeyac—and that left her miraculous image on the cloak (the "tilma") of Juan Diego the poor Indian she appeared to—is nothing less than the all-loving and all-powerful force of the complete divine Mother.

Let me now quote, in full, the astounding account of the Indian Juan Diego's first vision at Tepeyac in early December 1531 of "the woman clothed with the sun":

He went to the top of the hill, and he saw a lady who was standing and who was calling him to come closer to her side. When he arrived in her presence, he marveled at her perfect beauty. Her clothing appeared like the sun, and it gave forth rays.

And the rock and cliffs where she was standing, upon receiving the rays like arrows of light, appeared like precious emeralds, appeared like jewels; the earth glowed with the splendors of the rainbow. The mesquites, the cacti, and the weeds that were all around appeared like feathers of the quetzal, and the stems looked like turquoise; the branches, the foliage, and even the thorns sparkled like gold.

He bowed before her, heard her thought and word, which were exceedingly re-creative, very ennobling, alluring, producing love. She said, "Listen, my most abandoned son, dignified Juan; where are you going?"

And he answered; "My owner and my Queen; I have to go to your house [your church] of Mexico-Tlatatloco, to follow the divine things that our priests, who are the images of our Lord, give to us." Then she conversed with him and unveiled her precious will. She said, "Know and be certain in your heart, my most abandoned son, that I am the Ever-Virgin Holy Mary, Mother of the God of Great Truth, Teotl, of the One through whom we live, the Creator of persons, the Owner of what is near and together, of the Lord of Heaven and Earth.

"I very much want and ardently desire that my hermitage be erected in this place. In it I will show and give to all people all my love, my compassion, my help, and my protection, because I am your merciful Mother and the Mother of all nations that live on this earth who would love me, who would speak with me, who would search for me, and who would place their confidence in me. There I will hear their laments and remedy and cure all their miseries, misfortunes, and sorrows."

Every detail of this account in the *Nican Mopohua* is astonishing and de-ranges tradition. Firstly, the Virgin appears not to a member of the ruling "religious" class—the Spaniards who had just conquered Mexico with overwhelming brutality; she appears to a native Indian, a peasant. Secondly, she addresses Juan Diego with the ennobling, honoring tenderness of a true Mother: "dignified Juan Diego." In so doing through him, she symbolically restores to life and spiritual dignity a whole native people that Spanish Catholics (in the "name" of her son) had all but destroyed. Thirdly, the Virgin appears in a way that manifests not merely her transcendental glory but reveals her as the all-transforming Queen of Creation, as the Sacred Fire (in Hindu mysticism the Shakti, the feminine divine power) that lights up, creates, and sustains all living things. The "arrows of light" that shoot out from her divine beauty penetrate and transfigure all of nature: "The earth glowed with the splendors of the rainbow . . . even the thorns sparkled like gold." The woman "of perfect beauty" whose "clothing appeared like the sun" is clearly not only the Queen of Heaven but also Queen of Earth, not only an etherealized "heavenly" Mary—intercessor, mediator, and advocate—but the complete transcendent and immanent Divine Mother of all dimensions and worlds, the creative love-power of the entire cosmos, in whose radiance "heaven" and "earth" are united in a blaze of splendor.

Fourthly, and all-importantly, after giving Juan Diego (and through him all of us) this vision of her glory, the Virgin then goes on to define herself in a way that shatters all the conventional ways of defining her (and it is significant that this description of herself has been doctored in the later "Spanish Catholic" accounts of the apparition). The Virgin describes herself as "the Ever-Virgin Holy Mary" and then as the Mother not of Christ but of the Aztec god of great Truth, Teotl. She announces herself, in other words, as the "source" of the gods of the Aztec tradition that Catholicism was in the act of destroying. Teotl was one of the greatest of the Aztec deities: the place where the Virgin chose to appear—Tepeyac—was itself the site of a temple to Tonantzin, the Aztec divine Mother. The Virgin is announcing herself, then, as something far more and far greater than the radiantly subordinate figure of conventional Christianity. She is saying she is nothing less than the universal divine Mother, the Mother-Godhead, "source," by implication, of all theologies and all "Gods."

"The woman clothed with the sun," the Cosmic Mary, goes on in the text to be even more precise in her representation of herself. She says she is not only the Mother of Teotl, she is also the Mother of the "One through whom we live"—of the divine force that underlies and sustains all of life; the Mother of the "Creator of persons"—of the divine power that engenders all human beings in their unique individuality; the Mother of the "Owner of what is near and together"—that is, of the divine truth of interdependence between all things and beings; and the Mother of the Lord of Heaven and Earth—that is, of the "male" God that rules and unites all heavenly and all earthly dimensions. This is nothing less than the most inclusive imaginable description of the complete divine Mother and of the divine Motherhood of God as being the ultimate source of all beauty, truth, law, love, and power in the cosmos.

Having revealed herself in her "unedited" splendor, the divine Mother-Virgin then gives Juan Diego—and through him the world—a totally undogmatic account of her Motherhood of all beings. "I will show and give to all people all my love"; "I am . . . the Mother of all nations that live on this earth who would love me." She tells Juan Diego that she wants a "hermitage built for her at Tepeyac to enshrine and celebrate this universal Motherhood, where all the laments of those who love her—whatever their race, caste, sex, social status—can be heard and remedied. Symbolically, it is not in the places of established "Catholic" power that she calls for this temple of universal Motherhood to be built, but—outrageous in the historical context—on the site of an ancient Aztec temple to an Aztec divine Mother. Implicitly, here, the Virgin is calling to all Christians to throw away the prejudices that separate them from other revelations and to see the force that incarnated and incarnates in her and so births her son as linked to all manifestations of the Mother throughout the world and to all mystical traditions that celebrate the divine feminine.

The way in which the story of the apparitions at Guadalupe goes on to unfold from this point unveils, I believe, something of the working of the force of the divine Mother-Virgin.

Let us look at the story in some detail: Juan Diego, told by the Virgin to go and inform Bishop Zumarraga of Mexico City of her appearance and wishes, meets with a rebuff. He returns to Tepeyac where the Virgin again appears to him and stiffens his resolve to go back again to the bishop; again, Bishop Zumarraga does not believe him, and asks for a "sign."

Disheartened, Juan Diego goes back to his own home, where his uncle, Juan Bernardino, is found to be dying of smallpox. The third encounter with the Virgin at Tepeyac then takes place. At first, Juan Diego tries to avoid her; he wants to go and get a priest to give his uncle the last rites and so takes another path around Tepeyac. The Virgin meets him on this path and assures him that all will be well with his uncle. She then tells him to go to the top of the hill where he had seen her before and collect all the flowers he will find there.

The *Nican Mopohua* continues: "Juan Diego climbed the hill and when he arrived at the top he was deeply surprised. All over the place there were all kinds of exquisite flowers from Castile, open and flowering. It was not a place for flowers and likewise it was the time when the ice hardens upon the earth.

They were very fragrant, as if they were filled with fine pearls, filled with the morning dew."

Juan Diego gathers the flowers and takes them back to the Virgin, who touches them all, one by one. He then places them all in the hollow of his "tilma," his peasant cloak made of cactus fiber. The Virgin now tells him to go to the bishop with the flowers, saying, "These different flowers are the proof, the sign that you will take to the bishop. In my name, tell him that he is to see in them what I want." The Virgin continues to Juan Diego, "And you, you are my ambassador; in you I place all my trust. With all my strength I command you that only in the presence of the bishop are you to open your mantle and let him know and reveal to him what you are carrying. You will recount everything well; you will tell him how I sent you to climb to the top of the hill to cut the flowers, and all that you saw and admired. With this you will change the heart of the lord of the priests so that he will do his part to build and erect my temple that I have asked him for."

The rest of the story is well known. Juan Diego goes to the bishop's palace, eventually secures an interview with the bishop, tells him in detail how he had picked the flowers at the Virgin's instruction, and asks the bishop to receive them. The *Nican Mopohua* then informs us, "He unfolded his white mantle, the mantle in whose hollow he had gathered the flowers he had cut, and at that instant the different flowers from Castile fell to the ground. In that very moment she painted herself: the precious image of the Ever-Virgin Holy Mary, Mother of the God Teotl appeared suddenly just as she is today and is kept in her precious home, in her hermitage of Tepeyac, which is called Guadalupe." Amazed and chastened, the bishop and his attendants fell to their knees. At last, Juan Diego's story was believed, and the construction of the "hermitage" for the Image began soon after.

Juan Diego now returned home to find that his uncle Juan Bernardino was completely cured. The "Queen of Heaven" had appeared to him also and advised him to go and see the bishop. The *Nican Mopohua* relates, "She told him also that when he went to see the bishop, he would reveal all that he had seen and would tell him in what a marvelous way she had healed him and that he [the bishop] would call and name that precious image the Ever-Virgin Holy Mary of Guadalupe." Everything happened as the Virgin predicted; and the worldwide veneration of the Miraculous Image of Guadalupe began.

I have unraveled the story in detail because each of its twists reveals another aspect of the force of the Sacred Feminine, and in a way, I believe, that has profound implications for the future.

Firstly, it is clear from the way the story develops that, as we have already noted, the Virgin, the Mother, has chosen the poor, oppressed, and despised as her "ambassadors." Just as in the Magnificat, the historical Mary had proclaimed the messianic liberation of the poor, so here "the woman clothed with the sun" is making clear that her force and love are on the side of the oppressed, and reveals itself miraculously through them, through their courage, faith, and belief, and on their behalf.

Secondly, the revelation in the events of Guadalupe of the Mother's power shows that it brings healing of every kind. Not only is Juan Bernardino healed of his smallpox, but Juan Diego is also healed spiritually of his feeling of inferiority and uselessness. The Spanish bishop, too, is healed of his skepticism, elitism, and hard-heartedness. The Mother's perfect action of compassion heals the wounds of history not only in those oppressed by the powerful but in the powerful themselves.

Thirdly, the way in which the story unravels shows, I believe, how the full Mother wants her power acknowledged by the predominantly "male" and "patriarchal" church. Through a poor Indian and a miracle of "flowers," the Virgin changes the heart and will of the bishop and "compels" him to build her a church—or temple—at Tepeyac. Symbolically, the Mother is showing how the revelation of her power, majesty, and beauty can transform the heart of the patriarchal church and lead it to devote its efforts no longer to the pursuit of control but to creating a "temple," where the healing truth of her love can be experienced by anyone who wants it.

The apparitions of the Virgin at Guadalupe, then, not only unveil the splendor of the divine Mother in "the woman clothed with the sun"; they reveal with intricate beauty and tenderness how the power of the divine feminine works through encouragement, healing, and miracle to bring everyone to a higher awareness of their divine identity, equality, and of the possibilities for radical transformation that it awakens.

The great Marian apparitions of the last hundred and fifty years only continue this teaching. At Fatima, for example, the Great Sign that "the woman clothed with the sun" gives of her divine power is a spinning and hurtling of the sun itself, witnessed in wonder and terror by eighty thousand people—and this just after the Virgin has told the children, "The greatest sin is to rebel against the Motherhood of God and to refuse to recognize me as the Mother of all human beings." Again and again, as at Tepeyac, the Virgin in her apparitions has chosen the poor or the very young and innocent to be her "ambassadors" and the "mediums" through which she transmits her warnings and pleas for a worldwide transformation. Again and again, the Virgin repeats the messianic truths of the Magnificat—that only the humble shall be exalted, that God wants a revolution of the heart and society, that the new consciousness she is heralding is one that must alter all the conditions of human life. And just as at Tepeyac, the Virgin announces these truths not merely as the "Mother of God" of conventional dogma but as the indisputable Queen of Heaven and Earth, as, in other words, the full divine mother, pregnant with the new Christ-consciousness whose universal birth she has come to herald and prepare.

Learning from the Vision of the Mother in Other Mystical Traditions

To comprehend the Cosmic Mary in what Jesus has called "the totality of her messages," it is necessary to accept the challenge of the Virgin at Guadaloupe to bring to bear on our understanding of her all other world-revelations that celebrate the divine feminine. There is, of course, already within the Christian tradition—as I have shown at the beginning of this section—a line of Marian mystics stretching from the Desert Fathers through Romanus Melodus, St. Augustine, and Bernard of Clairvaux right up to Louis Marie Grignion de Montfort that, in a precise and devoted way, celebrates the Virgin's power and understands a great deal about her mystic role in birthing the inner Christ.

All of the mystics in this "lineage," however, are constrained by the patriarchal dogmas concerning her nature that tradition imposes on them. Even de Montfort—whose knowledge of the vast and secret ways in which the Sacred Feminine penetrates and transmutes the whole being is clairvoyant and profound—cannot declare Mary the full divine Mother. She remains a "human being," divinized, yes, but dependent on the "male" Trinity for all the powers and graces that radiate through her to the world. And even in de Montfort's most ecstatic pages we will not be able to find anything that matches the concrete reality of her glory as described in the *Nican Mopohua,* when the "arrows of light" that shoot out from her presence make "even the thorns sparkle like gold." De Montfort's Virgin—like St. Bernard's, Augustine's, and Dante's—is a transcendent queen but not the Queen of Nature, nor of the Creation, nor of the Body. The immanent, "embodied" power of the divine Mother is either ignored or muted.

Christian mysticism can no longer afford the subtle imbalance that this ignorance or muting of the full divine feminine implies. What must now be undertaken, and on a large, vivid scale, is a dialogue between Christian mystics and those of all the other mystical traditions that honor the divine Mother. Such a dialogue is bound to explode the patriarchal dogmas with which the Christian tradition has tried to contain the power of the Mother—which is perhaps why the majority of orthodox theologians oppose it with such venom. It will, however, realize the authentic message of the Virgin both in the Magnificat and in her apparitions, restore her to the heart of a transformed or redefined Trinity, and reveal the full, immanent, and transcendent passion and truth of Christ-consciousness.

From the great Hindu mother-mystics, like Jnaneshwar, Ramprasad, and Ramakrishna, the lover of Mary will learn of the Mother as the "Shining" of the Diamond of Godhead, the supreme power of creation and destruction, the force and divine consciousness which creates, sustains, destroys, and re-makes eternally all the worlds and universes. From the great Mahayana mystics, the Christian seeker will learn of her as the Void which births all things, as the emptiness which is the womb of all transcendent and immanent wisdom, as the saving compassion that "mothers" all Buddhahood, all enlightened thought and living. From the Taoist mystics, the Christian seeker will hear of the "Mother of the ten thousand things," of the mystery of the "Tao" from which all things are created and to whose subtle laws and rhythms all events in all worlds move. From the shamanic traditions and those of the Aborigines, Kogis, Yamomamis, and Native American Indians, the Christian worshipper of the feminine will learn of those aspects of the Virgin's power and grace that reflect themselves in the divine life of nature, in the intricate, earthy, and interdependent truths of the great web of life. From the traditions of the Jewish mystics, the Kabbalists in particular, the Christian seeker will come to know the Father-Mother whose eternal lovemaking creates all things at all times, and the "Shekhinah," the feminine presence that emanates from the Godhead through every atom of creation, binding it into a fiery sea of splendor. In the Sufi mystics, the Christian will meet a Mary who is revered as the Veil of Mercy of Allah. As Gilis informs us in his *Mary in Islam,* "In so far as Mary represents the origin of every conception and the limit of every understanding, the Virgin appears as the supreme veil that Allah has descended between him and his servants. This veil is one of mercy, with which he covers them and by which he graces them according to their different needs and states, his protection and his forgiveness."

Fusing, combining, "experiencing" all of these truths of the different world-traditions, the Christian mystic will then, at last, be able to begin to grasp the full beauty and glory of the Virgin's real power within the Christian revelation and to see exactly how all-infusing and all-encompassing is the maternal power that cries out in the Magnificat for the transformation of the world.

Mary as Queen of the Sacrament of Cana

This adventure into the wisdom of the mystical traditions concerning the Sacred Feminine will also illuminate for the Christian mystic the full—and radical—meaning of Mary's intervention at the marriage of Cana, will reveal Mary as what I call the "Queen of the Sacrament of Cana." The tantric traditions of Hinduism and Buddhism speak of a force of the divine Mother that illumines consecrated sexuality and reveals it as the site of an encounter with the divine and a place where enlightened consciousness can be tasted, known, and deepened.

At Cana, I believe, Mary is asking for a revelation of this tantric power and its potential for healing and transformation. Mary asks Jesus "at a marriage feast" to change "water" into "wine" (because the wine for the feast has run out). Traditional Christian mysticism has interpreted this, plausibly enough, as a call to Christ to divinize ordinary consciousness, to change the "water" of worldly awareness into Gnostic ecstasy, in which the Sacred Marriage of earth and heaven becomes clear.

Although authentic, this interpretation does not go far enough. What the Mother is revealing through Mary, I am convinced, is an aspect of the Christ-force that traditional Christian mysticism has either ignored or simply not had any access to, because of its tendency toward body hatred, contempt for sexuality, and a generalized denigration of earthly existence—what could be called the tantric aspect. What Mary is symbolically asking Christ to do at a marriage feast is reveal the power of the Christ-force to "divinize" sexuality, and so make a consecrated sexuality between devoted and faithful partners the site of an explosion of divine joy and divine knowledge, and a continually deepening source of direct awakening in the ground of life. At Cana, Mary reveals herself as the Queen of Tantric ecstasy, the force of embodied divine love that calls at the marriage feast of life for a wholly new vision of sexuality. This is the true "Sacrament of Cana," and when its full implications are embraced a worldwide healing of the body and of the many profound sexual wounds which a patriarchal interpretation of Christ has inflicted on humankind can take place.

Imagine a world in which the Mother and Christ are known to be united in sustaining and illumining a vast force of sexual joy and healing. This profound understanding would restore a noble mystical vision of the physical to the heart of life, promote the sacred honoring of women, heal men of their fear of the feminine and their homophobia. Those who dedicated their relationship to Mary and Christ and lived in humble acknowledgment of the tantric laws of fidelity, mutual honor, and respect would know in the heart-core of their lovemaking the energies that create the universe. Through the joy, freedom, and transforming insight such experience would release, beings would begin not only to imagine the Sacred Marriage between heaven and earth, heart and mind, body and soul, which is the ultimate truth of Christ, but to live it, and in the heart of their most important—and so most sacred—human relationships. Marriage—whether heterosexual or homosexual—would become what Mary and Christ have always wanted it to be: a mirroring of the Sacred Marriage of the masculine and feminine aspects of God that continually engenders the universe. The experience of such a "marriage" would enable the inner Sacred Marriage that births the inner Sacred Androgyne to take root in both partners.

Any couple who consecrates their love to Mary and Jesus will find that the Christ-fire enters and irradiates their lovemaking at every level. And this is not metaphor. The "green fire" of the Holy Spirit, what Hildegard of Bingen described as "viriditas," is nakedly visible when pure love is present, and its effects are palpable at every level: physically, in healing the pains and awkwardness of the body, those places where false shame and guilt have hidden for decades; emotionally, in revealing the all-encompassing dance of love in the universe; and spiritually, in slowly but astoundingly birthing both partners into the beginnings of Christ-consciousness.

What happens in the consecration of sexuality to Christ is that its essential Christ-heat is released. The Christ-heat that is the outstreaming of the completely open Sacred Heart and also the secret, life-sustaining energy of the body is now made alive, vivid, ecstatic, and above all conscious. It is seen and known as one force, one central, sacred, directly initiatory force that has no divisions or boundaries, and springs and flows and streams always from the Father-Mother. The aim of Tantra of Christ is to awaken this Christ-force, the force of divine human love, and to permeate and saturate consciousness and ordinary life with it, and so grow the "love body" spiritually, physically, and practically.

The restoration in the Mother of the tantric aspect of the Christ-force will permanently dissolve the hysterical body-hatred of the Christian tradition as it has developed. Consecrated human love will become Holy Communion, and Christ's words, "Take, eat. This is my Body," will reveal another dimension of miracle. The truth of what Matthew Fox writes in *The Cosmic Christ* will spread its flame of insight everywhere: "The Cosmic Christ might speak thus on the topic of sexuality. Let religion and the churches abandon their efforts to be 'houses of sublimation.' Instead re-enter the cosmic mystery that sexuality is and teach your people, young and old, to do the same, remembering justice, remembering responsibility as intrinsic to the mystical experience. All lovemaking (as distinct from 'having sex') is Christ meeting Christ. Love beds are altars. People are temples encountering temples, the holy of holies receiving the holy of holies. Wings of cherubim and seraphim beat to the groans of passions of human lovers, for the cosmic powers are there eager to enhance the celebration."

Mary as the Black Madonna

Perhaps the most powerful and all-embracing of all the symbols of the Virgin that is "returning" to our Christian consciousness to help us reimagine the power of the divine feminine is that of the Black Madonna. In its complex and majestic truth, I believe, all of the powers that need to be restored to the Mother in the revelation can be symbolized and worshipped. Seen in its full splendor, the image of the Black Madonna is one of the most moving and profound images of the divine Mother ever imagined by humankind, and a perfect image on which to focus devotion for Mary the full divine Mother in all of her aspects—as Queen of Heaven, Queen of Nature, Queen of Earth, and as a suffering, brave, dignified, mystical, and practical human divine being, who struggled and wept and prayed with us and who struggles, weeps, and prays with us and in us and for us still. The historical Mary of the Magnificat, the magnificence of "the woman clothed with the sun," the Queen of the Sacrament of Cana, the mystical Mother of all the different mystical traditions of the world—all of these powers and aspects and glories of the Mother can be seen concentrated in and emanating from the rich and many-layered divine presence of the Black Madonna.

The Black Madonna is the transcendent Kali-Mother, the black womb of light out of which all the worlds are always arising and into which they dissolve, the unknowable mystery behind all matter and all events, the "darkness" of divine love and the loving unknowing the divine Child embraces when his or her illumination is perfect. The Black Madonna is also the Queen of Nature and Tantra, the blesser and agent of all rich, fertile transformations in external and inner nature, in the outside world and in the intimacy of the psyche. And she is as well the human mother blackened by anguish and grief, but ennobled and made adamant by the secret mystical knowledge she has won from agony and is representing with dignity and is "voicing" as a perpetual appeal for justice and true change on every level. All of the different energies and powers of Mary are present in the Black Madonna in all of their different levels and dimensions and inner relations.

And because the fullness of the divine feminine is represented in this image, when we contemplate it fearlessly we are gradually initiated through it into the full nature of our Christhood in her. The human seared mother, the Miriam of the Magnificat, accompanies us in our worst anguishes and humiliations, representing that endurance and belief and surrender that are the clues to their transmutation into divine wisdom. The Queen of Nature and Tantra blesses us, and through our awed and grateful reception of that blessing transmutes into bliss and gnosis all the movements of our nature, making them whole and rich with her dark fecundity and strong with her strength that is rooted in the depths and mysteries of natural processes and rhythms, rhythms of creativity, transformation, and continual birth and rebirth. The transcendent and glorious dark Queen of Heaven, dark as the Virgin of Guadalupe but like her, wearing all the splendor of the sun and pregnant with the new, constantly inspires us and leads us forward and upward into the highest mysteries, while showing us in other of her aspects, which are also simultaneously present, how to ground, root, demonstrate, live, and embody them with naked courage.

As the Christ-Children of so complete and absolute and empowered a Mother, holy and unifying energies will be graced us, and all aspects of life on earth can be transformed. In her and his name, in the name and in the glory of the completely realized Father-Mother-Divine Child, nature will be saved and preserved and human life in all of its aspects changed forever into a mirror of divine love and justice.

And the Cosmic Christ will be born on earth at last.

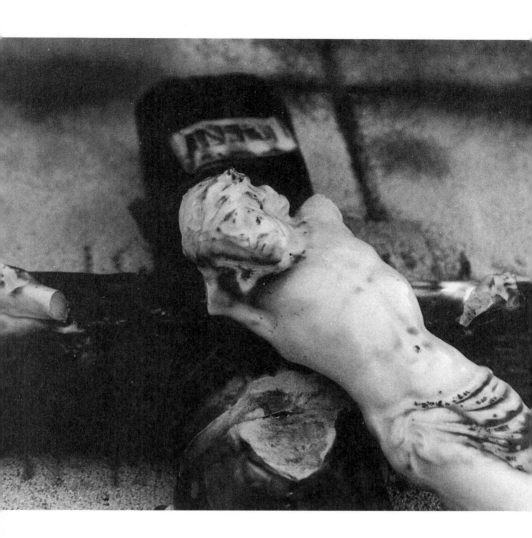

Part Four

The Direct Path to Christ:

Practices and Meditations

Introduction

❖ ❖ ❖

The fourth part of *Son of Man* has two connected sections—"Twelve Sacred Practices" and "Thirty-one Meditations on the Mystical Christ."

The first three parts have been an initiatory journey into the Cosmic Christ. Now, in the fourth part, "The Direct Path to Christ," I will present directly effective ways of uniting our being with the Cosmic Christ.

Just as Jesus took the direct path into Christhood—a path without intermediaries—so can we, if we dedicate ourselves to being "Christed" with determination, courage, a willingness to suffer whatever may be necessary for our transformation, and a commitment to incessant and increasingly fervent spiritual practice. As St. Paul has promised us in Romans 8:14–17: "For as many as are led by the Spirit of God, they are the sons of God. For ye have not received the spirit of bondage again to fear; but ye have received the Spirit of adoption, whereby we cry, Abba, Father. The Spirit itself beareth witness with our spirit, that we are the children of God; and if children, then heirs, heirs of God, and joint-heirs with Christ."

Claiming and living our "joint-heirdom" with Christ demands everything of us, and most especially that we strive to remain constantly in the presence of the Cosmic Christ so as to be infused at ever-deeper and more penetrating and empowering levels by his—and our own—bliss, peace, passion, wisdom, and divine power. In the "Twelve Sacred Practices," I offer in detail those spiritual exercises that I consider most immediately powerful in their ability to plunge us into the heart of Christ's all-encompassing, all-inspiring presence. I have chosen twelve because my intention is to provide an exercise for each month of the year; each exercise is designed to be practiced in two daily half-hour periods (one in the morning, the other in the late afternoon or evening) for an entire month. My hope is that by the end of the year anyone who follows these twelve practices seriously and with concentrated passion will have experienced their cumulative power and found out which ones work most richly for them, and in which emotional or spiritual circumstances. The direct path to Christhood demands of everyone who takes it that he or she become directly responsible for his or her spiritual evolution, under, and by the grace of, God. The most important tools in such a spiritual evolution are sacred practices that open the entire being to the love and power of the Cosmic Christ both within and without. Equipping yourself with those practices that are most effective is not a spiritual luxury; it is a necessity without which any profound evolution is impossible.

In the second section, "Thirty-one Meditations on the Mystical Christ," I present thirty-one mystical meditations by or on the Christ to provide sacred inspiration both for the preceding twelve practices and to be read and meditated on, on their own. This section can be used in two main ways—as a "reader" which will enable you to concentrate for yourself on the lessons and revelations of the book as a whole, or as a source of daily meditation to help you enter the presence of the Cosmic Christ when you begin whatever spiritual exercise you are practicing.

Through these sacred practices and meditations, may all human beings awake to the radiance of their divine identity! And may we each, through our own unceasing and striving and grace of the Father-Mother, come to birth the Cosmic Christ within us and so help the birth on earth of the Kingdom of God!

Section I
Twelve Sacred Practices

I am with you always, even unto the end of the world.

THE RESURRECTED CHRIST IN MATTHEW 28:20

Ask and it will be given you . . . for everyone who asks receives.

JESUS IN LUKE 11:9–10

According to your generosity you give to me
According to your majestic beauty you create me.

ODES OF SOLOMON

I no longer want to hear about you, beloved Lord, through messengers. I want to give myself completely to you. And I want you to give yourself completely to me.

SAINT JOHN OF THE CROSS

You will achieve nothing by your own efforts—yet God will not give you anything unless you work with all your strength.

THEOPHANE THE RECLUSE

The more deeply we press the Divine Object of our love into our hearts, and the more often we gaze upon him and intimately embrace him with the arms of our hearts, the more lovingly we shall be embraced by him here and in our eternal happiness.

HEINRICH SUSO

He prays constantly who unites prayer with the deeds required and mixes deeds with prayer. For the only way we can accept the command of St. Paul to pray constantly (1 Thessalonians 5:17) as referring to a real possibility is by saying that the entire life of the saint taken as a whole is a single great prayer.

ORIGEN

Liberator of my soul, I rejoice in ecstasy,
Knowing it is time for me to enter in and receive you.

ACTS OF THOMAS

Abbot Lot came to Abbot Joseph and said: "Father, to the limit of my ability, I
keep my little rule, my little fast, my prayer, meditation and contemplative si-
lence; and to the limit of my ability, I work to cleanse my heart of thoughts; what
more should I do?" The elder rose up in reply, and stretched out his hands to
heaven, and his fingers became like ten lamps of fire. He said: "Why not be ut-
terly changed into fire?"

SAYINGS OF THE DESERT FATHERS

Saying a Mantra

A mantra is a combination of sacred syllables that forms a nucleus of spiritual energy, and serves as a magnet or lens to focus spiritual power. In nearly all the major mystical systems—the Sufi, Hindu, and Buddhist, in particular—maintaining a constant and concentrated inner recitation of a mantra is seen as the simplest and most effective way of transcending the surface mind and entering the depths of the Spirit, where the mystery of divine presence is always alive.

This is true also of the ancient Christian mystical tradition. In recent years, the mantra tradition of the early Desert Fathers has been revived by, amongst others, John Main, Bede Griffiths, and Laurence Freeman. This tradition comes down to us in its most crystallized form in the tenth conference of the *Conferences* of the late fourth-century monk John Cassian. Cassian recommends the serious spiritual practitioner "take a single short verse and repeat it over and over again . . . every monk who wants to think continuously about God should get accustomed to meditating endlessly on it and to banishing all other thoughts for its sake." He advises us that "the mind should cling to it until, strengthened by the continual use of it, it casts off and rejects the rich and ample matter of all kinds of thought and restricts itself to the poverty of the single verse." This "restriction to the poverty of the single verse" effects, Cassian tells us, an extraordinary purification and empowerment of the spirit. "Those who realize this poverty," he writes, "arrive with ease at the first of the Beatitudes, 'Blessed are they who are poor in spirit for theirs is the Kingdom of Heaven.'"

Cassian's advice is repeated in the seventh century by John Climacus, who wrote, "Do not try to use many words lest your mind become distracted by the search for words. Because of one short sentence the publican in the Gospels received the mercy of God, the one brief affirmation saved the thief on the Cross. An excessive multitude of words in prayer disperses the mind in dreams, while one short word or sentence helps to silence the mind." As the English thirteenth-century *Cloud of Unknowing* reminds us: "We must pray in the height, length, and breadth of our spirit not in many words but in a single word."

Repeating a simple phrase or "single word" with single-minded calm in the depths of the heart unifies all the faculties of the being and gathers them together in the indwelling presence of God—and in an almost miraculously potent and fast way. As Bede Griffiths writes, "The function of the mantra is to collect the soul, to bring it back to its centre and unite the whole person—body, soul and spirit—with the spirit of God . . . the aim must be centering the body and soul in the depths of the spirit where the human spirit meets the spirit of God. St. Francis of Sales calls the spirit 'the fine point of the soul,' the point of self-transcendence where we go beyond ourselves and receive the divine spirit into our hearts . . . the repetition of the mantra is a way of keeping all faculties of soul and body centered on this point of the spirit" (*The New Creation of Christ*).

The mantra most commonly used in the early Christian tradition—perhaps even by the apostles and certainly by the Desert Fathers—was *Maranatha*. Maranatha is the mysterious word that ends St. Paul's first letter to the Corinthians and St. John's "revelation": it means, in Aramaic, "Our Lord, come" or "Come, O Lord" (*Mar* means Lord; *an*, our; *atha*, come).

When you say Maranatha, inwardly reflecting with the focused intensity of your entire being on the meaning of the sacred syllables "Our Lord, come" or "Come, O Lord," you will begin to see that they represent at once an invitation to Christ-consciousness to possess everything we are and transfigure it, and also an invitation of the Spirit of God to descend in a flame of charity upon the world and transform all existing conditions on earth. Maranatha is, then, both a plea for personal transformation and for a transformation of the world into the Kingdom. When you say it in the heart with these two meanings deeply intertwined, the Aramaic syllables grow fiery with every kind of visionary hope: you will find that the inner call of Maranatha, Our Lord, come, will concentrate within you all the desire of the soul for transcendent union with the Godhead, all the hunger of the heart to live in divine love, all the passion of the body to be awoken to its true resurrected being, and all the prayers of the unified self for the realization of the laws of the Kingdom on earth. Your whole being and its deepest hopes and desires will participate in the saying of the mantra; and through its practice an increasingly passionate and vivid experience of the Cosmic Christ will grow in you.

Another ancient mantra that is wonderfully powerful in evoking and sustaining the presence of the Cosmic Christ is *Abba*—the Aramaic word for

"Daddy" Jesus used. Abba suggests the trust and tenderness of his relationship with him. Saying Abba inwardly in the heart, then, imagining with all your powers the depth of Jesus' experience of the loving, all-protective presence of the Father, can help you enter more and more directly into that relationship. The word Abba itself is charged with the divine tenderness and self-abandonment of the Christ, and repeating it tenderly and abandonedly in the core of the heart can open your whole being to the fire of love.

If you want, you can work with a slightly longer phrase—such as the one Cassian recommends in the tenth conference (from Psalm 69, verse 2): *Come to my help, O God: Lord, hurry to my rescue.* Cassian tells us of this phrase: "It is not without good reason that this verse has been chosen from the whole of Scripture as a device. It carries within it all the feelings of which human nature is capable. It can be adapted to every condition and can be usefully deployed against every temptation. It carries within it a cry of help to God in the face of every danger. It expresses the humility of a holy confession. It conveys the watchfulness born of unending worry and fear. It conveys a sense of our frailty, the assurance of being heard, the confidence of help that is always and everywhere present." Working with it steadily, then, can deepen your sense of humility before God, and so increase your wonder at the awe of God's continual love.

Another slightly longer phrase that is always powerful in invoking and sustaining the divine presence is the one that St. Francis of Assisi is reported as using during long nights of continual prayer: *My God and my all.* When you say it in the heart, try to imagine St. Francis's total abandon of himself to God and the ecstasy, and surrender with which he must have said that simple phrase. You will be rewarded by a continually deepening sense of the fullness of God in all things around you and within you and by an always-stronger peace of acceptance.

What, then, is the best way of saying the mantra or short phrase in the two daily half-hour periods of practice? A good posture can greatly help the power of saying the mantra. Sit comfortably, with your spinal column, the nape of your head and neck in as straight a line as possible. When you recite the mantra inwardly, recite it calmly and slowly, savoring and concentrating on each syllable with your full attention. Some practitioners try to attune the recitation of the mantra to the rhythm of the heartbeat or the breath; if this arises naturally, welcome it, but never force anything. One way of making sure that the whole body as well as the spirit is gathered into the power of the practice is, when you breathe, to bring your breath *consciously* down from your head through the whole of your body—through the heart, belly, and genital centers, to the ends of both arms, and down to the soles of your feet. If done without strain but consistently, this can root the force of the mantra in the whole of the physical frame as well as the spirit, and lead to an ever-richer intuition of the fundamental unity of body and spirit.

What is essential, during the practice of the mantra, is to keep, calmly and consciously, returning to it. Thoughts will come and go: emotions—sometimes long-suppressed "dark" ones of fear, or trauma, or rage—will arise, especially as your practice becomes more focused. Do not suppress these thoughts and emotions, but do not identify with them either. The Fathers tell us that, in the case of thoughts, the best way of not being dominated by them is to imagine them passing like clouds in a perfect radiant blue sky, the sky of your inner divine nature. As for emotions—especially troubling ones—the most profound and healing way of encountering them is to allow them to unfold without fear within you and then surrender them whole-souledly to the sacred power inherent in the mantra. You will find if you do so, the emotions will gradually subside into acceptance and peace. Sometimes, if the emotions that arise seem particularly disturbing, it helps to take a few very deep breaths while saying the mantra and imagine its sacred force permeating the emotion that disturbs you with intense white light and dissolving it.

You will find that during your practice of mantra you will be constantly tempted to give it up, from distraction or boredom. Keep going. To say the mantra without ceasing in the face of boredom, distraction, and sometimes turbulent emotions is an act of spiritual humility, and, as Cassian tells us, "a practice of spiritual poverty," which, over time, can wear away the false self that always craves stimulation and excitement and open you to the vast and spacious timeless calm of the spirit. When practice becomes difficult, you need to practice with more and more conscious passion and focus; then you will discover that saying the mantra is helping you to die increasingly to the clamors and appetites of your mind and heart and concentrate more and more your full attention on the primacy of your divine self. After a while, you will find that saying the mantra will become more and more joyful for you and that it will even repeat itself without your consciously willing it in the depths of your heart, and even in your sleep. This is one of the signs, the Fathers and saints tell us, that our being is acceptable to the divine and that the Spirit is praying within us.

While the two half-hour periods during the day should be adhered to, you should also try to keep reciting the mantra inwardly throughout the day.

This will help you permeate your being, consciousness, and activity with the presence of God. Cassian advises us in his tenth conference: "Never cease to recite it in whatever task or service or journey you find yourself. Think upon it as you sleep, as you eat, as you submit to the most basic demands of nature. This heartfelt prayer will prove to be a formula of salvation for you. Not only will it protect you from all attacks of the Dark One, it will also purify you from the stain of all worldly sin and lead you to the contemplation of the unseen and the heavenly and to that fiery urgency of prayer that is indescribable."

The best advice given to a Christian mystic is St. Paul's in 1 Thessalonians 5:17: "Pray without ceasing." Keeping up a constant stream of mantra in your heart will transform your life, and if you persist, make you conscious of the Cosmic Christ within and without you at all times and give you an almost miraculous fearlessness in the face of extreme suffering or evil. Through the steady and tireless practice of the mantra, your entire consciousness will become fragrant with divine love. As Isaac the Syrian wrote: "When the Spirit takes its dwelling place in a man he does not cease to pray, because the Spirit will constantly pray in him. Then, neither when he sleeps, will prayer be cut off from his soul; but when he eats and drinks, when he lies down, and when he does any work, even when he is immersed in sleep, the perfumes of prayer will breathe in his heart spontaneously."

Saying the Name of Jesus in the Heart

Whatever ye shall ask of the Father in my name, He will give it to you.

JOHN 16:23

We should always be turning the name of Jesus around the spaces of our heart as lightning circles round the skies before rain.

HESYCHIUS OF JERUSALEM

This second practice builds on everything we have learned from building a solid and luminous practice of the mantra. In this practice, we concentrate entirely on saying the name of Jesus in the depth of the heart, that name that is, as St. Bernard of Clairvaux says, "honey in the mouth, music in the ear, a shout of gladness in the heart."

It is important to understand exactly what is meant by the heart in spiritual practice. When people in the West today speak of the heart, they normally mean the emotions and affections. However, in the Bible and in mystical practice, the heart has a vaster meaning. In this context, the heart is the primary organ of a person's being, whether physical or spiritual; it is the center of life, the determining principle of all our activities and aspirations. It includes the affections and emotions but also much else besides; it embraces everything that goes to comprise and create what we call a "person."

This is how the great Orthodox mystic of the fourth century St. Makarios describes this "heart": "The heart governs and reigns over the whole bodily organism . . . and when grace possesses the ranges of the heart, it rules over all the members and the thoughts. For there in the heart is the mind, and all the thoughts of the soul and its expectation; and in this way grace penetrates also to all the members of the body . . . Within the heart there are unfathomable depths. There are reception rooms and bedchambers in it, doors and porches, and many offices and passages. In it is the workshop of righteousness and of wickedness. In it is death; in it is life . . . The heart is Christ's palace; there Christ the King comes to take his rest, with the angels and the spirits of the saints, and he dwells there, walking within it and placing his Kingdom there."

As Theophane the Recluse, a great nineteenth-century Russian Orthodox master of prayer, tells us: "The heart is the innermost man or spirit, here are located self-awareness, the conscience, the idea of God and of one's complete dependence on him and all the spiritual treasures of the spiritual life." This "heart," then, is equivalent to man's spirit; it signifies the core or apex of our being, what the Flemish mystics—especially Ruysbroeck—call the "ground of the soul." It is here, in the "heart," that the human being comes face-to-face with God.

Other major mystical paths also recognize the exalted primacy of the heart in mystical experience. In the Hindu and Buddhist Chakra system, the heart-center—the Anahata—is the center of the psycho-spiritual being, the "chakra" or "center" that has to be opened for the being to know direct connection with the divine; it is in the "cave of the heart" (the "Hiranya-garbha") that the entire universe is said to be contained, alive and blazing in divine light. The heart, then, is the site of ultimate human divine realization, the place where transcendence and immanence meet in unity.

The same central significance is given to the heart in the Islamic mystical systems; Mohammed is reported as saying in one of his most important "hadiths," "The heart of the believer is the place of the revelation of God. The heart of the believer is the throne of God. The heart of the believer is the mirror of God." In another "hadith," Mohammed is reported as claiming that God told him, "I cannot fit into my heavens or into my earth but I fit into the heart of my believing servant." In his great mystical epic *Mathnawi*, the Persian poet tells us, "The mirror of the heart is limitless . . . Here, all understanding falls silent . . . for the Heart is with God or rather the Heart is God. . . . The reflection of each image shines out of the heart alone, as much in the many as in the One beyond it . . . polish the heart ceaselessly and you will soar above the color and perfume; you will contemplate Beauty ceaselessly; you will abandon the form and rind of consciousness and unfurl the flag of certainty."

Nothing is more important on the path to Christhood than awakening this vast heart, opening it to God, and keeping it open. Over the centuries, one of the most powerful ways of doing this has been simply to repeat in the heart-center the name of Jesus. Saint Catherine of Genoa was told by Jesus himself at the time of her conversion to "take the word Jesus from the

Hail Mary: May it be implanted in your heart and it will be a sweet guide and shield to you in all the necessities of life." When Catherine was comforting patients in the hospital she ran in Genoa, she would always urge them to "call Jesus, for there is no more powerful way of securing divine aid."

In every mystical tradition the divine name has transforming power, and its invocation is considered one of the supreme forms of the worship of God. Hindu mystics practice "japa"—the repetition of the name of God or Krishna or Durga or Shiva—in the heart to awaken their divine identity and drench their entire being with devotion; Sufi mystics in "dhikr" (remembrance of the name of God) repeat the holy names of Allah to be able to enter into ecstasy and the glory, or "Kibriya," of the presence. The Jews of the Old Testament had an overwhelming reverence for the name of God—the Tetragrammaton. According to later Rabbinic traditions, this reverence became so final that no one was allowed to pronounce the name aloud. Some Jewish sages even wrote that the contemplation of the letters of the name was sufficient to flood the whole being with sacred power.

For the Christian mystic, the holiest and most powerful of all divine names is that of Jesus himself. Those who have practiced saying the name of Jesus over and over again in the heart have come to experience directly that all the attributes, powers, passions, and graces of the living Christ flame out from the name as rays of light from a central sun. As Richard Crawshaw, a great English mystical poet of the seventeenth century, writes in his "Hymn to the name above every name, the name of Jesus":

> I sing the Name which none can say
> But toucht with an interior Ray;
> The Name of our New Peace; our Good;
> Our bliss; and Supernatural Blood:
> The Name of all our Lives and Loves . . .
> Sweet Name, in Thy each syllable
> A thousand Blest Arabias dwell:
> A thousand hills of Frankincense:
> Mountains of myrrh, and beds and spices,
> And ten thousand paradises . . .
> Happy he who has the art
> To awake them
> And to take them
> Home, and lodge them in his Heart.

For Crawshaw, and other mystics of the Name, repetition of the name of Jesus has the power to awaken the whole being to spiritual ecstasy and to immerse the entire self in the living truth of the Cosmic Christ.

The best way to learn the "art" of saying the name of Jesus is to practice it in two half-hour daily periods. Before you begin the practice, prepare yourself by reading a passage from the Gospels about Jesus or a poem in which his mystical beauty and power is celebrated. Don't begin the actual practice until you begin to feel a current of love for Jesus awaken in your heart.

To make the practice itself as rich as possible, the mystics suggest to us that each time we say the name of Jesus we try to imagine with all our might another of his sacred powers or attributes. Don't repeat the Name casually or hurriedly; say it once, slowly, concentrate entirely on whatever spiritual quality of Jesus you want to celebrate or invoke for yourself; only when you are satisfied that you have contemplated the quality or attribute you have chosen as richly as possible, and invoked it as deeply as possible into yourself, should you move on. Done in this way, the periods of practice of the Name become periods of passionate, inward contemplation of the nature of Christ-consciousness and sustained invocation of the radiance, tenderness, majesty, and intensity of the Christ-consciousness into every part of our being.

Just as when you practice the mantra, you should try to keep saying the Name as often as possible during the day, in all activities and circumstances. If you persist with this, a great secret will slowly become clear to you; the "Jesus" the heart is invoking and contemplating is also its own essential Christ-nature; its own essential enlightened fire-mind. Calling out the Cosmic Christ "without" awakens the Cosmic Christ "within."

In the later stages of the practice, you may also feel this Christ-presence directly—either as light, or as a warmth around the heart, or as a "sound" in the atmosphere surrounding you (a sound that is like the whirring of bees or the high-pitched soft buzz of telephone wires and which is known as the "Shabd" in Hindu mysticism). Do not dwell too much on these beautiful phenomena; they are meant as encouragements to go ever-deeper into the Christ-presence and not as ends in themselves.

As you come to end the practice, imagine the name of Jesus as a vast diamond of fiery white light with you at its center entirely illumined by its radiance. Send the light of the Name with great humility and love in all four directions to heal and transform all human beings, and to transform the whole earth into the Kingdom.

Saying the Jesus Prayer

⊠ ⊠ ⊠

The practitioner who has faithfully developed a strong mantra practice and begun to intuit through the practice of the Name the ecstatic depth of what is possible when, in Theophane the Recluse's words, "you stand with the mind in the heart before God," is now ready to undertake one of the most sublime of all mystical adventures—the saying of the Jesus Prayer: "Lord Jesus Christ, Son of God, have mercy on me." (Sometimes the words "a sinner" are added on the end.)

The roots of the Jesus Prayer extend far back to the ancient Jewish reverence for the name of God, and to two prayers that are reported in the Gospels: that of the blind man, "Jesus, Son of David, have mercy on me" and that of the publican, "God, be merciful to me a sinner." In Christian usage, "Son of David" became "Son of God" when the prayer developed its present form, probably in fourth-century Egypt. The first full text we have of the Jesus Prayer dates from the sixth- or seventh-century *Life of Abba Philemon,* an Egyptian hermit. From the sixth century onwards, there has been an unbroken tradition of saying the Jesus Prayer known as "Hesychasm."

It is Orthodox Christian mystics who have given us the greatest testimonies to the power of the Jesus prayer. Hesychius of Jerusalem wrote of it in the fourteenth century: "Truly blessed is he who cleaves with his thought to the Prayer of Jesus, constantly calling to him in his heart, just as air cleaves to our bodies or the flame to the candle. The sun, passing over the earth, produces daylight; the holy and worshipful Name of the Lord Jesus shining in the mind produces a measureless number of sun-like thoughts." The anonymous nineteenth-century Orthodox monk who wrote *The Way of a Pilgrim* wrote that when he practiced the Jesus Prayer "everything around me seemed delightful and marvelous. The trees, the birds, the earth, the air, the light seemed to be telling me that they existed for man's sake, that they witnessed to the love of God for man, that everything proved the love of God for man, that all things prayed to God and sang his praise . . . the prayer of my heart gave me such consolation that I felt there was no happier person on earth than I and I doubted if there could be any greater and fuller happiness in the Kingdom of heaven . . . Everything drew me to love and thank God: people, trees, plants, animals. I saw them all as my kinsfolk. I found in all of them the magic of the Name of Jesus."

Timothy Ware tells us in his magisterial introduction to *The Art of Prayer: An Orthodox Anthology* how to practice this all-powerful prayer:

The general division of prayer into three degrees—of lips, of the mind, and of the heart—applies also to the Jesus Prayer:

1. To begin with, the Jesus Prayer is an oral prayer like any other; the words are prayed aloud by the voice, or at least formed silently by the lips and the tongue. At the same time by a deliberate act of will the attention must be concentrated on the meaning of the Prayer. During this initial stage, the attentive repetition of the Prayer often proves a hard and exhausting task, calling for humble persistence.

2. In course of time the Prayer becomes more inward, and the mind repeats it without any outward movement of lips or tongue. With this increasing inwardness, the concentration of the attention also becomes easier. The Prayer gradually acquires a rhythm of its own, at times singing within us almost spontaneously, without any conscious act of will on our part. As Staretz Pathenii put it, we have within us "a small murmuring stream." All this is a sign that a man is now approaching the third stage.

3. Finally the Prayer enters into the heart, dominating the entire personality. Its rhythm is identified more and more with the movement of the heart, until finally it becomes unceasing. What originally required painful and strenuous effort is now an inexhaustible source of peace and joy.

Our practice of the Jesus Prayer should respect these three stages. Initially, then—for the first ten days of the month we assign to it—we should concentrate on saying the Jesus Prayer calmly, reverentially, out loud, meditating on the meaning of each word and on the way it unites two essential movements of Christian devotion: adoration and repentance. Adoration is expressed in the opening phrase, "Lord Jesus Christ, Son of God." Repentance is in the prayer for mercy that follows: "Have mercy on me." The prayer is at once an act of thanksgiving for the transformation that the Christ brings, an expression of grief at human limitation, and a call for its transmutation into Christ-consciousness through grace.

During this initial stage, do not let contemplation on the Jesus Prayer distract you from just saying it out loud as simply as possible. Before beginning the Prayer, establish peace within yourself and ask for the inspiration of the Holy Spirit, then simply begin. As Theophane the Recluse tells us, "The practice of the Jesus Prayer is simple . . . Standing with the consciousness and attention in the heart, cry out unceasingly: 'Lord Jesus Christ, Son of God, have mercy upon me.' Without having in your mind any visual concept or image, believing that the Lord sees you and listens to you."

During this first period of ten days, allow the recitation of the Jesus Prayer to become nonverbal and inward during moments of the day. Recite it inwardly during the activities and chores of the day. Do not force or strain; just repeat it within the heart.

This will prepare you for the second period of ten days in the month when the recitation of the Jesus Prayer will be entirely inward. During this time, pay special attention to the posture recommended by the Hesychast tradition: head bowed, chin resting on the chest, eyes fixed on the place of the heart. Again, don't strain. If you say the Prayer with this posture, however, you will find it easier to "drive" its awareness into the heart-center, easier to put the "mind" into the "heart," and easier, too, to "feel" the fire of love in the heart. Some Hesychasts recommend that you try to synchronize the prayer with your in-breaths and out-breaths; this can be dangerous without expert guidance and can also come to be a distraction from the actual "work" of the Prayer, which is permeating the entire being with the "perfume" of Christ-consciousness.

If the practice of the Prayer has been ardent and devoted, then in the last ten days of the month, just allow the Prayer to be repeated in the heart, as far as possible, during the set periods of practice and throughout the day. Do not worry if at moments the Prayer does not seem to be "going on." Unceasing prayer in the heart is a high stage of spiritual practice, and can require many months, usually years, of preparation. Just wait in reverent, calm silence, and you will find that the Prayer will begin again inside you, gathering all your powers into its circles of holy fire.

"What shall we say of this divine prayer?" asks the fifteenth-century Orthodox mystic St. Simeon of Thessalonica. "It is a prayer and a vow and a confession of faith, conferring upon us the Holy Spirit and divine gifts, cleansing the heart, driving out devils. It is the indwelling presence of Jesus Christ within us, and a fountain of spiritual reflections and divine thoughts. It is remission of sins, healing of soul and body, and shining of divine illumination; it is a well of God's mercy, bestowing upon the humble revelations and initiation into the mysteries of God."

Those who practice the Jesus Prayer humbly, indefatigably, with the full fervor of devotion and the full concentration of the mind in the heart, come to know the precise truth of all St. Simeon's claims. It is an extremely powerful way of always remembering the presence and always invoking its subtle fire. As Theophane the Recluse instructs all those who would use it on the Christ-path: "Delve deeply into the Jesus Prayer, with all the power that you possess. It will draw you together, giving you a sense of power and strength in the Lord, and will result in you being with him constantly whether alone or with other people, when you do housework and when you read or pray." And he adds, "Only you must attribute the power of this prayer, not to the repetition of certain words, but to the turning of the mind and heart towards the Lord in these words to the *action* accompanying the speech" (my italics). It is this *action* of turning the entire being constantly during the recitation of the Prayer to God that floods the whole being with grace and turns the "words" of the Jesus Prayer into instruments the Christ uses to turn us into him.

As Theophane the Recluse also reminds us, "The path to achievement of a systematic interior order is very hard but is possible to preserve this (or a similar) state of mind during the various and inevitable duties you have to perform; and what makes this possible is the Jesus Prayer when it is grafted in the heart. How can it be so grafted? Who knows? But it does happen. He who strives is increasingly conscious of this engrafting, without knowing how it occurs. Remain always in the presence of God, repeating the Jesus Prayer as frequently as possible."

PRACTICE NUMBER 4

The Practice of Centering Prayer

▦ ▦ ▦

Remembering all that has been learned so far of the nature of prayer, and of the necessity of "standing before God" with the "mind in the heart," let us now practice "centering" prayer in the two daily half-hour periods we have set apart for spiritual exercises.

This practice is designed to open the practitioner to the healing power or "contemplative" union with the Christ. At the beginning of the practice of centering prayer, sit comfortably and close your eyes, focusing your being wholly inward. Now choose one sacred word on which to direct your entire attention. Examples of words you might choose are Presence, Trust, Adoration, Divine, Love, Hope, Faith.

As Thomas Keating explains this form of prayer in *Open Mind, Open Heart*, the word you choose is sacred because it is the symbol of your intention to open yourself to the mystery of God's presence beyond thoughts, images, and emotions. It is not chosen for its content but for its intent. It is merely a pointer that expresses the direction of your inward movement toward the presence of God.

At the start of the practice of centering prayer, Keating says, "Introduce the sacred word you have chosen in your imagination as gently as if you were laying a feather on a piece of absorbent cotton." Then, keep thinking the sacred word in whatever way or form it arises. Unlike mantra practice or the Jesus Prayer, do not repeat the word continuously. The word can stop having any real meaning for you, or even vanish altogether from consciousness; don't grasp it or run after it. Accept it in whatever form it arises and relax any form of rigid desire for control.

Whenever during the practice you become aware you are thinking some other thought, return to the sacred word you have chosen as the expression of your decision to stay open to the Christ. What makes this form of prayer effective is not how clearly you say the sacred word or how often, but how tenderly and delicately you slip it into your imagination in the beginning of the practice and how quickly you return to it whenever you become caught in another thought or emotion.

Inevitably, thoughts and emotions will arise, sometimes in a distracting and insistent way. Just have the calm, unhurried courage to return again and again to the sacred word you have chosen. The more you allow thoughts and emotions to arise and pass, the more you will grow aware of the "gaps" of silence between them and of the luminous force and presence of that silence.

The more you do this practice, the more deeply you will experience this silence and the divine presence in it. The process of "centering" will be complete when you pass beyond the word you have chosen into pure awareness. When this starts to happen, let it; don't panic or imagine that you are not doing the practice "properly." To come into this silence beyond and above thought, which is the silence of the heart and of the Christ, is the goal of this form of prayer and its grace. As Thomas Keating writes, "What we are doing as we sit in centering prayer . . . is going beyond the sacred word into union with that to which it points—the Ultimate Mystery, the Presence of God, beyond any perception that we can form of him."

Keating defines five types of thoughts that might arise during centering prayer and suggests different approaches toward them.

The first type of thoughts he calls "the wool gathering of the imagination." These are the thoughts that the imagination just grinds out "because of its natural propensity for perpetual motion." Just accept these and pay as little attention to them as possible.

The second kind of thoughts Keating calls "thoughts with an emotional attraction to them." This is the kind of thought that calls for some kind of inner reaction. Just return to the sacred word gently and don't get angry with yourself for being diverted.

The third group of thoughts that Keating defines are "insight and psychological breakthroughs." What appear to be brilliant insights or psychological or theological breakthroughs may try to divert you from your essential task of keeping contemplatively open to the Christ. Do not under any circumstances pause to "follow" them; this kind of centering prayer demands a kind of ascesis, a fasting of the mind of its addictions, whether to habitual emotions or to any form of delight in its own perceptions. This "fasting," if done purposefully and with tactful skill, will open the practitioner to ever-deeper levels of silence, the silence of authentic presence that waits beyond all images, concepts, and "insights."

Keating's fourth kind of thoughts that may arise are what he calls "self-reflection": "As you settle into deep peace and freedom from particular thoughts, a desire to reflect on what is happening may arise." Such reflection immediately cuts you off from the presence; let it go and dive deeper into silence.

Keating informs us: "The tendency to reflect is one of the hardest things to handle in contemplative prayer. We want to savor the moment of pure joy, pure experience, pure awareness. We want to reflect on moments of deep peace or union in order to remember how we got there and thus how to get back." His advice? "Let this temptation go by and return to the sacred word . . . You will pass to a new level of freedom, a more refined joy." He reminds us that "the Presence of God does not respond to greed. It is totally available, but on condition that we accept it freely and do not try to possess it."

The fifth type of potentially disruptive thoughts that may arise during centering meditation Keating calls "interior purification." Any form of powerful meditation that transcends thinking sets off a process of dynamic purification: frightening thoughts and emotions and even long-suppressed traumatic memories may arise. The best way to handle these "eruptions" is not to attempt to deny or suppress them but to return gently to the sacred word.

Such "arisings" or "eruptions" of thoughts and emotions are not harmful, or "failures." In fact, they represent the bringing into consciousness of thoughts and drives and memories we need to claim and understand. As Keating says, "Through this process [of centering prayer] the undigested psychological material of a lifetime is gradually evacuated, the emotional investment of early childhood in programs for happiness based on instinctual drives is dismantled, and the false self gives way to the true self."

At the end of your practice period, dedicate all of the effects of your prayer to the illumination of all human beings and to the coming of the Kingdom on earth.

The practice of centering prayer reveals its power and great healing beauty only to those who persist in it. Do not be alarmed if at the beginning you find it hard, or frustrating, to keep returning to the word you have chosen, and try not to be surprised if, as your practice deepens, increasingly disturbing thoughts or turbulent emotions arise. Such "arising," as Keating has described, is part of the vast inner cleaning of the mind and heart that this practice makes possible, and is a sign that it is doing its work.

Just practice twice daily, steadily, with firm faith, and you will begin to experience at ever-greater depths the wonder of the silence of the Christ and of your own soul.

The Practice of Inner Conversation with Christ (or Mental Prayer)

▣ ▣ ▣

Nothing is more important on the Christ-path than developing as quickly and as profoundly as possible a living direct and unmediated intimacy with the Christ, a passionate friendship of the heart that can be called and relied on in all circumstances and conditions.

One of the most powerful ways of developing this passionate friendship of the heart is through the steady practice of what is known as "mental prayer"—which is, in essence, the use of inspiring scenes or events from Christ's life to arouse the spiritual imagination and to focus the will so that, awoken by love, we can speak to the Christ within and around us with spontaneous naturalness. The rewards of such a discipline—as many mystics down the centuries have told us—are extraordinary. Teresa of Avila, for instance, writes in her autobiography about a certain lukewarm period in her spiritual life: "I wish I could obtain leave to declare the many times I failed during this period in my obligation to God because I was not supported by the strong pillar of mental prayer."

Another great seventeenth-century Spanish mystic, Peter of Alcantara, writes: "In mental prayer, the soul is purified from its sins, nourished with charity, continued in faith, strengthened in hope; the mind expands, the affections dilate, the heart is purified, truth becomes real and obvious, temptation is conquered, sadness banished, the senses are made new, drooping powers revive, lukewarmness ends, the rust of vices is wiped clean. Out of mental prayer comes, like living sparks, those desires of heaven which the soul engenders when enflamed with the fire of Divine Love. The excellence of mental prayer is a sublime one, great are its privileges: to mental prayer heaven is opened; to mental prayer heavenly secrets are manifested and the ear of God is always attentive."

Very few of even the greatest saints find mental prayer easy at first. Distractions are normal, to be expected, and nothing to be ashamed of. We will need real persistence and courage if we are to continue and succeed. But success is certain to the determined. As Teresa of Avila says, "Besides the courage which we ought to have in the combat of mental prayer, we must also be firmly convinced that, unless we allow ourselves to be vanquished, our efforts will be crowned with joy."

The method of mental prayer that I and countless others have found most useful is one derived from Teresa of Avila's own practice. It has five simple stages and can easily be practiced twice a day in half-hour periods.

The first stage is known as "preparation." It is hard to begin an internal reconstruction or reimagination of a scene or incident from Christ's life without inspiring yourself. What I suggest you do to prepare your heart and mind for the conversation with Christ that is to come is to read a passage from a favorite mystic (or one of the passages I have given in Section Two of this part of the book). Sometimes it helps, too, to say the name of Jesus or the Jesus Prayer slowly and intensely—or to look at an image of Christ with your heart full of love.

When your mind is calm and your heart open you enter the second stage, which is the "preparation of the material." In this stage, you choose the scene you wish to imagine Christ in. Reread the scene slowly and with deep concentration in one or more of the Gospels, letting your imagination enter fully all the aspects of its drama. I almost always follow Saint Teresa of Avila's advice and choose a scene from the Passion to contemplate: I find this the clearest and most inescapable way of opening myself to the depths of Christ's love and to the depths of the love he is trying to birth in me. Saint Teresa's favorite topic of contemplations, we will see, was Christ being scourged at the pillar. I most often contemplate Christ in the Garden of Gethsemane, or Christ on the cross.

The secret of stage three, which now begins, and is known as "consideration of the scene," is to imagine yourself present, directly present, at the scene you have chosen. If you have chosen to imagine Christ being scourged, place yourself unflinchingly by his side and share his torment. If you have chosen to accompany Christ into the heart of the Agony in the Garden, try with all your powers of love and grief to experience with him his desolation and world-weariness. It helps immensely in this stage of "consideration" to ask yourself, as Saint Teresa recommends, some elementary questions: Why is Christ in this scene? What is he feeling? What does his feeling mean to me? How could my allowing myself to feel it transform my vision of Christ and so my life?

As you imagine the scene you have chosen, ask yourself questions like these and try, with intense concentration, to summon all the things you have learned or felt in the past about the event you are contemplating, so all your knowledge and feelings can be concentrated like a laser on the present moment. If you persevere, you will find that your imagination will cooperate with your will and will start presenting to you simple, blazing images, which will fire open your heart. When your heart is on fire with love, enter quickly the next and fourth stage of the practice.

This fourth stage is the whole point of the practice, its goal, its core, and its revelation. This is the stage known as "conversation," in which you talk out of the depths of your imaginative participation in the scene you have chosen with the living Christ. It is essential that in this stage you speak naturally and fearlessly. Teresa of Avila tells us; "With regard to the habit of speaking with your Divine Spouse, be confident that he will suggest to your heart what to say. You are not embarrassed when you speak to his creatures, why should words fail you when you wish to speak with your God? . . . The soul can picture itself in the presence of Christ and accustom itself to becoming enkindled with great love for his sacred humanity . . . ask him for the things it has need of, make complaints to him of its trials, rejoice with him in its joys . . . It has no need to think out set prayers but can use just such words as suit its desires and needs."

Let us listen to Saint Teresa herself as she reduces these principles to practice and gives us, in *The Way of Perfection,* a searing glimpse into her own inner conversation with the Christ scourged at the pillar: "Consider him bound to the pillar, become the Man of Sorrows, all his flesh torn to pieces, enduring this torture for the love he bears you; persecuted by some, covered with spittle by others, forsaken and abandoned by his friends, having nobody to take his part, shivering with cold, and reduced to such absolute solitude that you can, alone and without witnesses, come and mingle your sorrows with his, and console one another . . . Your heart will melt in tenderness in gazing on this state of your soul's Divine Husband, and if, not satisfied with looking upon him you feel inwardly moved to talk with him, do it; but be certain you do not use any studied language, but only simple words dictated by your heart; they are the most precious to him."

Then, in a wonderful passage, Saint Teresa goes on to expose the naked depths of her own inner conversation with Christ. The "simple words" her heart says "are the most precious to him": "O Lord of the world, and true spouse of my soul, you may say to him, how comes it that You are reduced to such extremity! O my Saviour and my God, how is it that you do not disdain the company of so poor a creature as I, and that I can be of any consolation to you; for it seems to me that I read upon your face that you are consoled in seeing me near you? How can it be, Lord, that the angels abandon you and that even your Divine Father does not console you? Since it is so, my beloved Master, and since you have submitted to this extreme suffering for love of me, what is this little that I suffer and of what can I complain? Shattered at seeing you in this horrible torment, I am resolved from this moment, beloved Master, to suffer all the tribulations that can rain down on me, and consider them as treasures in order to imitate you in something. Let us then proceed together, O Lord; I desire to follow you everywhere you go and pass through all that You pass through" (*The Way of Perfection,* chapter 26).

I quote Teresa of Avila here at length to show the different stages an authentic "conversation" can encompass. In her "conversation," Teresa moves, with the Christ scourged at the pillar, as we have seen, from grief at Christ's pain to amazement that her inner presence beside him can give him comfort; she then experiences grief at his aloneness, which leads to renewed wonder at the depth of Christ's divine love for her and for all beings; out of this wonder rises a resolution to suffer everything for and in Christ with Christ's own surrender to love and sublime beauty of soul. This interior movement, mapped out so simply and fervently by Teresa of Avila, shows us clearly, I think, how conversation with Christ can lead to a passion to become like Christ, to follow in Christ's footsteps of unconditional love and so be "Christed" in and with him.

There are times when we arrive at the fourth stage of this practice—the stage of "conversation"—that we feel so overwhelmed by the intensity or majesty of what we are contemplating that we can find nothing to say. We should not worry; we should fall silent and let the beauty or pathos of Christ inspire us. Sometimes the love for Christ that the practice evokes will become so intense that it leads us naturally into the silence of wonder or contemplation; if this is the case, rest in this wonderful silence and then speak from it simply, with tenderness. Subtle miracles of inner transformation take place every time you engage seriously with this practice of conversation; it is always wise to let the spirit find its own pace and rhythms.

The fifth stage—the "conclusion"—is a stage of profound thanksgiving. With your entire being, give thanks to God and the Christ that you can have such intimate and final contact with Jesus. Then, with no shame or fear, note where you wandered off during the practice or what blocks you encountered in attempting to open your heart to Christ and resolve to do better next time, so your practice of mental prayer can go on getting richer.

Finally, with joy, offer up all the sacred emotions and perceptions that have come to you during the practice to the redemption of humanity and the establishment of the Kingdom on earth.

Saying the Our Father

▨ ▨ ▨

The version of the Our Father that I have used from my childhood is that of the Old English Prayerbook, and is remarkable, I think, for its linguistic beauty and reverent rhythm. "Our Father, which art in heaven, hallowed be thy name, thy Kingdom come, thy will be done on earth as it is in heaven; Give us today our daily bread and forgive us our trespasses as we forgive those that trespass against us. Lead us not into temptation but deliver us from evil. For thine is the Kingdom, the power, and the glory, forever and ever. Amen."

There are other versions in use, of course, with slight variations. Employ whichever is most familiar to you, or the one you have come to love most. The Our Father is the one prayer Jesus gave humankind and so has a unique sacred significance for all those who take the Christ-path. As Louis Marie Grignion de Montfort writes in *The Secret of the Rosary,* "The beautiful order, the tender forcefulness and the clarity of this divine prayer pay tribute to our Divine Master's wisdom . . . The Our Father contains all the duties we owe to God, the acts of all the virtues and the petitions for all our spiritual and corporal needs."

Tertullian wrote that the Our Father was a summary of the New Testament. Teresa of Avila devotes the last chapters of her *Way of Perfection* to a moving mystical interpretation of the Our Father. In them, she writes, "Jesus taught it to each one of us and he is still teaching it; it is the central prayer. In so few words all contemplation and all perfection are enclosed."

Jesus did not only give us this prayer to use daily; he also taught us how to pray it. In Matthew 6:5–8, he tells us, "And when thou prayest, thou shalt not be as the hypocrites are; for they love to pray standing in the synagogues and in the corners of the streets, that they may be seen of men. Verily, I say unto you, they have their reward. But thou, when thou prayest, enter into thy closet, and when thou hast shut thy door, pray to thy Father which is in secret; and thy Father which seeth in secret shall reward thee openly. But when ye pray, use not vain repetitions, as the heathen do; for they think they shall be heard for their much speaking; be ye not therefore like unto them; for your Father knowth what things ye have need of before ye ask him."

Jesus' instructions are characteristically direct and clear; he tells us the Our Father is too sacred a prayer to be said in any way but intimately, in recollected privacy, with simple, unrepetitive concentration, and in trust that the Father hears and understands everything.

Before you start to practice the Our Father in the two half-hour periods I have suggested, prepare yourself. Origen tells us in his treatise *On Prayer,* "A person who is about to come to prayer should withdraw for a little, and so become more attentive and active . . . He should cast away all temptation and troubling thoughts and remind himself as far as he is able of the majesty whom he approaches, and that it is unholy to approach him carelessly, sluggishly, and disdainfully." So, as you prepare yourself to say the Our Father, recollect yourself, calm your mind, open your heart, and remember with humble wonder the glory and majesty of the one you will be speaking to.

Your actual recitation of the Our Father—whether you say it out loud or in the heart—should be as slow and concentrated as possible. Don't go on to the next phrase before you have thoroughly explored and savored the preceding one; if you find yourself rushing or skimping in intensity of concentration, have the humility to go back to the beginning of the prayer and start again. In this way, you will gradually school yourself in how to say the Our Father with unbroken attention, and an ever-deepening understanding of its infinite spiritual depths will result. Saint Teresa tells us in *The Way of Perfection* that if, in your practice period, you only say seven or eight complete Our Fathers, that will be enough; it will show, in fact, that you are truly meditating with all your powers on the meanings the prayer constantly evokes in your heart.

Teresa of Avila also gives us another crucial—and sublime—piece of advice. She tells us when we say the Our Father always to imagine "being beside Jesus as you say the prayer and saying it with him." All those who follow her instructions have found that praying the Our Father in this way takes them deep into the mystery of the Christ. As Teresa of Avila tells us, "Imagine the Lord near you and see with what love, what humility he instructs you. Believe me, separate yourself as little as you can from so wonderful a friend. If you take up the habit of keeping Jesus near you, if he sees that you are acting in this way out of love and that you are making efforts to please him . . . he will never abandon you, he will help you in all difficulties, you will find him everywhere."

Imagining with all your powers Jesus present beside you while you say the words of the Our Father gives great mystical intensity to your prayer. If you persist in this way, humbly, day after day, you will find that many unexpected insights and revelations will be given to you, and that your entire being will be flooded with the joy of Jesus' love and wisdom. You will find yourself being drawn deeper into the mystery of communion that Jesus describes in John 17:22–23: "And the glory which thou gavest me I have given them; that they may be one, even as we are one: I in them, and thou in me, that they may be perfect in one."

What I want to offer now is a few pointers on how to meditate on each phrase of the prayer culled from my own inner experience and from my reading of the great commentaries on the Our Father by Origen in his *Treatise on Prayer,* Teresa of Avila in her *Way of Perfection,* and Louis Marie Grignion de Montfort in his *Secret of the Rosary.*

Let me begin with the first two words of the prayer: "Our Father." Notice that the prayer begins not with a personal possessive, "My Father," but with the all-inclusive "Our." From the beginning of the prayer, then, you are acknowledging your interdependence with every other human being and every sentient creature in creation: you are acknowledging being one of millions of children of the all-loving Father, and you are implicitly praying not just for yourself but in unity with, and for, all beings.

So, as you offer yourself up to the Father at the beginning of the prayer, silently imagine that you offer also all other human beings and creatures to his transforming love. Begin the prayer in this way, and you will be praying it not merely as an individual soul in search of awakening but as a voice of the whole creation calling for its transfiguration in God.

When you say the word "Father," remember that Jesus called the Father "Abba," Aramaic for "Daddy." The whole prayer, then, is being said not to a stern, withdrawn Jehovah but to a forgiving, intimate Abba, who wants only your deepest good. You are saying the Our Father with and in Jesus to the source that he knew as—and wants you to know as—infinitely benign. Allow this knowledge to fill your spirit with tender faith and an unshakable confidence that what you are asking for will be granted to you—and to the whole creation through you—by a Father who is as extravagantly loving as the father in the parable of the Prodigal Son.

Allow the full mystery and beauty of the first two words of the prayer to expand in you before you continue. When you recite the next phrase "Which art in heaven," never imagine the Father in some ethereal other-where. The Father's glory and the Father's Kingdom are all around us and in us: everything in the creation is on fire with the Father's love. Teresa of Avila tells us that the heaven that is meant here is the heaven of the soul, where God is always present. She writes, "You know already that God is everywhere. Well, where the King is, the court is, that is obvious. Where God is, there is heaven. It is an indisputable truth that where the Divine Majesty is, there is all his glory. Saint Augustine reports you are aware that he looked for the Lord in many places but he found him at last in himself. Don't you think it would be some small advantage for a soul spread out everywhere to know this truth, to know that she does not need to go up to heaven to talk to her Eternal Father and experience all delight by his side, that she doesn't even have to raise her voice to speak to him? However quietly she murmurs, he will hear it, he is so close to her." She adds, "If I had understood as I do now how so great a King lives in this small palace of my soul, it seems to me I wouldn't have left it so often alone."

When you say, then, "Our Father, which art in heaven," try to gather your whole being into the "small palace of your soul" and feel the living presence that is always there; this divine joy and peace within you is the "heaven" where the Father is and reigns forever.

Going on to recite "Hallowed be thy name" in the atmosphere of this joy and peace will allow the full sacred splendor of the name of God to permeate your being. To really *mean* the words "hallowed be thy name," as Origen points out, means praying with your whole being that "the Kingdom of God may spring up in you, bear fruit and be rightly perfected." "The perfection of the hallowing of God's name and the perfect establishment of His Kingdom," he writes, "is not possible unless there also comes the perfection of knowledge of wisdom and of the other virtues." Praying for the Father's name to be sanctified and held sacred is praying to become the vessel of such a sanctification, so that, in Origen's beautiful words, "the Lord may walk about in you as in a spiritual garden."

To pray "Hallowed be thy name" is also to pray that the entire world become a place where the name of the Father is held sacred and to pray for all human hearts to be awakened as fast and as fully as possible to their source in the heart of light, the Father-Mother. Only through such a massive awakening can the planet now be preserved: only through such a "hallowing" of the name of Father can the Christ be born in each of us, through adoration and service and a continuing revelation of wisdom.

Now, as if prompted by the voice of this inner Christ, say, "Thy Kingdom come, thy will be done on earth as it is in heaven." The profoundest mystical meaning of this passage is that it is a plea to the divine to establish the full glory of the Kingdom in you and in the actual conditions of the world around you. In the Our Father, Jesus was praying—and is always praying—not merely for a personal transformation but also one that embraces the conditions of earth-life.

As you say these words, then, pledge yourself to a surrender to God's will and to the laws of Christing that will turn you into an instrument of love on earth: pray with all your heart and mind and soul for the establishment of justice on earth in every arena, for as Origen says, "Each member of the church must pray that he may make way for the Father: will intuit the same way that Christ made way for it . . . For it is possible for one united to him to become one spirit with him . . . so making way for his will so that as it has been perfected in heaven it may be so perfected on earth." He adds, "Let us ask that the will of God be fulfilled on earth as it is in heaven . . . so that we may, so to speak, make earth heaven, with the result that there will no longer be any earth, but all will become heaven. For if the will of God is done on earth as it is in heaven . . . the earth does not remain earth . . . we shall all be 'heaven.' "

Saying this part of the prayer in this way will initiate you progressively into one of the central secrets of Christ-consciousness: in Christing yourself, you come to act as an agent of transformation on earth, a humble revolutionary of love, an instrument of that divine will that hungers and labors for the establishment of the Kingdom in time.

Pray, then, as you say "thy will be done on earth as it is in heaven" for the preservation of the environment, the great opening of the heart that will lead to the elimination of all hierarchies and elites that keep billions poor and the whole planet enslaved to various fantasies of greed and power. As you pray, do not simply ask God to transform existing conditions; offer yourself up as an instrument and agent of the great birth, pledge yourself inwardly to plunge into action for love and in love in all the arenas of life. Don't pray vaguely: each time you recite the Our Father and come to this part of the prayer, make a particular concrete resolution to act for justice in the world, a resolution based in the facts of your everyday life.

To be active on love's behalf and a tireless agent of God's love and justice, you will need constant supplies of divine grace and divine energy; you will need to root your whole life and being in the source of infinite power that is the Father-Mother. In the next phrase of the prayer, "Give us this day our daily bread," know that you are praying not only for the physical necessities of life but also for a constant infusion of the "bread" of Christ-consciousness, of the

Christ's passion, truth, energy, power, and living charity. It is this "daily bread" of grace that you will need more than anything if you embrace the challenges and ordeals of following Christ. As Origen tells us, "The true bread is he who nourishes the true man, made in the image of God; and the one who has been nourished by it will come to be in the living likeness of him who created him . . . Daily bread, that is, bread for 'being,' is what corresponds most closely with a rational nature and is akin to 'being' itself. It procures health, vigor, and strength to the soul, and since the word of God is immortal, it shares its own immortality with the one who eats it . . . just as corporal bread distributed to the body of the person to be nourished goes into his being, so the Christ, the 'living bread which came down from heaven,' (John 6:51) is distributed to the mind and the soul and gives a share of its own power to the person who provides himself food from it."

If you have really surrendered yourself to the work of love, truly accepted the depths of surrender implied by the words "thy will be done," and in Teresa of Avila's words, "really become ready to suffer everything that his majesty is pleased to send you," then when you pray "give us today our daily bread" you will pray with your whole being to be fed from the source that Jesus himself was fed from so like Jesus you can endure everything that is necessary for a life of active charity with his patience, faith, courage, and boundless stamina. And you will discover daily, as Teresa promises, the "marvels that this Sacred Bread does in us." Through eating this bread, exhaustion will turn to hope; passive desolation will be transmuted into calm and lucid action. By flinging yourself entirely upon the mercy of the Father-Mother and acknowledging your total dependence on the source for everything you are and do in its Name, you will find that you will be fed directly by it and in the most direct, transformatory ways; your repeated, humble asking for "bread" will make you more and more transparent to its "reception," more and more able to "eat" its grace in all the contingencies of life.

The next phrase, "Forgive us our trespasses as we forgive those that trespass against us," takes us into the heart of Jesus' teaching on forgiveness. What is revealed to us here is that the Father forgives us insofar as we can find it in our hearts to forgive others; by forgiving others, we become fragrant to God and create within ourselves that loving emptiness that can in turn receive the grace of divine mercy. As Teresa of Avila makes vividly clear, forgiveness is Jesus' ultimate test of whether or not a soul is really dedicated to him. It is not ascesis or penitence or even intensity of devotion that Jesus selects as the ultimate sign of whether or not we sincerely belong to him and are authentically on the Christ-path but our capacity for forgiveness. Only a vast and unconditional divine love for humanity can forgive all its horrors; only continual and repeated forgiveness can give us the strength again and again to go into the inferno of the world and work for love and justice there without hatred and without the exhaustion that comes from being continually angry and despairing at human corruption.

Very few of us live in the atmosphere of all-forgiving, unconditional love for all beings; so when I say this part of the prayer, as well as inwardly asking God for forgiveness for all my faults, vanities, and mistakes, I also pray for the strength—the bread of Grace—to be able sincerely and fully to forgive others. I often repeat inwardly at this point the words of St. Francis of Assisi's poetic commentary on these words of the Our Father: "And whatever we do not forgive perfectly, so you, Lord, enable us to forgive to the full so that we may truly love our enemies and fervently intercede for them before you, returning no evil and striving to help everyone in you."

Most of us can remember enemies or ex-lovers and friends who have caused us terrible harm at one time or another. At this place in the Our Father, I find it helpful to pray each time for the strength to forgive one particular enemy and to wish him or her nothing less, in fact, than complete Christing. Nearly always I find when I do so I encounter a depth of resistance and still unhealed suffering in myself; this, too, I offer to the Father for healing. This is harsh, painful work, but the more sincerely you do it, the richer will be the rewards. Slowly, over time, you will find your fear of the harm your enemies have done to you diminishing; and with the diminishment of fear will come ever-greater and deeper courage to enact the will of love in the world. Armed with forgiveness, you will be able to plunge again and again without fear into the fire of loving action on behalf of all beings.

The next sentence of the prayer, "Lead us not into temptation but deliver us from evil," reminds us of all the necessary ordeals we will encounter on the path to Christhood. This is a problematic sentence, perhaps the most difficult to understand in the whole prayer, since in it Jesus seems to be suggesting that it is the Father who leads us into temptation, and so in some way permits evil.

For me, the most profound and helpful guide into the deepest truth of this plea is Teresa of Avila. She suggests that we approach these words not with a desire not to suffer, because, as she says, "the soldiers of Jesus Christ sigh after combat"—but with a passionate and humble hunger to be protected inwardly against all those temptations to vanity, pride, and self-inflation that can ruin us on the Christ-path. All forms of what she calls "vain glory" are especially harmful to us; only a radical humility, in fact, can make us continually aware of all inner dangers as they arise. So, in praying not to be led into temptation, we should pray for deeper humility. As Teresa tells us, "If we serve the Lord with humility he will never leave off coming to our help in times of necessity."

Such radical humility, Teresa and all other authentic Christ-mystics tell us, will guard us against those subtle mystical temptations that the dark one uses to try to abort the birth in us—temptations, as Teresa names them, of "false humility, excessive zeal for penitence, presumptuous confidence . . . and indiscreet austerities that make us believe we are more penitent than others." Such temptations are, in fact, the greatest evil, for they can cut us off permanently from the Christ within and without us. Teresa recommends, therefore, that in praying to be "delivered from evil," we simultaneously pray to be infused with "love" and "fear": for, as she says succinctly, "love will make us hurry up our path; fear will make us aware of where we put our feet."

Origen interprets "lead us not into temptation but deliver us from evil" a little differently, but in a way that can be seen as complementary to the profound mystical vision of Teresa of Avila. He writes, "Let us pray to be delivered from temptations, not by avoiding temptation—for that is impossible—but by not being defeated when we are tempted." He adds, "Let us pray that we do nothing to deserve being led into temptation by God's righteous judgment . . . in the times of relief between temptations, let us stand firm for their onset and let us be prepared for everything that can happen, so that whatever comes to pass, we may not be tempted as though unready, but may be prepared as those who have disciplined ourselves with extreme care."

Such rugged realism also pervades Origen's interpretation of the phrase "deliver us from evil." Afflictions will inevitably come, Origen tells us, and our task is to pray to open to them with faith and trust as Job did and so be "delivered" of their ultimate brutality. This, as Origen makes clear, necessitates a continual immersion in the divine presence: "Those are not set on fire who by the shield of faith quench all the fiery arrows sent against them by the Evil One . . . they do not allow the arrows of the Evil One to prevail by easily destroying them by the flood of divine and saving thoughts impressed from contemplations of the truth upon the soul of the one who has transformed himself to be spiritual."

It is a sign of Jesus' tremendous realism that the "praying" part of the Our Father ends with a reminder of the power of temptation and of evil. Jesus is aware that the enterprise of transforming this earth into the Kingdom is one that threatens all the powers of society and religion; he is aware that the one who follows him, who "hungers and thirsts after righteousness," as the Beatitudes say, will be beset by difficulties and torments of every kind. The last thing the tender warrior of the Christ-path can afford is any kind of naiveté about inner or outer evil.

We have come to the closing phrases of the prayer which evoke the splendor and might of the Father in whose Name we have asked for everything we need to sustain our deepest life and to Christ us. A sense of unshakable peace and power should pervade your saying of "For yours is the kingdom, the power, and the glory, forever and ever." Pour out your entire being in adoration and wonder and surrender to the divine beauty and divine will. When you say the "Amen"—"So be it" in Aramaic—know, with the certainty of illumined faith, that your prayers to be an instrument of love and for the establishment of the Kingdom on earth have brought their realization ever closer.

Before you begin to recite the prayer again, rest in the silence of the Kingdom and allow it to charge you with its clarity, wisdom, and passion for transformation.

The Practice of the Sacred Heart

▩ ▩ ▩

The path of Christ is the path of the Sacred Heart, of the heart that has become "sacred" because it has allowed itself to be wounded and pierced open by divine love to all the agony of humanity and the creation. Keeping your heart constantly in a state of all-embracing, all-suffering love is one of the hardest tasks of the Christ-path and perhaps the most essential; through such a pierced, open heart, divine graces, illuminations, and powers flow naturally. Keeping the heart in a constant fervent and poignant blaze of love for all beings is also the source of a continual dedication, in the face of derision, persecution, and ordeal to "serving the growing Christ."

The practice of the Sacred Heart that I am going to offer now is based on the vision of Jesus' heart by Saint Margaret Mary Alacoque. Margaret Mary was a nun of the Visitation at Paray-le-Monial in Burgundy; on the 27th of December, 1673, she saw the heart of Jesus in a vision. She was praying before the Holy Sacrament; suddenly, Jesus appeared to her and, leaning against her breast, revealed to her that in his passion to redeem all human beings he wanted his heart to be manifested everywhere "with all its treasures of love, mercy, graces and powers of sanctification." Then Jesus gave Margaret Mary a direct vision of his Sacred Heart in glory; it appeared to her, she relates, "as on a throne made entirely of fire and flames more brilliant and more radiant than a sun and as transparent as a crystal. The wound that it had received on the Cross appeared visibly in it. It was surrounded by a crown of thorns which signified the pricks that our sins gave it, and a Cross above it which signified that, from the first moments of his incarnation, that is to say from the first moment his Heart was formed, the Cross was planted in it." Jesus asked her for her heart, took it out of her chest, and placed it in his. Then he took it out of his heart, "like a burning flame," and put it back in her chest. From that day on, it is said, as a proof of the authenticity of her experience, Margaret Mary Alacoque always felt pain in the place of her heart.

In the first part of the practice of the Sacred Heart, begin by imagining with all your inner powers Margaret Mary's astounding cosmic vision of the

Christ's Sacred Heart. Reconstruct in your imagination every detail—the heart itself, "brilliant as a sun," "transparent as a crystal," on its throne of "fire and flames," with its open wound, a crown of thorns circling it and the cross above it. Experience the symbolic power of each image; the heart is brilliant as a sun because it is on fire with ultimate charity for all creation, and it is "transparent as crystal" because it is utterly pure of all selfishness or self-concern. It is not merely omnipotent and invulnerable; the wound of the crucifixion burns at its core, as a profound but fertile grief glows at the heart of all those mystics who have followed the Christ-path. The cross stands above it as a reminder of the terrible and glorious process of its birth in reality; a crown of thorns surrounds it, reminding us that the ultimate royalty of divine human love is always accompanied by selfless suffering.

The entire pain and agony of Christ-consciousness is enshrined in Margaret Mary's vision, and reconstructing it in your imagination with your own heart afire with love and wonder will, over time, take you deeper and deeper into the paradoxical marriage of extreme suffering and extreme joy that is at the core of Christ-consciousness.

One way I have found helpful in approaching the magnificence of the Sacred Heart on its throne of fire is to imagine it as a vast, exploding, blood-gold supernova, whose outspread fans of transparent fire embrace the entire universe. Once you have formed a clear and dramatic inner picture of this exploding cosmic heart, then imagine that it is always exploding, that in every moment it explodes again. Finally, imagine, with the whole of your being alight with awe, that this vast, constantly exploding heart is also in you, ready to blaze open, again and again, and embrace, again and again, the entire creation in its arms of transparent fire.

When you have reached this marvelous point in the practice, your whole being should be longing for transfiguration. Follow the vision of Margaret Mary Alacoque and imagine Jesus standing right beside you. Imagine that Jesus now does to you exactly what he did that December night to Margaret Mary; he reaches out toward you, takes your heart out of your chest, and plunges it into the molten pain and ecstatic tenderness of his own heart.

Everything at this moment of the practice depends on how deeply you allow yourself to experience this sacred initiation into the heart by the Cosmic Christ. Summon up all your powers of emotion, all your memories of mystic joy, and concentrate them all on the final intensity of this sacred act. Then imagine Jesus handing you back your heart "like a burning flame" and placing it back in your breast.

Your heart has now been transformed into a "burning flame" of the fire of the Sacred Heart of Jesus. Imagine it vividly within your chest, constantly leaping and burning. Now, humbly and with total sincerity, gazing up into the eyes of the resurrected Christ, who is still close beside you, say slowly the great prayer of Margaret Mary Alacoque to the Sacred Heart:

> I [your name] give and consecrate to the Sacred Heart of our Lord Jesus Christ myself and my life, my actions, sorrows and pains in order to make no use of no part of my being but to honor, love and glorify him. My irrevocable will is to belong to him, to do everything for him, to renounce absolutely and passionately everything that could displease him. Therefore, I choose you, O Sacred Heart, as the one and only object of my love, the protector of my life, the pledge of my salvation, the cure for my frailty and my inconsistency, the righter of all the faults of my life and my safe shelter at the hour of my death. O Heart so lavish, may you be my justification before God, your Father, and turn away from me the arrows of his just anger.
>
> O loving Heart, I put my confidence in you, because I am terrified of my malice and my feebleness but hope everything from your goodness.
>
> Destroy, then, everything that in me displeases or resists you. May your pure love drive you so deeply into the core of my heart that it never forgets you and is never separated from you. I beg of you whose generosity is boundless that my name be written in you, since my only happiness and glory is to live and die as your slave.

The second part of the practice of the Sacred Heart now begins. This second part involves very little imagery, just a plunge directly into the fire of the Sacred Heart so that everything in you can be penetrated by its passionate charity and its desire for the healing and transfiguration of all human beings.

Begin this second part—a direct heart practice—by going in silence to the core of your being, to that solitary place in the heart which is peace, stillness, and love. This is the "Virgin" space in the heart that no afflictions can destroy and no other loves can exploit: this is St. Francis de Sales's "fine point of the soul," the point where your spirit meets the Godhead without any interference.

When you have evoked for yourself this sacred space, imagine yourself seated in it, immersed wholly in, and surrounded on all sides by, a sea of flame, the flame of the Sacred Heart of Jesus. Allow this fire to penetrate your whole being and body. Know that not one part of your being—spiritual or physical—is now outside this sea of fire, not one toe or fingertip, not even the tiniest hair on your arms or legs.

You are now drowned consciously in the flame-sea of the Sacred Heart of the Cosmic Christ. Inevitably, even if you concentrate with your whole mind, heart, body and soul, thoughts, memories, and emotions of various kinds will arise. Do not identify with any of them. As each arises, imagine that you reach out and grab hold of each of them and drown them one by one in the sea of fire that surrounds you and penetrates each part of you and that you now are. In this way, you will merge every thought, memory, and emotion that arises directly with the love of the Sacred Heart and slowly saturate every movement of your emotional, mental, and spiritual being with its fire.

The feeling of love is infinitely more dynamic than the thinking process, so if you do this practice with total focus and sincerity, all thoughts, memories, and emotions will slowly vanish. Nothing will remain, the Nothing that is transparent to and soaked entirely through with the fire of the heart. In this Nothing of transparent fire, you will be one with the heart of the Christ. As you begin to surface into ordinary consciousness, dedicate your whole being and your whole life to being an instrument of the fire of the Sacred Heart, and pray for the Kingdom of the heart to flame out throughout reality.

A Heart Practice (adapted from an ancient Tibetan Buddhist meditation)

🔲 🔲 🔲

Nothing is more essential for the integration of the Christ-consciousness with daily life, I have found, than developing a strong heart practice, which we can use whenever we are afraid or tormented or trapped in the darkness of ordeal.

The heart practice I will give here was taught to me in Nepal by Tibetan adepts; I have used it continually with Christ to deepen my inner connection with him. I have found that its powers of consolation and direct psychological healing are extraordinary. In times of stress or danger, I have used it continually and discovered that saying it with sincerity and belief can serve to deepen faith immeasurably and keep you—whatever is happening around you—in the glory and calm of the Cosmic Christ.

I recommend practicing it for the customary two periods during the day, but also making sure that while you are devoting yourself to this particular practice that you repeat it many times during the day, especially in situations where you would not normally be thinking of doing an inner visualization—on the train to work for example, or in a few minutes of "dead" time in the office, or while walking to a shop or buying a paper. What doing the practice in this way through the day makes slowly possible is a continual experience of its effectiveness and a gathering intimacy with its power; the rewards of these are priceless.

In a cloudless bright sky in front of you invoke that representation of Christ that has most moved you and with whom you feel most deeply connected. If for some reason you cannot imagine the Christ, don't worry. Imagine him as a blazing sun or a star of brilliant white light.

It helps me at this initial stage sometimes to say a simple prayer so as to awaken love for Christ. Sometimes I do read a sacred poem or a passage from Scripture just to inspire my being. Sometimes just repeating "Jesus" in the heart can be very powerful in making the visualization come alive.

Open your heart now, as nakedly and as sincerely as possible, to the

Christ that stands shining in the cloudless spring sky before you. Keep nothing back. Know that you need feel no shame or guilt even if the emotions that you are feeling are dark ones. The Christ alive in love before you wants nothing but your healing and your flowering in every dimension. Know that he is listening to you with total attention and compassion and never for a moment judging you. Call now to Christ from the depths of whatever you are going through, say exactly what you are feeling and what you need, as simply as possible.

At this stage of the practice, what is essential is to be as frank and shameless and "unedited" as possible. Don't hide from any of the feelings inside you; expose them without fear to the Christ. Express them with perfect certainty that you are accepted in all your difficulty and darkness, and you will find almost immediately that whatever burden you are carrying will be lightened.

Imagine now that the image or representation of Christ that you have chosen begins to emit a stream of radiant white light. This light is the divine light, the power of divine love; it has absolute effectiveness in all situations and can heal and transform anything because it streams directly from the Godhead. Know this with profound faith and pray to the light to enter you and wash you free of all obscurities, all difficulties, all illnesses of soul or body.

Now imagine that in immediate response to your prayer the white light streaming from Christ enters you through the top of your head, and pours in pulsing, warm, sweet blissful waves down the full length of your body. Let the divine light of the absolute love of Christ enter you totally and wash you fresh and clean with its power of purification and healing, at least nine times; each time it enters you, call out inwardly to Christ with words of tender love. Allow the words you use to be as tender, affectionate, intimate, and grateful as possible, and you will find that your heart will expand more and more in peace and joy. Each time the divine light enters, try to offer up one more grief, worry, or dark impulse for healing and transformation.

The more fervently you participate with the cleansing power of the light, the more sincerely and passionately you invoke it and the more lucidly you offer yourself up for total purification, the deeper the peace and solace that will be given you. As this peace and solace deepens, allow yourself to relax into the bliss and protection of the presence of Christ more and more. The Tibetan who taught me the practice said: "At this point in the practice, picture yourself as a slab of butter left out in the burning sun. Melt away!"

As you feel yourself melting away more and more in the presence of

Christ's love, imagine that you "float up" quietly to where Christ is standing in the sky and that you embrace him. Rest against his heart, and imagine yourself totally dissolved in its sacred fire of peace. Rest in that peace for as long as you can.

When you feel yourself returning to ordinary consciousness, don't do anything brusquely or hurriedly. Try to allow whatever you have to do after the practice to be permeated by the calm and ease it has given you. As you begin to go about your life, say a prayer for all suffering human and sentient beings everywhere and wish them healing and sacred joy. Then, pledge to dedicate the new confidence and strength that the practice has given you to the establishment of the Kingdom on earth. Say something like: "Bless me into usefulness" or "O eternal love, use me as an instrument in the creation of your Kingdom."

The Rosary: Practicing the Presence of the Mother

In nearly all of her modern apparitions, the Cosmic Mary stresses again and again the importance of prayer. Again and again, she tells us that all graces and strengths stream to us through the openings that sustained and sincere prayer alone can create in our hearts and in the silent ground of our lives. Just as there is no richer or more direct way of coming into the presence of the Christ than the saying of the Our Father, so there is no faster or more powerful way of remaining in the presence of the divine Mother as Mary than saying the prayer she is said to have given herself to Saint Dominic in the thirteenth century—the Hail Mary (the words of the prayer will be given at the beginning of the next section, "The Practice").

Mary said at Fatima and repeated the same message at Banneux, Beauraing, and Medjugorje: "To all those who recite my rosary I promise my protection and many great graces." Many times over the last thousand years Mary has appeared to stress the sacred importance and miraculous saving power of the Rosary. In these last terrible times, it seems, she wants to make even more certain that we understand that saying the Rosary is the most clear, swift, and effective way of uniting the soul to the Mother and so enabling the birth of the Christ-consciousness. Its simplicity and profundity make this practice available to everyone, whatever their level of awareness; it can be done, like the Our Father, anywhere and in any circumstance. If for the purposes of our practice we devote two half-hour periods to its calm and concentrated recitation, it is only so as to deepen our grasp of its power, so that the entire day can be perfumed by its secret recitation and illumined by the sacred intimacy with the Mother that it brings.

There is a complex and a simple way of saying the Rosary. The complex way consists of fifteen decades of Hail Marys divided into three distinct parts that each contain five decades. Each of the three parts relate the Hail Mary to different sacred mysteries in the path of Christ. This is a beautiful and mystically powerful way of saying the Rosary and of experiencing the sacred intertwining of Mary's and Christ's mission and consciousness. Anyone who wants to explore the fullness of its mystery should read de Montfort's masterpiece *The Secret of the Rosary,* and follow precisely its guidelines, hints, and instructions.

But there is a simpler way of saying the Rosary, which is more suited to the urgency and pressure of modern life and which has been used over the ages by many lovers of the Mother. It is just as powerful as the grander and more complex version when done with real love. After all, what is essential is to pray to the Mother with an open heart; the form is secondary. Mary herself said at Medjugorje in 1985: "I do not need a hundred Our Fathers and Hail Marys; it is better to say one with a real desire to encounter God." This simple way is to say the Hail Mary itself one hundred and fifty times, or as many times as possible, repeating after every ten recitations, perhaps, an Our Father or a spontaneous prayer to the Mother.

Mary the Mother is particularly present to us in the Hail Mary as many of the saints whose lives have been transformed by it testify. Saint Bernardine of Siena wrote, "Each time we hail Mary, she hails us in turn, for she is entirely full of tenderness and courtesy, and she always replies to our salutations by one of her own, in deepest kindness. If we were to hail her a thousand times, she would hail us back a thousand times." Saint Bernard of Clairvaux tells us the following story: he had a habit of saluting each of his statues of Mary as he passed them; one day he was astounded when he heard one reply, "Hail Bernard!"

Remember, then, that Mary is completely and intimately present to anyone who salutes her with love, and that salutation echoes directly in her Sacred Heart, the heart of the divine Mother herself. Knowing this can only give us the greatest confidence, hope, and trust; the trust of a child in the presence of a Mother that wants for it every profound good.

The Practice

The words of the Hail Mary as given by the Virgin herself to Saint Dominic are as follows: "Hail Mary, full of grace, the Lord is with you. Blessed art thou amongst women and blessed is the fruit of thy womb, Jesus. Holy Mary, Mother of God, pray for us sinners now and in the hour of our death. Amen."

Each simple phrase is packed with the deepest spiritual truth; the Hail Mary only yields its secrets after many years of constant recitation. What I want to offer here is my own interpretation, which has come to me in meditation and reflects the vision I have proposed of the Cosmic Mary as the birther of the Christ-consciousness.

When I say "Hail Mary," the person I am praying to is at once Miriam, the mystical social revolutionary of the Magnificat and Mother of Jesus and also the divine Mother, the Cosmic Mary, "the woman clothed with the sun." Whenever I begin the prayer, I try to imagine with all the power of my being the full glory and tenderness and radical passion for transformation of the full divine Mother, and I turn my whole self toward her in deep trust and in full knowledge that I am seen and known by her and loved unconditionally. As I do so, I always ask her to birth the Christ in me, to transform me into her divine Child. Here I often use an ancient prayer to Our Lady of Chartres: "O Immaculate Virgin, who births into grace and glory all the chosen of God, deign to receive me into your maternal breast and to form me in you so that I may resemble Jesus."

From the beginning of the Hail Mary, I make certain that I am committing myself to the divine Mother to be formed by her into the Christ. When I say "Hail Mary," I surrender my whole being in dark faith to her transforming power.

The next phrase, "Full of grace, the Lord is with you," has come to mean to me that the Cosmic Mary is full of the infinite power of divine grace, capable as the Mother of effecting total transformation. In calling her "full of grace," I remind myself of the power of her vast love.

When I say, "The Lord is with you," I envision the deep meaning of this phrase in two related ways. To me, "the Lord is with you" means that the Christ-consciousness is with her, the Cosmic Christ stands silent and eternally by her side, inseparable from her, at one with her will and one with her love. I also believe it means "the Lord"—the Cosmic Father—is with you. The Cosmic Mary comes accompanied by the transcendent Father; her power and his are one: her force is an aspect and expression of his; Mary as the Mother of creation is one with the timeless and spaceless transcendent Father, full of his grace and brimming over with his power as well as her own. For me, seeing Mary in this complete way (and completed by the Father aspect of God) only deepens my wonder at her divine maternity. Wherever she is, the entire Godhead is present, perfectly expressed through her love, beauty, power, majesty, and bliss.

The next phrases, "Blessed art thou amongst women" and "Blessed is the fruit of thy womb, Jesus," take me directly into the heart of the mystery of the birthing of the Christ-consciousness by the force of the Mother. The words make it clear that this mystery is the "gift" of the Sacred Feminine: "blessed art thou amongst women" not only signifies Mary as the holiest of women but also underscores and underlines her blessedness as the vessel of the Sacred Feminine in creation.

The next phrase, "and blessed is the fruit of thy womb, Jesus," is for me perhaps the richest and deepest of the entire prayer, for it makes clear what is the supreme secret of the Christ-path: that Christ-consciousness is the "fruit" of the "womb" of Mary the Mother. By being in the "womb" of the Mother, enclosed in all her strength, powers, and virtues, we ripen into the full Christ, we become her fruit, the fruit of her transcendent and immanent Tree of Life. Whenever I come to this phrase, I try to bring to my contemplation of it everything that I have learned of the inner relation of the Sacred Feminine to the Christ-consciousness and pray that the powers, strengths, and passions for justice and transformation of the earth of the Mother may deepen their hold on me so that more and more of my being can be "mothered" into Christhood.

For me, the next phrases, "Holy Mary, Mother of God," reveal the entire secret of her real identity. Traditionally, the description of Mary as "Mother of God" has been intended to "limit" her identity, to make it "dependent" on that of Christ's. The very formulation, however, reveals a different truth. "Mother of God" can mean "Mother of Jesus," and so a human mother selected by grace to birth the Son of the Father. But a far richer and more profound mystical interpretation can also radiate from it: "Mother of God" can mean "source of God, 'the Light-Void' out of which 'God' is formed": "Mother of God" can mean, in fact, the final Godhead out of which "God" is born. This final Godhead is what I worship when I say the Hail Mary; I worship the Mother-void, the ultimate Mother-source of Godhood, the birthing power of the entire cosmos as focused through the figure of "the woman clothed with the sun." It is this transcendent and immanent force that is creating and sustaining the entire universe, and it is in an entire "opening"—in bliss and trust and surrender of will—to this force of immense power and boundless love that the Christ-consciousness is born.

When I ask this maternal Godhead to "Pray for me now and at the hour of our death," I do so knowing that this vast cosmic power loves all beings with fathomless love and is my Mother and will pray for me because she wants my every good and most glorious transformation. When I say, "And at the hour of our death," I use the repetition of the phrase to remind myself of death and of the urgency of using every moment in this life to "form" myself in her womb, and also of the vulnerability that I—and every other human being—lives. Knowing that what is essential at the moment of death is to have the whole being turned consciously toward God, toward her, when I say this phrase I pray to her to be entirely present in all her mystical tenderness and glory when I die so I can pass over into the truth without fear or any attachment.

After I have finished the prayer, I try to open my heart entirely to the Mother in silence and pray in whatever words then come most naturally to be "born" in her womb as the Christ-Child I (and all other beings) essentially am.

The interpretation I have given here of the Hail Mary is not in any way intended as "final": it is part of a journey that I have been taking for several years into the mysterious depths of this prayer, and I have written it here as an invitation to all others on the Christ-path to "use" the prayer as a way of entering into the presence of the divine Mother and her birthing power.

The Practice of the Presence of the Mother, by Performing All Our Actions with Mary, in Mary, through Mary, and for Mary

▩ ▩ ▩

The aim of this practice is to bring you constant presence of the divine Mother by making you aware of her sustaining, inspiring, guiding, and transforming power and love at each moment of the day. It requires total gift of self and total concentration on Mary as the Cosmic Mother of the Christ-consciousness and is immensely powerful as a way of working on all aspects of being.

The two half-hour practice periods of the day should be devoted to sustained prayer to Mary, and acts of repeated dedication of the entire being—body, soul, heart, and mind to her to do with what she wants.

When I am doing this practice, I begin by saying slowly and with as much sincerity and devotion as I can the following prayer:

> O Mary, my divine Mother, by your grace and your love
> Turn all my speech and talk to mantra,
> Making all the actions of my hands gestures of blessing.
> May all eating and drinking this day be offerings to you,
> May all lying down be prostrations to you,
> May all pleasures I enjoy be as dedications of my entire self to you,
> May everything I do be instinct with profound worship of you.

I find that praying to live each moment of the day in divinized Mother-consciousness is a very profound practice; with each phrase of the prayer I consecrate a different part of my being to her. When I say, "Turn all my speech and talk to mantra," I offer up to her the spiritual communication center in my throat for her blessing and purification; when I ask her to make all actions of my hands gestures of blessing, I imagine her white divine light infusing and irradiating my hands so they become instruments of love and healing. When I ask, "May all eating and drinking this day be offerings to you," I promise to dedicate consciously to her every meal and to eat each meal with gratitude for her grace to me expressed through the food, and to eat the food as a divine Child, strengthening myself for service to other beings in the world. When I pray, "May all lying down be prostrations to you," I lie down on the floor and imagine my whole body laid on an altar to her and offered up to her transforming passion of love, dedicated in its every breath, thought, appetite, and movement to expressing on earth her rhythm, her harmony, her tenderness, the work of her beauty. When I say, "May all pleasures I enjoy be as dedications of my entire self to you," I evoke slowly the pleasures I may experience during the day, and I turn my whole self inwardly to her in them, all pledging to recognize her as their source and her bliss as the secret presence uniting all their joys.

Said in this way, this prayer becomes a way of praying for Christ-consciousness. What is authentic Christ-consciousness but service of the Mother aspect of the Godhead and the creation at each moment? All of life is the gift of the Mother, and through life she is ceaselessly feeding truth, bliss, and love to those of her children who work to be awake. Saying the prayer I have given, then, with the full powers of your spiritual imagination, will remind you of the core truth of the Christ-life that it is lived with the sensitivity, refinement, strength, patience, and radiant humility and self-offering of the Sacred Feminine.

When I have said the prayer eight times (eight is the sacred number of the Mother in many mystical systems), deepening my understanding of it each time and each time finding other parts of my being to offer up to her, I then read slowly and prayerfully the wonderful words of de Montfort, who pioneered this practice in his *The Secret of Mary*. De Montfort writes:

Act with Mary: The essential practice of this devotion is to perform all our actions with Mary . . . We must have habitual recourse to our Lady, becoming one with her and adopting her intentions, even though they are unknown to us. Through Mary we must adopt the intentions of Jesus. In other words, we must become an instrument in Mary's hands for her to act in us and do with what she pleases, for the greater glory of her son.

Act in Mary: We must always act in Mary, that is to say, we must gradually acquire the habit of recollecting ourselves interiorly and so form within us an idea or a spiritual image of Mary . . . She will be a burning lamp lighting up our inmost soul and inflaming us with love for God . . . If we do anything at all, it will be in Mary, and in this way Mary will help us to forget self everywhere and in all things.

Act Through Mary: We must never be without her when praying to Jesus.

Act for Mary: We must perform all our actions for Mary, which means that as slaves of this noble Queen we will work only for her . . . in everything we must renounce self-love because more often than not, without our being aware of it, selfishness sets itself up as the end of all we work for. We should often repeat from the depths of our hearts: Dear Mother, it is to please you that I go here or there, that I suffer this pain or that injury.

Having contemplated the profound wisdom hidden in these simple words of de Montfort—and I find that every day I devote myself to them, I uncover richer and deeper meanings in them—I end this next part of the practice by reading de Montfort's description of the power of this devotion to remind myself at the deepest level of why I am doing it; "This devotion faithfully practiced produces countless happy effects in the soul. The most important of them is that it establishes, even here on earth, Mary's life in the soul, so that it is no longer the soul that lives, but Mary who lives in it . . . Mary's soul becomes identified with the soul of her servant . . . When, by an unspeakable but real grace, Mary most holy becomes Queen of a soul, she works untold wonders in it. She is a great wonder-worker especially in the interior of souls. She works there in secret, unsuspected by the soul, as knowledge of it might destroy the beauty of her work . . . She causes Jesus to live continually in the soul and that soul to live in continuous union with Jesus. If Jesus is equally the fruit of each individual fruit of Mary for each individual soul as for all souls in general, he is even more especially her fruit and her masterpiece in the soul where she is present . . . Mary becomes all things for the soul that wishes to serve Jesus Christ. She enlightens his mind with her pure faith. She deepens his heart with her humility. She enlarges and inflames his heart with her charity, makes it pure with her purity, makes it noble and great through her maternal care."

In the final sate of the practice, I rest my whole being in the presence of the Mother, in silence and in trust, and try to clear my mind of all thoughts and emotions so as to be as naked as possible to her love. I close the practice by reciting the Hail Mary once, very slowly and with everything that I have experienced during the practice, infusing it with truth and power.

As I said at the beginning, the point of the two daily practice periods is to turn your entire attention to her and dedicate the entire day to her as a celebration of her spirit, guidance, and truth. The really difficult—and truly transforming—power of the practice, however, lies in how many times you remember it during all the various activities of the day. Every time you have any spare time, dedicate it to thinking of her. I find carrying around a small image of her, or a picture, helps. What I have found also helpful is resolving each day to practice as far as I can one of the virtues of the Sacred Feminine—to devote myself especially that day to cultivating patience, for example, or working deeply on seeing the way my pride or arrogance deforms my vision and so deepening humility.

A wonderful way to end the days on which you do this practice of presence of the divine Mother is, just before you go to sleep, to offer up your sleep and dreams for her to use for your instruction. Ask to remain as lucid to whatever message she wishes to give you through them as possible; you will find that if you do this regularly, you will be helped to become more conscious of how you act and react in daily life and more aware of the spiritual rhythms of her work within you. This heightened awareness will enable you to gather each day more and more harmoniously into her light-rhythm.

The practice of the presence of the Mother demands and gives everything. It cannot be done halfheartedly or with anything less than alert and humble concentration. Its rewards are nothing less than the growth of the awareness of the Christ within, of the compassion, strength, and joy of the divine Child of the Father-Mother living a timeless life in time, dying each day a little more completely into what St. John of the Cross describes as "the tenderness of the life of God."

The Practice of Giving and Taking (adapted from the Tibetan Buddhist practice of Tonglen)

▨ ▨ ▨

This supremely beautiful and effective spiritual exercise helps you develop and use the Christ-power of compassion to establish yourself in the light of love and send love and healing to others. If done with sincerity and faith, it can transform the ground of your being, awaken you to the glory of the Christ within you, and make you a powerful agent of divine healing in the world. Its informing principle is simple: in the course of the practice, you "take on" the pain, terror, and sadness of others, as Christ did (and does), and then "give out," as Christ did and does, all peace, all love, all help, all possible forms of healing.

There is nothing to fear: the pain, terror, and sadness you take on in this practice will not destroy you or "invade" you. What your intention to take them on will do is wear away your attachment to your false self, the self that keeps you separate from others in life and so from your profoundest Christ-self. Every time you do this practice with a sincere intention to help another person who is suffering or ill or a whole group of people in need of divine truth or succor, you will also be offering up your own separate false self for purification. The rewards of this offering up of your false self will become slowly obvious: you will grow humbler, more transparent to the suffering of others, and less willing to turn away from them because, through doing the practice, you will come to know that you are not impotent in the face of the overwhelming grief of the world but able, in and through Christ, to be an agent of healing.

To do the practice of Giving and Taking with truth and calm, you have first of all to experience your own inner Christ and the power he has to heal yourself.

Begin the practice of Giving and Taking by sitting down in front of a large mirror in which you can see yourself clearly. The person in the mirror is your biographical self, with all its sadnessess, fears, and difficulties; the person looking at your biographical self is the Christ in you, fearless, all-loving, calm, awake. Imagine this with all the intensity and faith you can muster; allow the Christ in you to look at your biographical self candidly, but mercifully. See clearly from your Christ-self all your biographical self's weaknesses and needs; do not judge them, but see them all without shame, and with detached compassion.

Now imagine that all the fears and needs and desolations your biographical self is harboring within itself issue from the stomach of the image in the mirror in the form of a ball of black smoke. Visualize this ball of black smoke clearly. Then breathe in the ball of black smoke that you have imagined into your open and calm Christ-heart, and imagine it dissolving there completely, as smoke would in a cloudless, shining blue sky.

Breathe in the black ball of smoke issuing from your biographical self, the image of you in the mirror: breathe back at your biographical self all the peace, bliss, joy, and healing power of your inner Christ.

Do this at least nine times, very calmly and with great concentration; each time your sense of the power of your Christ-nature to dissolve fear and pain and heal suffering in its sky-like spaciousness should become more and more powerful. Every time you imagine the black ball emerging from the stomach of your biographical self, see it clearly; see clearly, too, how it dissolves in the shining blue sky of our open Christ-heart. Do not begin breathing back to the self in the mirror the Christ-light until you have seen that the black smoke has dissolved completely in the sky of the heart and nothing but sky remains.

At the end of this first part of the practice, rest in the peace of your Christ-nature; feel its calm and strength penetrate your entire body, heart, mind, and soul. At this point, I find it helpful sometimes to say slowly and prayerfully a verse from the Gospel. One I often use is these words of Jesus from John 14:27: "Peace I leave with you, my peace I give unto you; not as the world giveth, give I unto you. Let not your heart be troubled, neither let it be afraid."

When you feel calm and strong in your Christ-nature, turn with faith and joy to the second part of the practice.

In this part of Giving and Taking, select a person you know who is in psychological or physical pain. Imagine them clearly in your heart's eye, and meditate for a few moments on all the difficulties they must be experiencing and all the grief and fear they must be undergoing.

Now imagine that all their psychological or physical anguish comes out of their stomach in the form of a black ball of smoke. As you breathe in, breathe in that black ball of smoke, and as you breathe out, imagine that you are breathing out the divine light of Christ to the person you are concerned for. Breathe in slowly and calmly and imagine the black ball of smoke dissolving completely in the open sky of your Christ-heart as you do so. When you breathe out the divine light of Christ, imagine as you do so the person you have chosen to help completely irradiated by it, and healed of everything that afflicts them.

In the third part of the practice, turn in your heart to confront the agony of the whole planet. Imagine the animals dying in the burning forests, the women and children murdered in wars, the horror of the lives of the poor on each continent. Imagine the full danger the planet faces from environmental destruction, and the possibility of nuclear annihilation.

Imagine now that the whole earth gives off a ball of black smoke, in which these horrors are concentrated. Imagine that you are now the Cosmic Christ, as large as the universe. Take that black ball of smoke into your Sacred Heart and dissolve it in its sky-pure transparence. Breathe in the earth's black smoke, and imagine it dissolving utterly in your heart: breathe out the light of the heart, and imagine the whole earth bathed in its all-healing glory. Do this nine times slowly, with total concentration.

At the end of the half-hour period, say a prayer for the healing of all the pain of all human and sentient beings everywhere and dedicate all the joy and peace you have felt during the practice to the creation of Christ's Kingdom on earth. Imagine that through the practice the grace of Christ has turned you into a living light-diamond: send the lights of the diamond-being that love has made you to all the four directions of the universe, and to all beings in all dimensions.

Birthing the Divine Child in the Mother

❖ ❖ ❖

This practice introduces anyone who does it with sincerity to that radiant wholeness of being and that complete "healed" integration of body, spirit, heart, and mind that the divine Mother is trying to birth in all of us; it introduces you, in fact, to the full health, power, vigor, and heart-centered truth of the divine Child, the Christ in you. That is why I call it Birthing the divine Child in the Mother.

Before beginning it, read and meditate for ten minutes on Logion 22 from the Gospel of Thomas:

> Jesus saw some babies nursing. He said to his disciples, "These nursing babies are like those who enter the Kingdom." They said to him, "Then shall we enter the kingdom as babies?"
>
> Jesus said to them, "When you make the two into the one, and when you make the inner like the outer and the outer like the inner, and the upper like the lower, and when you make male and female into a single one, so that male will not be male nor female be female; and when you fashion eyes in place of an eye, and a hand in place of a hand, and a foot in place of a foot, and a likeness in place of a likeness, then you shall enter the kingdom."

To help your meditation on this divinely inspired and extremely precise teaching on the nature, range, and effect of divine Child-consciousness, it might help you to read what has been written about Logion 22 in the section on Sacred Marriage in the Map in Part Two of this book. Then, turn to Logion 22 itself and read it slowly, bringing to each phrase the full presence of your inner spiritual experience. Pause continually to pray to the Christ and to Mary for clarity; try to penetrate the full majesty of the truth of unity and integration of every part and force and quality of being that logion is speaking of. Try, too, to imagine with devotion and joy what it would be like to be such a healed, integrated being living a human divine life with full awareness and full possession of body, heart, spirit, and mind in the living light. I find that it helps in this first stage of the practice to pray to become a divine Child and to say inwardly, "Make me, O divine Mother, your whole and healed divine Child"; or "Birth me in you, and bring me into your wholeness"; or "Light the fire of your Sacred Heart in my mind, in my heart, in my mind and in every cell of my body and let me come to live in its unity and in the all-transforming, all-unifying power of its love."

After this period of intense and loving meditation, start the visualization that I am going to give now with perfect faith that it can act as an instrument of the birthing power of the divine Mother. Know that it can and will, if you do it regularly, and with ardor and humility, birth more and more completely in you the divine Child you essentially are and free you of all concepts, ideas, and psychological and physical disturbances that prevent you from attaining effortless trust and effortless being-in-her.

Before you begin the visualization, pray that you can be born as a divine Child to be of use to all sentient beings and be a complete instrument of the birth of the Kingdom; it is essential to dedicate your birth in this way to the benefit of all beings.

Now, with exaltation and trust, imagine Mary the divine Mother standing, in whatever form you worship her most readily, above your head with her palms outspread. The form of Mary that I find most powerful is that of the Virgin of Guadalupe, because it is in this image, as I have written in Part Three, "Christ and the Sacred Feminine," that I find the full transcendent and immanent glory of the Cosmic Mary represented.

Imagine the Virgin of Guadalupe, or whatever image of Mary moves you most, surrounded by blazing golden light, smiling with infinite tenderness and compassion. From her outspread palms above your head now begins to pour a living glittering stream of soft golden light. Know that this golden light has within it every power of divine love, every power of gnosis, healing, and integration; this golden light is the irradiation of the sun of eternal glory that the Mother is, and it contains, crystallizes, and focuses simultaneously and spontaneously all her powers of revelation and care. Know this with your whole being and surrender your whole being to its operation in calm and trust.

Now allow the stream of golden light from her outspread palms to enter you through the top of your head as you envisage the light entering you. Pray to it and Mary to heal, purify, clarify, and irradiate everything in you and bring every part of you—your body, heart, mind, and soul—into a living unity of peace, bliss, and power.

Let the golden light now fill your head. As it does so, pray particularly for your powers of vision and understanding of the sacred to be aroused. Sometimes you may feel a tickling between the eyebrows; this is the light starting to awaken what in Eastern mystical traditions is called the Third Eye, the spiritual eye at the center of the forehead, which is opened slowly through prayer, meditation, and service and which, when completely open, sees the divine world directly and knows the whole universe as the living dance of light-consciousness.

Once you have let the golden light fill your head and have invoked it to open your spiritual eye, and keep it open, invite it down into your throat. In the Eastern mystical systems, the spiritual center in the throat "controls" communication of every kind. Allow the light now to open that center as sunlight opens a shy rose. Imagine the rose of effortless communication of truth and love opening in your throat, slowly but certainly, as the divine sunlight of her gold light is trained on it.

Your head and your throat are now gently on fire. Take that golden fire down into your shoulders and along your arms to the very tips of your fingers, imagining, as you do so, that every cell in that part of your body awakens to its essential divine strength and life.

Now take the light down into the heart. As you do so, remember that the heart is the core and guide of your divine human being; awakening its boundless love and all-embracing sky-like charity—which are one with the love and charity of Christ and Mary—is the most crucial aspect of the birth you are allowing her to prepare in you. So as you take the golden light of the Mother down into your heart, pray to the Mother to open your Sacred Heart completely and to reveal the whole universe blazing in its subtle fire, and to keep your heart open-in-her forever. As you do so, start to feel how, through her grace, your light-opened heart aligns head and emotion, mind and psyche, intellect and passion. Pray for this supreme sacred balance of heart and mind, soul and body, "heaven" and "earth," inner and outer, upper and lower, "male" and "female" to become ever deeper and ever richer in you, and to carry you to ever-more profound realizations of the truth of unity.

By opening your vision, communication, and heart centers through the grace of her golden light, you have now begun the birth and established yourself in the presence of love. Relish that ecstatic and blissful presence and call out to it inwardly in words of welcoming adoration. Know that the Child is being born in you, and thank and adore the birthing Mother with all your awakened Sacred Heart.

Now, with full faith, trust, and confidence, begin the next movement of this sacred practice. Take the golden light down into the rest of your body, uniting it and all of its conscious and subconscious movements, hungers, and desires with the conscious love-power of the light. First, take the golden light down into your belly, allowing it to become "pregnant" with the light's full sweetness. In the belly there is a spiritual center that ensures balance in the deepest sense, a balance that helps the work of the Sacred Heart in grounding gnosis, and earthing the action of the light in the real. As you take the light into the belly then, pray to it to mature and deepen this earthing and grounding power, so that you can incarnate in all of your emotions, acts, and thoughts more and more of the Mother's love and force.

Confident that you are established in sacred balance and in divine love, now fearlessly lower the full force of the Mother's light into the genital area, invoking as you do so the Cosmic Mary as the Queen of the Sacrament of Cana, the Tantric Queen of Heaven and Earth, who wants every aspect of your being to flower in light and joy. A great deal of human ignorance, pain, and violence comes from sexual wounding, from the wounded millennia of body-hatred inflicted on all of us, nearly always in the name of "religion." The Mother of the Christ that is her divine Child wants all of our instincts to be consecrated to God. Know that one of the transforming freedoms that the Cosmic Christ wants to give to humanity is that of a sanctified sexuality, a sexuality that provides a direct way of delighting in the divine energies that engender and sustain the creation and a direct initiation into the mysteries of divine human love. So, as you lower the golden light of the Mother into your genital area, pray to her to remove all of your guilt, all of your shame, all of the fears and blocks in you that prevent you from consecrating your sexual nature. Ask her to transform your sexual nature into an instrument of divine human love, to grow love's body in you, not by repressing your physical desires but by divinizing them.

Now take the golden light of the Mother even farther down—down the thighs, through the kneecaps, down the back of the legs, and down through the ankles to the end of the toes. In the Eastern mystical systems, the "centers" governing the life of the subconscious are hidden in the lower part of the body. So as you draw the light down throughout the lower part, pray to the Mother to clarify and divinize all the secret movements of your subconscious, to make all its darkness conscious, and to open up all the traumas and humiliations and fears that are hidden there to the direct light of divine healing.

Every part of your body, heart, mind, and soul are now alight in the golden fire of the divine Mother. Harmoniously and blissfully relish the sweet power of being that now streams in you and from you; savor the balance between all dimensions you now are. Be grateful to her for the birth-in-her of your whole and healed transformed human divine being.

Now, slowly and with tremendous joy, take the golden light back up through every center, one by one, blessing each one with its healing power again. Let the light travel up into your head and then sit like a large, pulsing fireball on your head. Balance it there for a long, grateful, blissful moment, and then, with an inward shout, drop it into the heart, and let the heart explode with divine passion.

Imagine as your heart explodes that it is a birthing supernova of divine fire and that radiation from its birth expands and extends throughout the universe.

Rest calmly and humbly in this birthing power that has now been born in you. Imagine the entire creation being caressed by the flames of the love of your exploding heart and pray with your entire body, heart, mind, and soul united now in one vast fire: "Let the Christ be born everywhere! Let the Kingdom of Christ come! Let the rule of the divine Child begin on earth! Let ruined nature be green again and love be awakened in its full power in the heart and body of every sentient being!"

Section II
Thirty-one Meditations
on the Mystical Christ

◈ ◈ ◈

Introduction

The following thirty-one meditations on the mystical Christ have been taken from the full range of the Christian tradition, beginning with certain luminous self-revelations of Jesus himself and ending with an apocalyptic and prophetic passage from one of the twentieth century's most prescient mystics, Bede Griffiths. In between, arranged chronologically, are excerpts from the writings of some of the greatest and most fearless practitioners of the Christ-path, amongst them Gregory of Nyssa, Julian of Norwich, Meister Eckhart, John Ruysbroeck, St. John of the Cross, Teresa of Avila, and Therese of Lisieux.

Each excerpt illustrates or expands one or more of the crucial themes of the first three parts of *Son of Man*. Read together, the selection is intended to be a presentation and unfolding of the full range, glory, passion, and power of the Christ-force, as experienced by those who have lived directly in its fire. Since there are thirty-one meditations, one can read one each day of any month, perhaps before or after the two daily half-hour periods of spiritual practice needed for the Twelve Sacred Exercises.

Nothing is more essential on the Christ-path than, at all times and in all circumstances, and as intensely and focusedly as possible, to maintain a constant fervor of inspiration. Such fervor is the key to keeping the mind and heart on fire with love of the divine and open to the gnosis and grace that are streaming from the mind and heart of the Christ to all humanity. The passages that I have selected here are the ones that over many years I have come to love and need the most in my own journey toward Christ.

The best way to read each passage is in the heart slowly, with concentration, and with profound devotion. Savor each phrase and invoke continually the wisdom and insight of Christ-consciousness in this way and your reading will be transformed into a way of meditating directly on the Christ. Before each reading, prepare your mind and heart to be receptive by sitting in silence or saying a mantra. After each reading, dedicate whatever perceptions or joy the meditation has given you to the coming of the Kingdom on earth.

You will find that if you repeatedly read the passages this way, separately or together, they will, over time, engender an increasingly rich understanding of the Christ within, and will help you in your daily task of integrating the thoughts, emotions, and actions of your lives with the truths and transforming energies of divine love.

As you read and meditate on these passages and strive to infuse your life with their illuminations, keep alive in your heart the urgent summons of Teresa of Avila:

> *Christ has no body now on earth but yours*
>> *no hands but yours*
>> *no feet but yours,*
> *Yours are the eyes through which he is to look out*
>> *Christ's compassion to the world*
> *Yours are the feet with which he is to go about*
>> *doing good;*
> *Yours are the feet with which he is to bless men now.*

"I Am the Living Bread"

Verily, verily, I say unto you, he that believeth on me hath everlasting
life.

I am that bread of life.

Your fathers did eat manna in the wilderness, and are dead.

This is the bread which cometh down from heaven, that a man may
eat thereof, and not die.

I am the living bread which came down from heaven: if any man eat
of this bread, he shall live for ever: and the bread that I will give
is my flesh, which I will give for the life of the world. . . .

Verily, verily, I say unto you, except ye eat the flesh of the Son of man,
and drink his blood, ye have no life in you.

Whoso eateth my flesh, and drinketh my blood, hath eternal life; and
I will raise him up at the last day.

For my flesh is meat indeed, and my blood is drink indeed.

He that eateth my flesh, and drinketh my blood, dwelleth in me, and I
in him.

As the living Father hath sent me, and I live by the Father: so he that
eateth me, even he shall live by me.

This is that bread which came down from heaven: not as your fathers
did eat manna, and are dead: he that eateth of this bread shall
live for ever.

Gospel of John 6:47–51, 53–58

"I Am the True Vine"

I am the true vine, and my Father is the husbandman.

Every branch in me that beareth not fruit he taketh away: and every branch that beareth fruit, he purgeth it, that it may bring forth more fruit.

Now ye are clean through the word which I have spoken unto you.

Abide in me, and I in you. As the branch cannot bear fruit of itself, except it abide in the vine; no more can ye, except ye abide in me.

I am the vine, ye are the branches: He that abideth in me, and I in him, the same bringeth forth much fruit: for without me ye can do nothing.

If a man abide not in me, he is cast forth as a branch, and is withered; and men gather them, and cast them into the fire, and they are burned.

If ye abide in me, and my words abide in you, ye shall ask what ye will, and it shall be done unto you.

Herein is my Father glorified, that ye bear much fruit; so shall ye be my disciples.

As the Father hath loved me, so have I loved you: continue ye in my love.

If ye keep my commandments, ye shall abide in my love; even as I have kept my Father's commandments, and abide in his love.

These things have I spoken unto you, that my joy might remain in you, and that your joy might be full.

Gospel of John 15:1–11

"I in Them and Thou in Me"

Jesus lifted up his eyes to heaven, and said, Father, the hour is come; glorify thy Son, that thy Son also may glorify thee: As thou hast given him power over all flesh, that he should give eternal life to as many as thou hast given him.

And this is life eternal, that they might know thee the only true God, and Jesus Christ, whom thou hast sent.

I have glorified thee on the earth: I have finished the work which thou gavest me to do.

And now, O Father, glorify thou me with thine own self with the glory which I had with thee before the world was.

I have manifested thy name unto the men which thou gavest me out of the world: thine they were, and thou gavest them me; and they have kept thy word. . . .

Neither pray I for these alone, but for them also which shall believe on me through their word;

That they all may be one; as thou, Father, art in me, and I in thee, that they also may be one in us: that the world may believe that thou hast sent me.

And the glory which thou gavest me I have given them; that they may be one, even as we are one:

I in them, and thou in me, that they may be made perfect in one; and that the world may know that thou hast sent me, and hast loved them, as thou hast loved me.

Father, I will that they also, whom thou hast given me, be with me where I am; that they may behold my glory, which thou hast given me: for thou lovedst me before the foundation of the world.

O righteous Father, the world hath not known thee: but I have known thee, and these have known that thou hast sent me.

And I have declared unto them thy name, and will declare it: that the love wherewith thou hast loved me may be in them, and I in them.

Gospel of John 17:1–6, 20–26

"The Hymn of Christ"

Before he was arrested . . . Jesus assembled us all and said, "Before I am delivered to them, let us sing a hymn to the Father, and so go to meet what lies before us." So he told us to form a circle, holding one another's hands. Jesus stood in the middle and said, "Answer amen to me." So he began to sing the hymn,

Glory to You, Father, Amen.
Glory to You, Mother, Amen.
Glory to You, Word, Amen.
Glory to You, Wisdom, Amen.
Glory to You, Spirit, Amen.
Glory to You, Holy One, Amen.
Glory to Your Glory, Amen.

Praise to You, Father, Amen.
Praise to You, Mother, Amen.
Praise to You, Eternal Spirit, Amen.

I will be saved, and I will save, Amen.
I will be loosed, and I will loose, Amen.
I will be wounded, and I will wound, Amen.
I will be born, and I will bear, Amen.
I will eat, and I will be eaten, Amen.
I will hear, and I will be heard, Amen.
I will be understood, and I am understanding, Amen.
I will be washed, and I will wash, Amen.
I will pipe, dance, all of you, Amen.
I will mourn, beat all your breasts, Amen.
The Holy Eight sing in choir with us, Amen.
The twelfth Number dances on high, Amen.
The entire universe belongs to the Dancer, Amen.
If you do not dance, you don't know what is happening, Amen.
I will flee, and I will remain, Amen.
I will adorn, and I will be adorned, Amen.
I will be united, and I will unite, Amen.

I have no house, and I have houses, Amen.
I have no place, and I have places, Amen.
I have no temple, and I have temples, Amen.
I am a lamp to you who see me, Amen.
I am a mirror to you who know me, Amen.
I am a door to you who knock on me, Amen.
I am a Way to you who travel with me, Amen.

Acts of John 94 (Seers Version)

"The One Who Reveals"

His disciples said, "Lord who is the one who seeks and who is the one who reveals?"
The Lord said, "The one who seeks is the one who reveals. . . .
The one who speaks is also the one who hears,
and the one who sees is also the one who reveals."

Dialogue of the Savior

"I Am You and You Are Me"

I stood on a high mountain and saw a Mighty Man and with him a dwarf and heard as it were a voice of thunder, and drew closer to hear it: and it spoke to me and said, "I am you and you are me; wherever you are I am there, and I am scattered in all things; from wherever you want to you gather Me, and gathering Me you gather yourself."

The Gospel of Eve

"Only Through Direct Knowledge"

Become zealous about the Lord.
The first condition of the Lord is faith:
Its second is love;
And its third is works.

From these proceed life.
The world is like a grain of wheat.
When a person sowed it,
He believed in it;
When it grew, he loved it
For he looked forward
To thousands of grains in the place of one;
When he worked it,
He was saved,
Because he prepared it for food.
And again he kept back some grains to sow.

So it is possible
For you to receive the kingdom of heaven;
Unless you receive it through direct knowledge
You will never be able to discover it.

Apocryphon of James

"If You Do Not Know Yourself,
You Will Not Know Anything"

Know who Christ is, and acquire him as a friend, for this is the friend who is faithful. He is also God and Teacher. This one, being God, became man for your sake. It is this one who broke the iron bars of the Underworld and the bronze bolts. It is this one who attacked and cast down every tyrant. It is he who loosened from himself the chains of which he had taken hold. He brought up the poor from the Abyss and the mourners from the Underworld. It is he who humbled the haughty powers; he who put to shame the haughtiness through humility; he who has cast down the strong and the boaster through weakness; he who in his contempt scorned that which is considered an honor so that humility for God's sake might be highly exalted: and he has put on humanity. . . .

For no one who wants to will be able to know God as he actually is, nor Christ, nor the Spirit, nor the chorus of angels, nor even the archangels, as well as the thrones of the spirits, and the exalted lordships, and the Great Mind. If you do not know yourself, you will not be able to know all of these.

Open the door for yourself that you may know the one who is. Knock on yourself that the Word may open for you.

Teachings of Silvanus

"From Dove to Dove, and from Glory to Glory: the Law of the Constant Transformation in Christ of the Soul"

The divine nature is simple, pure, unique, immutable, unalterable, ever abiding in the same way, and never goes outside of itself. It is utterly immune to any participation in evil and thus possesses the good without limit, because it can see no boundary to its own perfection, nor see anything that is contrary to itself. When therefore it draws human nature to participate in its perfection, because of the divine transcendence it must always be superior to our nature in the same degree. The soul grows by its constant participation in that which transcends it; and yet the perfection in which the soul shares remains ever the same, and is always discovered by the soul to be transcendent to the same degree.

We see the Word leading the bride up a rising staircase, as it were, up to the heights by the ascent of perfection. The Word first sends forth a ray of light through the windows of the Prophets and through the lattices of the Law and the commandments. Then he bids the bride draw near to the light and then to become beautiful by being changed, in the light, into the form of the dove. And then, even though she has enjoyed her share of good things as far as was in her power, he nonetheless continues to draw her on to participate in transcendent beauty as though she had never tasted of it. In this way, her desire grows as she goes on to each new stage of development; and because of the transcendence of the graces which she finds ever beyond her, she always seems to be beginning anew.

For this reason the Word says once again to His awakened bride: "Arise"; and when she has come, "Come" (Song of Songs 2:13). For he who is rising can always rise further; and for him who runs to the Lord the open field of the divine course is never exhausted. We must therefore constantly arouse ourselves and never stop drawing closer and closer in our course. For as often as he says "arise," and "come," he gives us the power to rise and make progress.

In this light you must understand the sequel. In bidding the bride to become beautiful even though she is beautiful, he reminds us of the words of the Apostle who bids "the same image" to be "transformed from glory to glory" (2 Cor. 3:18). This means that though what we find and grasp is always glory, no matter how great or sublime it may be, we always believe it to be less than what we hope for. Similarly, though the bride is a dove because of her previous perfection, she is ordered to become a dove once more by way of being transformed into what is more perfect.

Gregory of Nyssa

"You Fill Me with Words of Truth"

You fill me with words of truth,
    that I may proclaim You and Your Way!
Like flowing waters, truth flows from my mouth,
    and my lips declare Your fruits.
You cause Your knowledge to abound in me,
    Your mouth, O Christ, is the true word,
    and the door of Your light.
The Most High has given You to generations,
    who are the interpreters of Your beauty,
the narrators of Your glory, and the confessors of Your purpose,
    and the preachers of Your mind, and the teachers of Your
    (works).
For the subtlety of Your word is inexpressible,
    and like Your expression so also is Your swiftness and Your
    (acuteness),
for limitless is Your path.
You fall and You remain standing,
    You know the descent and the Way.
For as Your work is, so is Your expectation,
    for You are the light and the dawning of thought.
And by You the generations speak to one another,
    and those who were silent acquire speech.
And from You came love and harmony,
    and they speak one to another whatever is theirs.
And they are stimulated by the word,
    and know who made them, because they are in harmony.
For the mouth of the Most High speaks to them,
    and Your exposition is swift through him.
For the dwelling place of the Word is in human beings
    and Your truth is love.
Blessed are those who by means of You have recognized everything,
    and have known the truth. Hallelujah.

Odes of Solomon 12

"In Every Last Part"

We awaken in Christ's body
as Christ awakens our bodies,
and my poor hand is Christ,
he enters my foot, and is infinitely me.

I move my hand, and wonderfully
my hand becomes Christ, becomes all of him
(for God is indivisibly
whole, seamless in his Godhood).

I move my foot, and at once
He appears like a flash of lightning.
Do my words seem blasphemous?—Then
open your heart to him.

And let yourself receive the one
who is opening to you so deeply.
For if we genuinely love Him,
we wake up inside Christ's body

where all our body, all over,
every most hidden part of it,
is realized in joy as him,
and he makes us, utterly, real,

and everything that is hurt, everything
seemed to us dark, harsh, shameful,
maimed, ugly, irreparably
damaged, is in him transformed

and recognized as whole, as lovely,
and radiant in his light
we awaken as the Beloved
in every last part of our body.

Symeon the New Theologian (translated by Stephen Mitchell)

"Mystical Union with Christ"

"I beg you, O daughters of Jerusalem . . . that you stir not up nor make the beloved to awake till he pleases" (Song of Songs 2:7). The divine Bridegroom, in his passionate desire not to disturb the rest of his beloved, leaves her to sleep in his embrace and allows nothing to disturb this sweetest of all slumbers. I cannot contain myself for joy at the sight of the divine majesty deigning to come down to our weakness in so intimate and delightful a union, in which the supreme God contracts marriage with the soul exiled here below and desires to bear witness to that love towards her with which he is consumed. This, I have no doubt, is what heaven is like! I read in the Bible—and the soul, the bride of Christ, realizes the whole truth of these words—that it is impossible to express the happiness that is lived there. But the soul is also incapable of telling the joy that she now feels united with the Bridegroom. What more shall the soul receive, I ask you, that here below enjoys God so intimately that she feels herself clasped in his embrace, warmed on his breasts, and so carefully guarded for her sleep not to be broken before she awakens?

Bernard of Clairvaux

"This Wild Inhuman Need"

If all the world's creatures were to mourn me
Still no one could ever describe to them
This wild inhuman need I wander in.
Any human death would be far more tender
Than living without you in this darkness.
Everything I think—and am—runs after You
Like a bride hungry for her husband.

Mechthild of Magdeburg

"All in Christ"

She was swept away, into an indescribable light, and in this divine
light she saw a Man, beautiful above all children of men . . . and in
this Man and in this divine light, she saw the elements and the creatures and the things which are made from them, both small and great,
stand out in such brilliance, that each of them, however small, appeared a hundred times more brilliant than the sun . . . even the
smallest grain of corn or pebble. And the light of the present world
compared with this brilliance would have seemed dark like the moon
when she is covered by a dark cloud. And created things appeared so
clearly in this radiance that each could be distinguished by its quality;
a green grain, a red rose. But among all the elements and created
things, the earth was the most magnificent. And this because God
took his body from the earth; . . . and because during the Lord's Passion the earth was drenched with the blood of the Saviour . . . All this
was in this Man, in Christ.

Agnes Blannbekin

"To Live in Christ"

We must be continually aware that noble service and suffering are proper to man's condition; such was the share of Jesus Christ when he lived on earth as Man. We do not find it written anywhere that Christ ever, in his entire life, had recourse to his Father or his omnipotent Nature to obtain joy and repose. He never gave himself any satisfaction, but continually undertook new labors from the beginning of his life to the end. He said this himself to a certain person who is still living, whom he also charged to live according to his example, and to whom he himself said that this was the true justice of Love: where Love is, there are always great labors and difficult pains. Love, nevertheless, finds all pains sweet: Qui amat non laborat; that is, he who loves does not labor.

When Christ lived on earth as Man, all his works had their time. When the hour came he acted: in words, in deeds, in preaching, in doctrine, in reprimands, in consolation, in miracles, and in penance; and in labors, in pains, in shame, in calumny, in anguish, and in distress, even to the passion, and even to death. In all these things he patiently awaited his time. And when the hour came in which it befitted him to act, he was intrepid and powerful in consummating his work; and he paid, by the service of perfect fidelity, the debt of human nature to the Father's divine truth. Then mercy and truth met together, and justice and peace kissed each other (Psalm 85:10).

With the Humanity of God you must live here on earth, in labors and sorrow, while within your soul you love and rejoice with the omnipotent and eternal Divinity in sweet abandonment.

For the truth of both is one single fruition. And just as Christ's Humanity surrendered itself on earth to the will of the Majesty, you must here with Love surrender yourself to both in unity. Serve humbly under their sole power, stand always before them prepared to follow their will in its entirety, and let them bring about in you whatever they wish.

Hadewijch of Antwerp

"Hell Is the Highest Name of Love"

Hell is the seventh name
of this Love wherein I suffer.
For there is nothing Love does not engulf and damn,
And no one who falls into her
And whom she seizes comes out again,
Because no grace exists there.
As Hell turns everything to ruin,
In Love nothing else is acquired
But disquiet and torture without pity;
Forever to be in unrest,
Forever assault and new persecution;
To be wholly devoured and engulfed
In her unfathomable essence,
To founder unceasingly in heat and cold,
In the deep, insurmountable darkness of Love.
This outdoes the torments of hell.
He who knows Love and her comings and goings
Has experienced and can understand
Why it is truly appropriate
That Hell should be the highest name of Love. . . .
For she ruins the soul and mind
To such a degree that they never recover;
They who love no longer have virtues to do anything
But wander in the storms of Love,
Body and soul, heart and thought—
Lovers lost in this hell.
If anyone wishes to face this, he must be on his guard,
Since for Love nothing succeeds
But the constant acceptance of caresses and blows.
The offerings of veritable Love must be sought
In the depths of the heart possessed of fidelity.
If we act thus, we must conquer.
Though we are far off, we shall reach knowledge.

Hadewijch of Antwerp

"Christ the Mother"

I saw the blessed Trinity working. I saw that there were these three attributes: fatherhood, motherhood, and lordship—all in one God. In the almighty Father we have been sustained and blessed with regard to our created natural being from before all time. By the skill and wisdom of the Second Person we are sustained, restored, and saved with regard to our sensual nature, for he is our Mother, Brother, and Savior. In our good Lord the Holy Spirit we have, after our life and hardship is over, that reward and rest which surpasses for ever any and everything we can possibly desire—such is his abounding grace and magnificent courtesy.

Our life too is threefold. In the first stage we have our being, in the second our growth, and in the third grace. For the first I realized that the great power of the Trinity is our Father, the deep wisdom our Mother, and the great love our Lord. All this we have by nature and in our created and essential being. Moreover, I saw that the Second Person who is our Mother with regard to our essential nature, the same dear Person has become our Mother in the matter of our sensual nature. We are God's creation twice: essential being and sensual nature. Our being is that higher part which we have in our Father, God almighty, and the Second Person of the Trinity is Mother of this basic nature, providing the substance in which we are rooted and grounded. But he is our Mother also in mercy, since he has taken our sensual nature upon himself. Thus "our Mother" describes the different ways in which he works, ways which are separate to us, but held together in him. In our Mother, Christ, we grow and develop; in his mercy he reforms and restores us; through his passion, death, and resurrection he has united us to our being. So does our Mother work in mercy for all his children who respond to him and obey him . . .

A mother's is the most intimate, willing, and dependable of all services, because it is the truest of all. None has been able to fulfill it properly but Christ, and he alone can. We know that our own mother's bearing of us was a bearing to pain and death, but what does Jesus, our true Mother, do? Why, he, all-love, bears us to joy and eternal life! Blessings on him! Thus he carries us within himself in love.

And he is in labor until the time has fully come for him to suffer the sharpest pangs and most appalling pain possible—and in the end he dies. And not even when this is over, and we ourselves have been born to eternal bliss, is his marvelous love completely satisfied.

Julian of Norwich

"Cries of Jubilation"

Christ's love is both avid and generous. Although he gives us all that he has and all that he is, he also takes from us all that we have and all that we are and demands of us more than we can accomplish. His hunger is incomparably great: He consumes us right to the depths of our being, for he is a voracious glutton suffering from bulimia and consuming the very marrow from our bones. Still we grant him all this willingly, and the more willingly we grant it, the more does he savor us. No matter how much of us he consumes, he cannot be satisfied, for he is suffering from bulimia and so has an unquenchable appetite. Even though we are poor, that does not matter to him, for he does not wish to leave us.

First of all, he prepares his food by burning all our sins and transgressions. Then, when we have been purified and roasted in the fire of love, he opens his mouth as wide as a vulture ready to devour everything, for by consuming our sinful life he wishes to transform it into his own life, which is full of the grace and glory which he keeps always ready for us if only we are willing to deny ourselves and renounce our sinful ways. If we could comprehend Christ's passionate desire for our salvation, we would not be able to refrain from casting ourselves down his throat. Although these words of mine sound strange, those who love know what I mean.

Jesus' love of us is so noble that at the very moment it consumes us it also wishes to nourish us. Although he absorbs us completely into himself, he gives us himself in return, together with a spiritual hunger and thirst which make us want to savor him eternally. To satisfy our spiritual hunger and heartfelt affection, he gives us his body as our food, and when we eat and consume it with fervent devotion, his glorious, warm blood flows from his body into our human nature and into all our veins. In this way, we become enflamed with love and heartfelt affection for him, and our body and soul become thoroughly flooded with longing and spiritual savor. He thus gives us his life full of wisdom, truth, and instruction, so that we might follow him in all the virtues. He then lives in us and we in him. He also gives us his soul with its fullness of grace, so that we might always stand firm with him in love, in virtue, and in the praise of his Father. Above all this he reveals and promises us his divinity for our everlasting enjoyment. What wonder is it, then, if those who experience and savor this should break forth in cries of jubilation?

John Ruysbroeck

"The Eternal Coming of the Bridegroom"

When we have become seeing, we are able to contemplate in joy the eternal coming of the Bridegroom . . . What, then, is this eternal coming of our Bridegroom? It is a perpetual new birth and a perpetual new illumination: for the ground from where the Light shines and which is Itself the Light, is life-giving and fruitful: and so the manifestation of the Eternal Light is renewed without interruption in the hiddenness of the spirit. Here all human works and active virtues must cease; for here God works alone at the apex of the soul. Here there is nothing else but an eternal seeing and staring at that Light, by the Light and in the Light. And the coming of the Bridegroom is so swift, that he comes perpetually, and he dwells within us with his abysmal riches, and he returns to us afresh in his Person without interruption; with such new radiance, that he seems never to have come to us before. For his coming consists, outside all Time, in an Eternal Now, always welcomed with new longing and new joy. Behold! the delights are fathomless and limitless, for they are himself: and this is why the eyes by which the spirit contemplates the Bridegroom are opened so widely that they can never close again.

John Ruysbroeck

"On the Few Lovers of the Cross of Jesus"

Jesus has many who love his Kingdom in Heaven, but few who bear his Cross. He has many who desire comfort, but few who desire suffering. He finds many to share his feast, but few his fasting. All desire to rejoice with him, but few are willing to suffer for his sake. Many follow Jesus to the Breaking of Bread, but few to the drinking of the Cup of his Passion. Many admire his miracles, but few follow him in the humiliation of his Cross. Many love Jesus as long as no hardship touches them. Many praise and bless him, as long as they are receiving any comfort from him. But if Jesus withdraw himself, they fall to complaining and utter dejection.

They who love Jesus for his own sake, and not for the sake of comfort for themselves, bless him in every trial and anguish of heart, no less than in the greatest joy. And were he never willing to bestow comfort on them, they would still always praise him and give him thanks.

Oh, how powerful is the pure love of Jesus, free from all self-interest and self-love! Are they not all mercenary, who are always seeking comfort? Do they not betray themselves as lovers of self rather than of Christ, when they are always thinking of their own advantage and gain? Where will you find one who is willing to serve God without reward?

Seldom is anyone so spiritual as to strip himself entirely of self-love. Who can point out anyone who is truly poor in spirit and entirely detached from creatures? His rare worth exceeds all on earth. If a man gave away all that he possessed, yet it is nothing. And if he did hard penance, still it is little. And if he attained all knowledge, he is still far from his goal. And if he had great virtue and most ardent devotion, he still lacks much, and especially the "one thing needful to him."

And what is this? That he forsake himself and all else, and completely deny himself, retaining no trace of self-love. And when he has done all that he ought to do, let him feel that he has done nothing.

Let him not regard as great what others might esteem great, but let him truthfully confess himself an unprofitable servant. For these are the words of the Truth himself: "When you shall have done all those things that are commanded you, say, "We are unprofitable servants." Then he may indeed be called poor and naked in spirit, and say with the prophet, "I am alone and poor." Yet there is no man richer, more powerful or more free than he who can forsake himself and all else, and set himself in the lowest place.

Thomas à Kempis

"The Divine Birth"

God gives birth to the Son as you, as me, as each one of us. As many beings, as many gods in God.

In my soul, God not only gives birth to me as his son, he gives birth to me as himself, and himself as me. I find in this divine birth that God and I are the same: I am what I was and what I shall always remain, now and forever. I am transported above the highest angels; I neither decrease nor increase, for in this birth I have become the motionless cause of all that moves. I have won back what has always been mine. Here, in my own soul, the greatest of all miracles has taken place—God has returned to God!

Meister Eckhart

"The Marriage"

Now then let us deal with the divine and spiritual marriage, although this great favor does not come to its perfect fullness as long as we live.

The first time the favor is granted, his Majesty desires to show himself to the soul through an imaginative vision of his most sacred humanity so that the soul will understand and not be ignorant of receiving this sovereign gift; with other persons the favor will be received in another form. With regard to the one of whom we are speaking, the Lord represented himself to her, just after she had received Communion, in the form of shining splendor, beauty, and majesty, as he was after his resurrection, and told her that now it was time that she considered as her own what belonged to him and that he would take care of what was hers, and he spoke other words destined more to be heard than to be mentioned.

It may seem that this experience was nothing new since at other times the Lord had represented himself to the soul in such a way. The experience was so different that it left her indeed stupefied and frightened: because this vision came with great force . . . You must understand that there is the greatest difference between all the previous visions and those of this dwelling place. Between the spiritual betrothal and the spiritual marriage, the difference is as great as that which exists between two who are betrothed and between two who can no longer be separated.

I have already said that even though these comparisons are used, because there are no others better suited to our purpose, it should be understood that in this state there is no more thought of the body than if the soul were not in it, but one's thought is only of the spirit. In the spiritual marriage, there is still much less remembrance of the body because this secret union takes place in the very interior center of the soul, which must be where God himself is, and in my opinion there is no need of any door for him to enter. I say there is no need of any door because everything that has been said up until now seems to take place by means of the senses and faculties, and this appearance of the humanity of the Lord must also. But that which comes to pass in the union of the spiritual marriage is very different. The Lord appears in this center of the soul, not in an imaginative vision but in an intellectual one, although more delicate than those mentioned, as he appeared to the apostles without entering through the door when he said to them, "Pax vobis." What God communicates here to the soul in an instant is a secret so great and a favor so sublime—and the delight the soul experiences so extreme—that I don't know what to compare it to. I can say only that the Lord wishes to reveal for that moment, in a more sublime manner than through any spiritual vision or taste, the glory of heaven. One can say no more—insofar as can be understood—than that the soul, I mean the spirit, is made one with God. For since his Majesty is also spirit, he has wished to show his love for us by giving some persons understanding of the point to which this love reaches so that we might praise his grandeur. For he has desired to be so joined with the creature that, just as those who are married cannot be separated, he doesn't want to be separated from the soul.

The spiritual betrothal is different, for the two often separate. And the union is also different because, even though it is the joining of two things into one, in the end the two can be separated and each remains by itself. We observe this ordinarily, for the favor of union with the Lord passes quickly, and afterward the soul remains without that company; I mean, without awareness of it. In this other favor from the Lord, no. The soul always remains with its God in that center. Let us say that the union is like the joining of two wax candles to such an extent that the flame coming from them is but one, or that the wick, the flame, and the wax are all one. But afterward one candle can be easily separated from the other and there are two candles; the same holds for the wick. In the spiritual marriage the union is like what we have when rain falls from the sky into a river or fount; all is water, for the rain that fell from heaven cannot be divided or separated from the water of the river. Or it is like what we have when a little stream enters the sea, there is no means of separating the two. Or, like the bright light entering a room through two different windows; although the streams of light are separate when entering the room, they become one.

Teresa of Avila

"On the Creation"

A bride who will love you
My Son
I want to give you
  Who, because of her great value,
  Deserves to share your company
  And eat bread at our table
  (This one I too eat at)
  So she can know
  The Good I have in you
And so she can rejoice with me
  In your grace and full beauty.

I am grateful,
Father,
Said the Son
  And I will show my shining
  To the bride you gave me
So she can see by its radiance
How great my Father is
And how the being I possess
Streams to me from Your being.
  I will hold her in my arms
  And she will burn in your love
  And with eternal delight
  She will exalt Your goodness.

John of the Cross

"On the Creation II"

"Let it be done, then,"
the Father said,
"For your love has deserved it."

And after saying these words,
He created the world
A place for the bride
Fashioned with great wisdom
And divided into two rooms,
One above and one below.

And the lower part of the place
Was made of infinite differences,
But the one above was adorned
With glorious jewels
So the bride might know her Bridegroom.

And in the higher sphere,
The order of angels was unfurled
But human nature was placed in the lower,
For in his making man was a lesser thing.

And although beings and places
Were divided in this way
All are part always of one body
Which is named the bride
For the love of one bridegroom
Has made them all one bride.

Those above possessed the bridegroom in ecstasy
And those below lived in hope rooted in the faith
Which He infused in them
When He said that one day
He would raise them up
And raise them from their dereliction.

So no one would insult them any more
For he would himself come with them
And live with them

And God would be man and man would be God
And he would talk with them
And eat and drink with them.

And he would remain with them constantly
Until the end of the world
And when that end came
He and all of them would join together
In eternal song
For he was the Head of the bride he had
Whom he would take tenderly into his arms
And there give her his love
And so when they were joined as one
He would lift her to the Father.

And there the bride would rejoice
In the same joy
That God rejoices in.

For as the Father and the Son
And he who proceeds from them
Live in one another
So it would be with the bride;
Absorbed within God
She will live the life of God.

John of the Cross

"Home of Heaven"

Holy region of Light,
Field of pure joy, that never fails
From snow or brutal sun,
Glowing, always fertile, earth
Eternal Giver of consolation.

With purple and with snow adorned,
His glorious head crowned,
The Good Shepherd, without sling or crook,
Leads towards your pastures
The flock he loves and protects.

He walks, and his serene flock
Follows after to where he feasts them
On roses that can never whither,
And on a flower that is reborn forever
The more they feed from its splendor.

Sometimes on to the mountain
Of Final Good he guides them, and sometimes
He bathes them in veins of faithful joy
And always keeps open table for them
Their shepherd and their field in one, and all good luck.

And when from its highest sphere
The Sun streaks the summit with Light
He, radiant and at rest,
Surrounded by his flock, enchants
In tender tones their holy ear.

On his strong clear pipe he plays—
Eternal sweetness floods the soul
Turning the world's gold to ash
And she, in burning ecstasy, plunges
In boundless and perfect Good.

O sacred Sound and voice!
If only an atom of you
Could find and touch my senses

And drag my soul out of herself
And transform all of it into you, O Love!

Then she would know, sweet husband,
The place where you rest—
And, free at last from this jail
Of anguish, and one with your flock,
She would no longer be astray or lost.

Fray Luis De Leon

"Mary the Way to Christ"

What then can we do to make our hearts worthy of him? Here is the great way, the wonderful secret. Let us, so to speak, bring Mary into our abode by consecrating ourselves unreservedly to her as servants and slaves. Let us surrender into her hands all we possess, even what we value most highly, keeping nothing for ourselves. This good Mistress, who never allows herself to be surpassed in generosity, will give herself to us in a real but indefinable manner; and it is in her that eternal Wisdom will come and settle as on a throne of splendor.

Mary is like a holy magnet attracting Eternal Wisdom to herself with such power that he cannot resist. This magnet drew him down to earth to save mankind, and continues to draw him every day into every person who possesses it. Once we possess Mary, we shall, through her intercession, easily and in a short time possess divine Wisdom.

Mary is the surest, the easiest, the shortest, and the holiest of all the means of possessing Jesus Christ. Were we to perform the most frightful penances, undertake the most painful journeys, or the most fatiguing labors, were we to shed all our blood in order to acquire divine Wisdom, all our efforts would be useless and inadequate if not supported by the intercession of the Blessed Virgin and a devotion to her. But if Mary speaks a word in our favor, if we love her and prove ourselves her faithful servants and imitators, we shall quickly and at little cost possess divine Wisdom.

Note that Mary is not only the Mother of Jesus, Head of all the elect, but is also Mother of all his members. Hence she conceives them, bears them in her womb and brings them forth to the glory of heaven through the graces of God which she imparts to them. This is the teaching of the Fathers of the Church, and among them St. Augustine, who says that the elect are in the womb of Mary until she brings them forth into the glory of heaven.

Louis Marie Grignion de Montfort

"Mary and the Second Coming of Christ"

It is through the Very Holy Virgin that Jesus Christ came into the world to begin with, and it is also through her that he will reign in the world. . . .

I say with the saints: the divine Mary is the terrestrial paradise of the New Adam, where he was incarnate by the operation of the Holy Spirit to work incomprehensible miracles; she is the great, divine world of God where there are ineffable beauties and treasures. She is the magnificence of the Most High where he has hidden, as if in his own breast, his only Son . . . Oh! How many great and hidden things all-powerful God has made in this wonderful woman. . . .

Until now, the divine Mary has been unknown, and this is one of the reasons why Jesus Christ is hardly known as he should be. If then—as is certain—the knowledge and reign of Jesus Christ arrive in the world, it will be a necessary consequence of the knowledge and reign of the Very Holy Virgin, who birthed him into this world the first time and will make him burst out everywhere the second.

Jesus Christ is for every person who possesses him the fruit and the work of Mary. . . . When Mary has put down her roots in a soul she engenders there miracles of grace that she alone can work, for she alone is the fecund Virgin who has never had and never will have any equal in purity or fecundity. . . . Mary has produced, with the Holy Spirit, the greatest thing that has ever been—or will ever be—the God-man, and she will produce the greatest things that shall be in these last times. The formation and education of the heroic saints that will come at the end of the world are reserved for her; for only this singular and miraculous Virgin can produce, in union with the Holy Spirit, singular and extraordinary things. . . .

Mary must break out more than ever in these last times in pity, force, and grace. Her power over the demons will flash out everywhere. . . . It is a kind of miracle when a person remains firm in the middle of the fierce torrent of these times, and stays uninfected in the plague-ridden air of our corrupt era. . . . It is the Virgin, in whom the Serpent has never had any part, that works this miracle for those beings who love her well.

Anyone who knows Mary as Mother and submits to her and

obeys her in all things will soon grow very rich; every day he or she will amass treasures, by the secret power of her philosopher's stone. "He who glorifies his Mother is like one who amasses treasure." . . . It is in the bosom of Mary that the young become old in light and holiness and experience and wisdom. . . .

Mary is the dawn that precedes and reveals the Sun of Justice. . . . The difference between the first and second coming of Jesus will be that the first was secret and hidden, the second will be glorious and dazzling; both will be perfect, because both will come through Mary. This is a great and holy mystery that no one can understand; "let all tongues here fall silent."

Louis Marie Grignion de Montfort

"The Spectre"

The Spectre is the Reasoning Power in Man; and when
    separated
From Imagination, and closing itself as in steel, in a
    Ratio
Of the Things of Memory, It thence frames Laws and
    Moralities
To destroy Imagination! the Divine Body, by
    Martyrdoms and Wars.
Teach me O Holy Spirit the Testimony of Jesus! let me
    comprehend wondrous things out of the Divine Law.

William Blake

"I Will Sing the Canticle of Love"

My one thought, Jesus, is to love you. I can neither preach the Gospel nor spill my blood—but what does it matter? Others labor while I, a little child, stay close to you and love you for all those who are in the battle.

How shall I show my love, since love proves itself through acts? I will sing the canticle of love by each word and look, each tiny, daily sacrifice. I wish to profit from the smallest actions and do them all for love. I wish to suffer for love's sake and to rejoice. If my roses have to be gathered among thorns, I will sing; the longer and fiercer the thorns, the sweeter will be my song.

I love you, Jesus, and bear in mind always the words of St. John of the Cross: "The least act of pure love is of more value than all other works put together."

Therese of Lisieux

"Prayer to the Cosmic Christ"

From Patriarchy's lack of authentic curiosity,
From Patriarchy's separation of head from body,
From Patriarchy's separation of body from feelings,
From Patriarchy's preoccupation with sex,
From Patriarchy's fear of intimacy,
From Patriarchy's reptilian brain,
From Patriarchy's anthropocentrism,
From Patriarchy's cosmic loneliness,
From Patriarchy's crucifixion of Mother Earth,
From Patriarchy's envy and manipulation of children,
From Patriarchy's abuse of women,
From Patriarchy's homophobia,
From Patriarchy's righteousness,
From Patriarchy's idolatry of nationhood and national security,
From Patriarchy's forgetfulness of beauty and art,
From Patriarchy's impotence to heal,
From Patriarchy's sado-masochism,
From Patriarchy's parental cannibalism and devouring of its children,
From Patriarchy's lack of balance,
From Patriarchy's savaging of the earth,
From Patriarchy's quest for immortality,
From Patriarchy's ego,
From Patriarchy's waste of talent and resources, human and earth,
From Patriarchy's human chauvinism,
From Patriarchy's compulsion to go into debt to finance its bloated
        lifestyles,
From Patriarchy's matricide, spare us O Divine One.

Matthew Fox

Christ had to go through death in order to enter into the new world, the world of communion with God. We have to go through death with him. It is the only way. This is the challenge that faces the world today. We are passing out of one world, the world of Western domination, and entering a new age in which the logical, rational mind of Greek philosophy and Roman law, the economic and political order, the science and technology of the West, will pass away. Our patriarchal culture is passing away at this present moment.

Something new is emerging. Nobody knows exactly what form it is going to take. It is a moment of trauma, of birth. We are waiting until all the present forms and structures pass away, and we shall see the whole universe in space and time and the whole of humanity redeemed by Christ standing in the fullness of reality.

Bede Griffiths

About the Photographs

⊠ ⊠ ⊠

Cover: Municipal Cemetery of Ars, France, a small village of Beaujolais famous for its saint-priest John-Mary Vianney, "the cure of Ars."

p. vi: Chapel of Our Lady of Guadalupe, Santa Fe, New Mexico.

p. viii: "The Teaching Christ," Cathedral of Chartres, France.

p. xvi: EH Studio. This religious card is said to be a "miraculous" portrait of Jesus, which appeared on the negative of a picture of an altar, in Italy.

p. i: Vezelay (Burgundy, France), Basilica of St. Mary-Magdalene. A relic of the saint was brought back by the crusaders. The basilica (and the city itself) are built around the relic.

p. 87: Carmel Monastery of Cristo Rey, San Francisco, California.

p. 101: San Juan Batista, California.

p. 129: Père Lachaise Cemetery, Paris.

p. 195: Montmartre Cemetery, Paris.

p. 296: Friedenau Cemetery, Berlin, Germany.

p. 297: Laeken Cemetery, Belgium.

I would like to dedicate all the photos in this book, in love and gratitude, to the memory of my grandfather Oscar Van Weynendaele.

About the Author

Andrew Harvey is a poet, novelist, mystical scholar, seeker, and teacher. He is the author of over thirty books, including the novel *Burning Houses; The Essential Mystics; The Return of the Mother; The Way of Passion: A Celebration of Rumi;* and the bestselling *Hidden Journey* and *A Journey in Ladakh*.

Eryk Hanut is a photographer, and the author of several books, including *I Wish You Love: Conversations With Marlene Dietrich* and two other collaborations with Harvey, *Light Upon Light: Inspirations From Rumi* and *Mary's Vineyard*, winner of the 1997 Benjamin Franklin Award. They live in Nevada.